PENGUIN CANADA

THE NAKED INVESTOR

JOHN LAWRENCE REYNOLDS has written extensively on financial and investment matters and has collaborated with former cabinet minister Brian Tobin and Air Canada CEO Robert Milton to produce acclaimed books on politics and business. His book *Free Rider: How a Bay Street Whiz Kid Stole and Spent $20 Million* won the National Business Book Award and was optioned as a motion picture. He has also won two Arthur Ellis Awards for best mystery novel and a National Magazine Award. He lives in Burlington, Ontario.

D0973679

ALSO BY JOHN LAWRENCE REYNOLDS

NON-FICTION

Straight from the Top (with Robert Milton)

All In Good Time (with Brian Tobin)

Money Management for Canadians (contributor)

Free Rider: How a Bay Street Whiz Kid Stole and Spent $20 Million

Mad Notions

RRSPs and RRIFs for Dummies

Ballroom Dancing: The Romance, Rhythm and Style

FICTION

Haunted Hearts

Solitary Dancer

Gypsy Sins

Whisper Death

And Leave Her Lay Dying

The Man Who Murdered God

JOHN LAWRENCE
REYNOLDS

THE
NAKED
INVESTOR

WHY ALMOST
EVERYBODY BUT YOU
GETS RICH ON YOUR RRSP

PENGUIN
CANADA

PENGUIN CANADA

Published by the Penguin Group

Penguin Group (Canada), 10 Alcorn Avenue, Toronto, Ontario, Canada M4V 3B2
(a division of Pearson Penguin Canada Inc.)

Penguin Group (USA) Inc., 375 Hudson Street, New York, New York 10014, U.S.A.
Penguin Books Ltd, 80 Strand, London WC2R 0RL, England
Penguin Ireland, 25 St Stephen's Green, Dublin 2, Ireland (a division of Penguin Books Ltd)
Penguin Group (Australia), 250 Camberwell Road, Camberwell, Victoria 3124, Australia
(a division of Pearson Australia Group Pty Ltd)
Penguin Books India Pvt Ltd, 11 Community Centre, Panchsheel Park, New Delhi – 110 017, India
Penguin Group (NZ), Cnr Airborne and Rosedale Roads, Albany, Auckland, New Zealand
(a division of Pearson New Zealand Ltd)
Penguin Books (South Africa) (Pty) Ltd, 24 Sturdee Avenue, Rosebank, Johannesburg 2196,
South Africa

Penguin Books Ltd, Registered Offices: 80 Strand, London WC2R 0RL, England

First published 2005

1 2 3 4 5 6 7 8 9 10   (WEB)

Copyright © John Lawrence Reynolds, 2005

Author representation: Westwood Creative Artists
94 Harbord Street, Toronto, Ontario M5S 1G6

Manufactured in Canada.

LIBRARY AND ARCHIVES CANADA CATALOGUING IN PUBLICATION

Reynolds, John Lawrence
The naked investor : why almost everybody but you gets rich
on your RRSP / John Lawrence Reynolds.

Includes index.
ISBN 0-14-301623-7

1. Registered Retirement Savings Plans. 2. Retirement income—Planning.
3. Financial planners—Canada. I. Title.

HD7129.R488 2005   332.024'01   C2004-905322-1

Visit the Penguin Group (Canada) website at **www.penguin.ca**

For my sister Alice Boucher

No lesson seems to be so deeply inculcated by the experience of life as that you should never trust experts. If you believe the doctors, nothing is wholesome. If you believe the theologians, nothing is innocent. If you believe the soldiers, nothing is safe. They all require to have their strong wine diluted by a very large admixture of insipid common sense.

—LORD SALISBURY, LETTER TO LORD LYTTON, JUNE 15, 1877

Experto credite
(Trust one who has gone through it)

—VIRGIL, 70–19 BC

CONTENTS

INTRODUCTION

In the spring of 2000 a middle-aged couple decided to obtain independent financial planning advice. The couple had accumulated substantial RRSP investments, owned an almost mortgage-free home, operated a personal corporation that generated more tax benefits than profits, and was looking for assistance in managing their assets.

The husband wanted to concentrate on writing books and tapering off a lucrative career as a marketing consultant. The wife wanted to expand her time gardening and pursuing other interests. Both wished to travel more widely, launch Registered Educational Savings Plans for their grandchildren, establish a cash-flow strategy, and deal with certain nagging debts, including one built up within the personal corporation and secured by the equity in their home.

The couple's chartered accountant had provided excellent advice over the years and continued to do so. But the husband believed a fresh eye could always uncover new opportunities and options. Over the years, the couple had encountered a financial advisor at social functions for an arts group they supported.

"Come in and visit me some time," the advisor suggested. "I'll do an analysis of your situation and make a proposal. If you don't like our ideas, it won't cost you a cent. If you do like them, and let us handle things, the analysis fee is $750."

"We can't lose," the husband said to his wife a few days later, showing her the advisor's business card. She noted an alphabet of letters after the advisor's name. "Let's go downtown and talk to him, see what he suggests," the husband said.

She agreed, and during three visits over the next month, each visit extending more than an hour, they provided the advisor with copies of their income tax statements, details of their RRSP investment portfolios, and information he requested that seemed to have little connection with their concern about solving cash-flow problems, such as, "How much life insurance do you carry?" and "What are the terms of your wills?"

A week or so after their final visit, the advisor called to say his report was ready. When could the couple come down to review it?

At the advisor's office, the husband and wife were surprised to be handed copies of an inch-thick computer-generated report, many of the pages bright with multicoloured pie charts. They sat stunned while the advisor flipped quickly past the charts as though they were more decorative than informative. He then summarized the lengthy report as follows.

"Sell all your bonds now—they're too risky."

The bonds in the couple's RRSPs were all federal- and provincial-guaranteed, with maturity dates extending from 5 to 10 years into the future. Purchased in the early 1990s when interest rates were relatively high, the bonds had proven an excellent investment, and their market value represented about half of the couple's total RRSP value.

"Sell all the mutual funds you have accumulated over the years."

These were primarily value-based and indexed funds investing in major Canadian corporations and managed by companies such as AIM-Trimark, Templeton, and Dynamic.

"Move into growth-oriented mutual funds, the ones that are technology-based—that's where to build wealth in the future." The advisor provided a list of such funds, noting that they were "no load—all your money goes into the fund instead of into sales commissions." All the funds, however, charged high management fees with a deferred sales charge (DSC) extending over seven years. (The explanation and implication of these terms are provided in Chapter 4.)

"Purchase $400,000 each in new term insurance with a 20-year guarantee on premiums."

The couple already carried policies totalling $300,000 in benefits, and their children were grown, with families of their own. The annual premiums for the new policies approached $10,000. No explanation for these recommendations was provided beyond the comment, "This is what you need to build your retirement nest egg."

The couple thanked the advisor for his assistance, asked for time to ponder the recommendations, exited his office as swiftly as possible, and drove home, appalled at his proposals. None addressed their original concerns. Moreover, reviewing his report and their most recent RRSP statements that evening, they estimated that the advisor stood to earn from $30,000 to $40,000 if they implemented every proposal in the plan. The money would accrue to the advisor from the following:

1. The Sale of the "Risky" Government Bonds

Commissions as high as 2 percent are not uncommon in bond markets. These commissions, earned by discounting the bond price, are rarely if ever reported to the investor and would have placed about $5000 in the advisor's pocket.

2. The Purchase of High-MER (read: "expensive to own") Mutual Funds by the Advisor

Paid for with cash from selling the existing mutual funds in the couple's RRSPs, the new funds would have paid the advisor as much as $15,000 in sales commissions.

3. The Payment to the Advisor, by the Mutual Fund Companies, of Trailing Fees

These would be paid annually for as long as the couple retained the new mutual funds. The husband estimated these payments at $2500 each year; over five years, about $12,500 would have flowed into the advisor's pocket.

4. Sales Commissions on the $800,000 Life Insurance Policies
Estimated at $8000 in the first year.

The couple informed the advisor that they would not be following his recommendations and refused his several telephone pleas to give him a chance to "rethink things a little differently."

Within a few weeks of the couple's encounter with the "independent" financial advisor, stock markets began to fall. The value of mutual funds recommended by the advisor, heavily weighted toward high-tech and health services companies, suffered the worst. Had the couple invested their entire RRSP savings accrued over 25-plus years, as the advisor proposed, perhaps 80 percent of its value would have vanished with the market decline. It took over three years for prices to begin a recovery, but by mid-2004 they had still not achieved their earlier value. Whenever and if ever they returned to the price levels of early 2000, the couple would have lost at least several years of potential growth.

When tech stock prices began sliding, so did interest rates, which meant the value of the couple's bonds increased with every rate reduction (bond prices move in the opposite direction to interest rates). Had the couple sold their bonds when the advisor prompted them to, several thousand more dollars in potential earnings would have been lost.

Nothing the advisor did or proposed was illegal or even, in some quarters, considered ill-advised. The fact remains, however, that if the couple had followed his counsel, he would have been at least $30,000 wealthier. Meanwhile, the value of the couple's RRSPs would have been reduced by hundreds of thousands of dollars and they would have little recourse to recover their losses. An attempt to do so would take years of investigation and substantial upfront legal fees.

While industry organizations claim to protect small investors and work to replace losses as a result of advisor malfeasance or bad advice, they are sluggish to respond, loathe to replace losses, and protective of the investment industry. Had any of the relevant groups—the provincial securities commissions, the Investment Dealers Association of Canada, the Ombudsman for Banking Services and Investment, the Mutual Fund Dealers Association of Canada, among others—chosen to pursue an inquiry, the advisor would claim in his defence that he could not have foreseen either the collapse of stock market prices, especially the technical sector, or the resulting drop in interest rates. Nor was he bound by rule or law to reveal how much he stood to earn from commissions paid to him as a result of selling the bonds and old mutual funds, purchasing a new stable of mutual funds, and brokering the term insurance.

The losses suffered, the couple might have been lectured, were part of the risk that all investors must assume. When you invest in markets, prices can go down as well as up; that's the risk you take. This is the common defence of ineffective advisors. The industry wants you to accept dramatic loss as a potential outcome of every investment decision associated with long-term planning for your retirement, *and it is a lie.*

There is a difference between risk and uncertainty. Risk can be measured and accounted for; uncertainty cannot. Risk can be balanced according to rules capable of being absorbed by every Canadian mature enough to open his or her own RRSP, and their mechanics can be grasped in the time it takes to sip a cup of coffee. Risk and uncertainty are very different. No one can anticipate uncertainty. Everyone can understand and account for risk.

In essence, the couple would have taken all the risk and lost. The advisor would have taken no risk and won.

The experience of this couple is not as rare as the investment industry claims. Too many trusting RRSP investors stand naked in the market while their advisors convince them they are wearing a superbly fitted and highly fashionable suit of clothes. Canadians need to be educated about methods employed by the financial and investment industry to enrich itself in an atmosphere with minimal transparency and accountability. That's my primary reason for writing this book. Here are seven others:

1. Because, in addition to losses suffered by investors through inappropriate advice, borderline-legal activities and out-and-out fraud occur with alarming frequency in the industry, destroying the life's work and dreams of Canadians while fraudsters escape with little more than a slap on the wrist.

2. Because neither the various regulatory bodies nor the industry appear to be addressing the problem effectively.

3. Because Canadian law can be construed as favouring large investment firms over individual citizens.

4. Because too many interests, including the legal profession and certain sectors of the media, support grey aspects of the financial and investment industry and overlook the concerns of small investors.

5. Because a loss of trust by citizens in the investment industry will harm Canada's economy.

6. Because prudent investment decisions made on the basis of a few simple rules, according to the investor's best interests, are still the best way to achieve long-term financial security.

7. And because the middle-aged man who sought assistance in financial planning, only to discover that the licensed, highly qualified, commission-earning advisor based every decision solely on generating benefits for himself ... was me.

You Are David, They Are Goliath, and You Don't Have a Slingshot

In 1987, at age 60, Armand Laflamme and his brother sold the door and window manufacturing business they had built from scratch. After almost half a century of mostly manual labour, Armand deserved a comfortable retirement, financed by his share of the $10 million selling price of the company.

Things went wrong from the start. Instead of receiving $5 million, Armand received only $2.2 million, the balance tied up and eventually lost in financial complications with the company's buyer. Still, $2.2 million represented a substantial nest egg for a man with a grade four education and, following the guidance of his son, Armand contacted securities dealer Burns Fry (now BMO Nesbitt Burns), where his account was assigned to a man named Jules Roy.[1] Neither Armand nor his son had any investment experience, and they were persuaded by Roy to sign a number of blank documents, which Roy would complete at a later date. Armand Laflamme transferred $2 million to Roy at Burns Fry, confident that he had placed his assets in the hands of a licensed financial advisor employed by a reputable investment firm.

A year later, Roy moved to Prudential-Bache Commodities Canada Ltd. From there he sent another set of blank documents to

Laflamme and requested that Laflamme sign them—the details again to be completed by Roy—transferring his account to Prudential-Bache. Laflamme agreed; after all, Prudential-Bache was as large and reputable as Burns Fry.

Within a few weeks, Armand Laflamme was stunned to learn that his $2 million balance had not only declined by more than $200,000 but that Roy was managing the account on margin—that is, borrowing money from the brokerage (at a relatively high interest rate) and adding the borrowed money to Laflamme's assets in order to purchase larger quantities of securities, many of them outright speculative in nature. Trading larger volumes of securities generated, of course, larger commissions for the broker. Laflamme, through his daughter, instructed Roy to cease margin trading, limit stock market investments to $500,000, and place the balance in safe instruments such as bonds and guaranteed investment certificates (GICs).

The instructions were ignored. Losses mounted, securities were traded without Laflamme's knowledge or approval, and the value of Armand Laflamme's hard-earned nest egg continued to dwindle. On March 2, 1990, Laflamme pulled what little remained of his account out of Prudential-Bache and began court action to recover at least a portion of his losses. The effort took 10 years.

The first court decision, handed down six years after Laflamme launched his suit, resulted in a decision in his favour by the Superior Court of Quebec. In his ruling, Justice Lebrun found Roy and Prudential-Bache "entirely liable" and listed "quite unmistakeable and clearly proved" faults that included—

- Failure by Roy to act in accordance with the client's objectives (i.e., generate a retirement income)
- Failure by Roy to comply with the client's specific instructions
- Failure by Roy to deal with the client in good faith and in accordance with good practice

- Conducting extremely large numbers of transactions for the sole purpose of generating commissions for Roy and the brokerage
- Failure by Prudential-Bache to exercise proper supervision over Roy
- Roy being in a conflict of interest, as Roy's supervisor received a 50 percent share of the defendant's commissions

It was a devastating judgment that included instructions for Roy and Prudential-Bache to repay Laflamme $1.5 million lost as a result of Roy's actions.

But Prudential-Bache was not finished. It appealed the decision and won, managing to reduce the damages payable to a paltry $70,000. To those outside the legal community, the basis of Roy and Prudential-Bache's appeal reads like an example of extreme cynicism. After a year of dealing with Roy, the appeal judge determined, Armand Laflamme would have generated enough investment knowledge to be considered experienced and qualified to assess Roy's investment tactics and should have taken responsibility for the advisor's actions. Thus, the brokerage was not responsible for any losses after that point.

While the appeal court ruling did not use the same terminology, the context and meaning appears in numerous defences launched by advisors and brokerage firms when facing client charges of malfeasance: "You are the author of your own misfortune."

Armand Laflamme may have been confounded by the ruling, but he was not yet finished. He and his legal counsel went to the Supreme Court of Canada, which agreed to hear the case on the basis that it related to the liability of a securities dealer acting as a portfolio manager. In a scathing review, the Supreme Court overturned the appeal court's judgment, restoring most (but not all) of the original amount decreed. Roy and his brokerages were ordered to pay Armand Laflamme and his family $924,374 plus interest and costs.

A substantial portion of Armand Laflamme's retirement nest egg, earned through 50 years of labour, was returned to him 13 years after it had been placed in the hands of a professional financial advisor employed by a reputable investment firm. It was May 2000. At age 74, Armand Laflamme could finally begin to enjoy his retirement without the trauma of watching his money dribble into the hands of a commissioned-based advisor while fighting legal battles with a giant brokerage.

In mid-2000, when my wife and I received the inappropriate advice from the financial advisor whose goal appeared to be to enrich himself at our expense, I had written a guide to RRSP and RRIF investing and had begun a book tracing the criminal trial of a man charged in a major investment fraud. The charges involved Bay Street broker Michael Holoday, and the story was the basis of my book *Free Rider: How a Bay Street Whiz Kid Stole and Spent $20 Million.*

Free Rider taught me much about the investment industry that I had not fully appreciated. Until details of Holoday's activities were revealed and the impact they made on his victims assessed, I had focused exclusively on the benefits of assembling and maintaining a portfolio within an RRSP in preparation for retirement. That was the bright side of investing for the future. Holoday's tale, and the flood of experiences that poured my way during and after his trial, provided a glimpse of the darker sides.

One of these sides is represented by Armand Laflamme's experience. As he discovered during more than a decade of battling egregious treatment by a qualified financial advisor and a national brokerage, the industry will fight to the last writ to protect itself from precedent-setting legal losses and any admission of culpability. Its arguments against admitting responsibility can defy logic and plumb new depths of cynicism. Consider the Prudential-Bache defence based on the idea that Armand Laflamme, with a grade four education and no investing experience, would have acquired sufficient insight in the one year of dealing with his broker to make effective assessments and decisions regarding the performance of his account entirely on his own. How does this correlate with the industry's declaration that its advisors undergo extensive education, rigorous training, and constant assessment of their professional skills, backed by years of experience? It does not, except perhaps in the brief of a win-by-any-means lawyer.

Contributing to an RRSP on a regular basis is a wise thing to do, as everyone from federal politicians to banks and brokerage firms keeps telling us. As prudent and obedient Canadians, millions of us have done so, managing by fortune, diligence, and perhaps even good advice to accumulate RRSPs with balances in the mid-six-figures. Each year, about six million Canadians dump an average of $5000 into their RRSP plans, generating $30 billion in cash looking for a place to reside for several years. The old adage about your home representing the largest asset you will acquire in your lifetime may no longer be true. Now your RRSP could outstrip your home in value, and it is liquid.

This liquidity, unfortunately, is more accessible to others than it is to you—others in this case being people within the investment industry whose careers and income depend on how much of your RRSP assets they can move first into the coffers of their firm and eventually into their own pockets. With the exception of fraud and outright theft, these earnings are obtained legally through mutual fund fees, brokerage commissions, and other avenues.

The nature of the system provides a means for the industry to generate income by acting according to its primary interests, with the interests of the investors playing a largely secondary role. In effect, hundreds of billions of dollars salted away by Canadians for their retirement represent a vein of gold to be mined for by financial advisors, mutual fund sponsors, and financial institutions in ways that most RRSP owners fail to recognize.

Too many RRSP and RRIF owners have discovered that the investment industry is designed to protect itself, which it manages to do with remarkable success; indeed, it protects itself more effectively than it protects its clients. Proving that a broker, financial advisor, or financial planner has made decisions that favour himself at the expense of the trusting client is difficult because the advisor or broker can explain and justify almost any recommendation in ways that the client can neither anticipate nor dispute. When complaints to an investment firm about inappropriate handling of an account lead nowhere, the distressed client might press on, only to find herself bounced among a half dozen or more organizations ostensibly created to protect her interests. Representatives of each might nod with empathy before suggesting that the client's case really belongs with another agency, starting a game of circle tag in which the client is always "It."

If and when a client, sufficiently motivated and probably obsessed, manages to attract legal attention to her cause, she will likely never see her claims presented in court. Instead, her case will be referred to arbitration, where she may hope for a settlement of perhaps 50 cents on the dollar. The public will never hear the terms, for such agreements invariably include the condition that no details be revealed. Should the client discuss her settlement openly, she could be required to pay a substantial penalty that usually includes the return of any money received plus punitive damages. This demand for secrecy is never made by the investor; total confidentiality is stipulated by the investment industry, and its insistence on non-disclosure represents an effective method of concealing the extent of investor dissatisfaction and investor abuse.

Dig deeply enough into investor and regulator concerns and you will discover two sides to the Canadian investment industry.

One presents a benevolent face shining with trust, wisdom, and the assurance that it wants to assist Canadians in building themselves a solid financial future. Like a kindly mentor, the industry explains that individual investors are ill equipped and thus unable to make major investment decisions on their own. Only with professional assistance, investors are gently lectured, can they achieve the financial security they seek and deserve.

The other, less charitable, side is frantic in its efforts to find ways of securing ever-larger portions of client RRSPs. It strives to do so not from enhanced performance or service but through marketing efforts that prey on the insecurities, aspirations, and trust of RRSP owners. When not conceiving new ways of siphoning funds from investors, the industry keeps busy diluting demands for reform and greater accountability.

Slowly, things are beginning to change, sparked to some degree by events beyond Canada's borders, such as the crusading activities of New York State Attorney General Eliot Spitzer. Demands for change are even beginning to resonate among the industry's own practitioners, including proposals to elevate financial advisors to true professional status by replacing sales commissions with direct fees. An equitable system will arise, however, only when Canadian RRSP owners grow fully aware of industry techniques to make itself wealthy first, treating the wealth of its clients almost as an afterthought.

The purpose of this book is to shine light on the circumstances behind these events and equip you to deal with similar situations, especially if your primary interest in investing is to provide the kind of retirement income your parents counted on receiving from employers' pension plans.

Defenders of the investment industry claim that the incidents you'll encounter on the following pages are "anecdotal," as though the word were synonymous with falsehood. The industry prefers statistical data, on the basis perhaps that accounts of real people pale against hard facts spat from a calculator. But statistical data will never reveal the actual number of victims, many of them senior citizens, who believe little can be done to correct errors made in their names by trusted advisors. As noted earlier, the industry—and much of the legal profession that represents investors and advisors at the same time, albeit in different cases—seeks to conceal the scope of its problems.

Among the first things a lawyer specializing in charges made against an advisor or brokerage will tell you is, "Don't talk about your case with anybody." The lawyers will claim the advice is given solely to improve the prospect of obtaining a favourable settlement, a questionable assertion when made by someone who is in court this week arguing on behalf of a brokerage and advisor against a wronged investor, and back in court next week making a case on behalf of an investor against an advisor and brokerage. And among the last things you will be told when advised to sign a settlement, whether or not it meets your reasonable expectations, is the same: "Don't discuss it with anybody or you could forfeit the money you receive."

When victims draw attention to the price they paid for bad advice, inappropriate investments, altered records, fraudulent statements, and other activities that may enrich the advisor at the client's expense, they encounter a system that often either favours the sales side of the investment industry or simply refuses to get involved.

Too harsh a condemnation? Hold your judgment until after you read about—

- The daughter of a 90-year-old widow who was told by a senior official with the Investment Dealers Association of Canada that no actions would be taken on her mother's claim about advisor malfeasance because, "Your mother might die before we get around to her case, and we have limited resources to deal with claims."

- The realtor who returned from vacation to discover his six-figure portfolio depleted through unauthorized broker transactions and a $70,000 debt, leading to years of frustrating and fruitless efforts in civil court to obtain redress.

- The nearly blind widow with poor English skills whose RRIF was depleted by half in just two years after her advisor moved her into high-risk investments. The brokerage defended itself by noting that she had failed to object to changes in the value of her portfolio, ignoring her many complaints that she could not understand the statements.

- The retired United Church minister and his wife who not only lost every penny of borrowed money in a supposedly safe tax-sheltered investment but were harangued for years by Canada Customs and Revenue, which demanded $100,000 in back taxes, interest, and penalties after declaring the investment was not tax-exempt after all.

- The 62-year-old woman who, when she asked about steep declines in the value of her RRSP portfolio, triggered a tantrum from her advisor, who shouted that she was ungrateful for all the work he was doing on her behalf.

- The businesswoman concerned about differences between the inflated value of her portfolio, as provided by the broker, and its shrunken value, as indicated by brokerage statements. When she did precisely what investors are advised to do in these situations and called the brokerage compliance officer for assistance, she was referred back to the broker for an explanation. Her broker turned out to be one of Canada's biggest stock fraud artists.

No matter how much it tries, the investment industry cannot claim that stories such as these are rare and anecdotal, because no one knows the precise number of such incidents. Until investors grow educated and wary, and the industry's feckless self-regulated organizations grow responsive, the situation will become worse, and the number of personal financial disasters will increase. Why? Because employers are turning from defined-benefit programs, in which the corporation assumes responsibility for managing employee pension funds, to defined-contribution programs, where responsibility for managing portfolios is assigned to the RRSP owners. The value of these RRSP accounts is measured in hundreds of billions of dollars, and the earnings from these assets, and frequently the assets themselves, are more accessible to brokers and financial advisors than to the RRSP owners.

The stories you encounter on these pages are true, although a few subjects asked me to respect their privacy (and, often, their embarrassment) by changing their names and, in some cases, details of their circumstances. Study all the statistics you wish, but until you have watched an elderly man be moved to tears over the way in which his life savings have been squandered by an accredited advisor, with neither the advisor's firm nor the investment industry demonstrating serious interest in addressing his loss, your data will remain a column of cold figures, and the scope of the situation will remain obscure.

Industry representatives, including financial planners, financial advisors, registered representatives, mutual fund salespeople, brokers, and owners of all the various designations assigned to people licensed to trade securities, insist that most of its members are honest and hard working. They are correct, inasmuch as most people *everywhere* are basically honest. But they should not deride these stories nor minimize the scope of unnecessary losses suffered by RRSP and RRIF owners through mismanagement of their assets. Effective, hard-working financial planners and advisors will *welcome* this book, because the crooked members of any profession are the enemy of the honest.

The lessons on these pages are not meant to encourage you to hide your life savings under a mattress or salt them away in bank accounts where they earn miserly income. The best way to build for your future is to invest your savings, especially your RRSP assets. Doing this effectively and safely requires you to maintain the attitude of a child strolling through the forest on her way to Grandma's house. Enjoy the scenery, smell the roses, and look forward to a lovely time in a safe and cozy cottage. Just be sure to stick to the well-worn path, and never assume that everyone you meet in the woods is anxious to help you get to Grandma's safely.

With that approach, you also may succeed in surviving the same near miss that prompted this book.

OF FOXES AND HEDGEHOGS:
LEARNING TO DO ONE THING WELL

Joe Killoran has the attitude and, some might say, obsession of a dedicated whistle-blower and conspiracy buff. In places ranging from the office of the prime minister of Canada to storefront brokerage firms, Killoran is considered a pain in the ass, a consumers' rights defender, a financially focused Don Quixote, or a combination of all three. To those who feel abused by the investment industry, however, he is a champion for investor rights and industry standards, if slightly mad, as most crusaders are.

We meet in a sandwich bar near Toronto's Pearson International Airport, where Killoran, an articulate man with the demeanour of a fugitive, relates his story. Bright and well educated—he earned an MBA from the Ivey School of Business—Killoran worked as a broker with Merrill Lynch Canada and as a pension consultant with Canada Life, where his experiences converted him into a self-appointed Lone Ranger dedicated to protecting the public from the investment industry.

"I am hated and despised by the investment industry," he almost boasts. "They say I rant about abuses. They are wrong. I don't rant. I just keep repeating the facts that people need to hear. I don't rant any more than the advertisements, repeated month after month, persuading people to put their investments in mutual funds that enrich the person selling the funds but do nothing for the investor."

For three years during the 1990s, Killoran published *The Frugal Bugle,* an investor bulletin featuring articles on financial planning amid warnings about questionable practices in the investment industry. Refusing to accept advertisements because it would have compromised his editorial integrity, Killoran eventually had to abandon his foray into publishing and accept a job as marketing communications consultant with a leading planner/advisor at a large bank-owned brokerage. He lasted less than a year.

"During the 1996 'hunting season,'" Killoran recalls, "all the mutual fund companies started making sales pitches to brokers and advisors, each promoting their funds to be pushed on our clients. One of the fund operators, a guy with a reputation for running one of the biggest fund companies in the country, showed up with a brand-new batch of funds marketed under his name. He gathered 50 or 60 brokers, plus a couple of managers, in a meeting room and said, 'You all know me. We've taken some trips together. Look over your books of business and you'll find some funds you sold with deferred sales charges seven to nine years ago that are now free and clear to be redeemed with no deferred sales charges.' He meant that clients wouldn't complain about paying a deferred sales charge when the broker talked them into selling the funds. Then he said, 'These clients are prime candidates to be switched to my new funds, and you'll get a new 5 percent sales commission too!'"

Killoran shakes his head at the memory. "It didn't matter if these new funds matched or suited the needs of the client. He wanted us to push his product. These were immature funds. They had been launched only a year before, so they had no track record to point to, no basis for recommending them in the clients' interests. Essentially, he was suggesting that we churn the accounts, but nobody in the room stood up and said, 'Hey, that's not acceptable!' They all just sat on their hands. It's all part of the unwritten code of silence among financial advisors. To be an advisor, your licence must be sponsored by your employer, and if the sponsorship is yanked, you're out of a job. That's why everybody in the business is compromised from telling the truth about inappropriate securities industry practices."

To Killoran, the fund manager's pitch was inexcusable. When Killoran submitted a scathing response to a request from the Ontario Securities Commission for commentary on mutual fund marketing practices, he was fired from the brokerage. Seven years later, in the fall of 2003, he remained unemployed, earning money here and there as a substitute teacher and counting on his wife's salary as a school principal to cover most family expenses. His unpleasant situation was at odds with the one that might have been predicted for him when he was a defenceman for St. Michael's College hockey team. Perhaps the same bulldog tenacity that earned him the sobriquet Killer Killoran on the ice propels him today, but the physical power has faded. Joseph Killoran looks and acts like a beleaguered man.

During his battle for investor rights, Killoran helped present a data-screening computer program to the Ontario Securities Commission. The program could identify and track brokers churning clients' accounts, a practice brokerage houses claim is difficult to detect. "I met [Ontario Securities chairman] David Brown in August 1998 and proposed the program to him," Killoran recalls, "explaining how it would protect people from churning, showing how it could be applied by one of the leading mutual fund companies, and why the brokerages should use it. Brown said, 'We don't give awards to whistle-blowers.' Then he stood up and walked away."

Over lunch, Killoran rhymes his way through a score of individuals, some notorious, some obscure, some of near celebrity status in the industry (including his own cousin, Arthur Labatt who, breaking with family tradition, left the brew company to co-found Trimark

Funds, then sold Trimark to AIM Funds, pocketing his self-made half-billion-dollar fortune). Joe Killoran believes he is more than blackballed by the investment industry; he suspects he is also targeted, which may explain his edgy manner when we finish lunch and say goodbye in the parking lot.

Upon returning home after meeting Killoran, I find a telephone message from him, his voice more jarring than before. He wants to know if anyone knew we were meeting that day, because his car inexplicably died at 120 km/h on his way back to Oshawa, died for no reason at all that his mechanic could determine. Had I told anybody about meeting him near the airport? Was I followed to our meeting? Had someone tampered with his car? Could this be another warning from the industry for him to shut up? Killoran worries it may be. He worries he is despised so much that his car's mechanical failure was an omen of things to come.

To fully appreciate the manner in which the financial and investment industry taps into your retirement savings, you need to recognize how the industry functions, and weigh some unpleasant facts.

In spite of efforts to position themselves as wise and contemplative professionals, brokers and financial advisors are essentially middlemen. Like all middlemen, they don't actually create anything. Rather, they provide a service, earning an income by moving products from source to end user. Dress it up with graphs and jargon, but the description still applies: When you deal with a broker, financial planner, or mutual fund salesperson, you're dealing with a middleman.

Here's another down-to-earth way of seeing things: When public corporations and bond issuers deliver profits to the investment industry in the form of stocks and bonds, the industry immediately takes its profit. Small investors, including those trying desperately to build a nest egg for their retirement or their children's education, divide whatever is left over.

Taking things a step farther, your interests and the interests of Bay Street and its spinoffs are diametrically opposed, because the bigger the slice of the pie you take, the less remains for the investment industry. This is why brokerage and mutual fund firms dislike people, like Joe Killoran, criticizing the way they make money. When it comes to paying you through potential investment gains, the industry shouts over the sound of brass bands and dancing cheerleaders. When it comes to paying themselves, they tend to whisper or change the subject.

A second fact to file: Almost every organization dedicated to providing investment counsel is involved, to some extent, in a conflict of interest. This salient truth, which the industry would prefer also not to discuss, was recognized in the United States when the Securities and Exchange Commission (SEC) dropped the hammer on half a dozen of the world's largest investment firms. These firms, the SEC determined, were beholden both to public companies seeking cash from investors and to investors seeking returns on their money. The brokerage firms underwrite the issues of private shares, committing to purchase sizeable blocks of the securities before adding a sales commission and selling the shares to investors. So far so good. But SEC evidence showed that the firms were promoting shares in companies whose prospects were so unpromising that they were described by brokerage personnel as "dogs." Supposedly objective analysts within the brokerage firms would "assess" these same shares as an excellent investment, hang a "Buy" sign on them, then watch brokers and financial advisors promote the securities to their clients— at which point the mutts were transmogrified into pedigree Best of Show winners. This process carried the role of middleman to new highs, or lows if you prefer.

Brokerages in Canada function under the same conflict cloud, as do self-regulating organizations created to protect investor interests. Provincial securities commissions such as the Ontario Securities Commission claim their goals are *to foster fair and efficient capital markets and to provide protection for investors from unfair, improper, or fraudulent practices.*[1] Fostering fair and efficient capital markets means nothing less than attracting outside capital from corporations and organizations that seek cash from investors to finance their operations. This kind of capital, especially given the current globalization environment, is remarkably fluid and more than a trifle skittish about excess regulation. If Sam Zillionaire decides that a sector in Canada is imposing too many rules on the way he can sell his shares or bonds, and on the way he can treat his minority shareholders, he'll take his money where the laws are less stringent, the regulations are more flexible, and the enforcers are quick to wink at the odd non-compliance issue. In such an environment, no securities commission or regulatory organization can claim it puts investor concerns first, since any perceived imbalance may frighten off capital. How well is equilibrium maintained between capital sources and the interests of small investors? According to a growing number of small investors and industry critics, not well at all.

Another fact to consider: Much of the investment industry holds you and every other retail investor in contempt. If you truly value your RRSP as the primary source of retirement income, the industry trumpets, you must actively invest the funds and not salt them away in a low-paying bank savings account or a batch of lethargic GICs. Most Canadians grasp this concept and agree. Then, dropping the other shoe, the industry stops patting your head and begins slapping your hand, insisting that you are not competent to manage your own RRSP portfolio. You don't have enough time to make your own investment decisions, it suggests. And if you have, you will inevitably make nothing but bad choices, it scolds. Do you know any other business where it is *de rigueur* to insult the customer?

The financial and investment industry proclaims love and concern for small investors at the drop of a Dow Jones Average, yet almost every service institution at its disposal favours the industry's interests over those of small investors. These include mammoth associations and organizations representing chartered banks, mutual fund companies, dealers, brokerages, investment counsellors, insurance agents, and financial planners. All pay lip service to investor protection, but their actions too often appear directed toward maintaining the status quo. No association comparable to the industry's own self-regulated, self-serving organizations plays a similar role on behalf of investors. Beyond the sluggish pace of the civil law courts and industry regulators, only a few lone voices like Joe Killoran's are shouting into the wind, railing against unfairness and abuse.

Small investors need the investment industry every bit as much as it needs them. This book is not about how to destroy the industry's effectiveness, minimize its benefits, or maximize its operating complexity. It is about the need to introduce openness into the relationship.

Whom Do You Trust? Maybe Only Yourself

Up to this point, the focus in this book has been on brokers, financial advisors, and financial planners because they are investors' primary source of contact, and because the vast majority earn their income from sales commissions. As you will discover as you continue reading, brokers are not the only drain on your investment growth. In some cases, they're not even the most critical. There are other wolves in the forest, some less benign perhaps but all basing their livelihood on that large portion of money that follows a serpentine route from the creators of investment wealth into your account and out again. They include—

- Mutual fund operators who prove that the best way to get rich is not to invest in a mutual fund—it's to own one
- Fraud artists in Armani suits who equate a licence to trade securities with authorization to steal
- Securities analysts who tout shares in corporations that they themselves wouldn't touch with a 10-foot pole
- Celebrity investment advisors whose role is more closely linked to sideshow barkers and carnie shills than to the once-grey process of investing
- The Investment Dealers Association, provincial securities commissions, and other self-regulating organizations whose structure and indolence could teach the federal bureaucracy a thing or two about avoiding decisions
- Canada's chartered banks, which treat retail investors the same way the proverbial slaughterhouse treats hogs—harvesting everything but the *oink*
- Packaging experts who add little more than glitz to an existing product, charge you for the extra packaging, reduce your potential earnings with high fees, call it a "wrap account," and convince you it's a bargain

One way or another, they are all middlemen. Their products are created by others who need your money to finance their operations, and who promise to reward you with dividends and potential capital growth. The middlemen bring both sides together and handle the cash transactions. That's a reasonable service. The problem arises because Canadian investors generally have no idea how extensive the middleman system is. They do not realize how many hands slip into the pockets of their RRSPs to withdraw a little money here and a little money there until, over the long run—and what other savings plan runs longer than retirement preparation?—untold thousands of dollars have seeped from their nest eggs.

Wherever substantial amounts of cash begin to flow, the shorelines of the money river grow crowded with people ready to scoop out a portion for their own benefit or, in the case of more outrageous fraud artists and embezzlers, divert the entire stream into their ponds. This appears obvious to almost everyone except the average investor. Two reasons for this are obscurity and trust, and the investment industry nurtures both.

Of the hundreds of billions of dollars invested in their RRSPs, most Canadians have little idea about the nature and structure of these investments—the ones not ensconced in sleepy bank savings accounts—or their performance levels. Amid internet access and extensive media coverage of investment markets, this is inexcusable. The average investor's knowledge is moving in the opposite direction from the amount of cash the average Canadian is investing. *We're putting more money in places we understand less.* A 1980 investment industry study indicated that just 10 percent of adults in the United States had direct contact with securities markets; barely 20 years later, the estimate had risen to 50 percent because more and more Americans were relying on their own investment programs, fuelled by federal government tax incentives, to generate retirement income.[2] Given the cultural and economic similarities between the United States and Canada, and the determination of Canadians to generate a self-sufficient retirement income, the figures in Canada are likely identical. No evidence exists, however, to indicate that the awareness of either Americans or Canadians of the investment industry's operations has risen by nearly the same degree.

Knowing What You Don't Know

Here's a quiz to measure your awareness of the investments you own, in or outside your RRSP:

1. Can you name all the mutual funds you own?
   Yes ❏   No ❏

2. Do you know how much you pay, as a percentage of each fund's value, to own these funds?
   Yes ❏   No ❏

3. Can you invest 100 percent of your RRSP in foreign equities?
   Yes ❏   No ❏   Don't Know ❏

4. Are there twice as many mutual funds in Canada as there are stocks on the Toronto Stock Exchange?
   Yes ❏   No ❏   Don't Know ❏

5. Is there a risk that advisors recommend mutual funds to clients on the basis of sales commissions rather than on their suitability to the client's needs?
   Yes ❏   No ❏   Don't Know ❏

6. Do you know the method used to generate a commission for your broker on every bond you buy?
   Yes ❏   No ❏

7. If you find a serious discrepancy in your RRSP account statement—missing money or a transaction you did not authorize—and your broker disputes your claim, do you know whom to call?
   Yes ❏   No ❏

8. Do you know which of these popular financial commentators is licensed to provide investment advice and guidance: Garth Turner, Brian Costello, Jerry White, Gordon Pape?
   Yes ❏   No ❏

If you answered No or Don't Know to any of the above, you are right where the investment industry wants you. The less you know about investing, the more valuable you are to that industry. You have the money and it has the knowledge. Eventually, if you are not careful, the roles will be reversed.

The investment industry will publicly dispute but privately admit the following statement: *When seeking reasonable long-term growth from your RRSP and assurances that the assets will remain available when you retire, you may not need a broker or financial advisor if you can grasp a few logical rules that are unassailable in their effectiveness.* These rules are proven, they are simple, and they are included in Chapter 12 as part of the rather basic but effective analogy of a road trip. They are not designed to increase the value of your RRSP to the point where your net worth rivals that of Bill Gates, but that's not the goal of most Canadians (though it may be their wish). *The rules are designed to keep your RRSP moving at a steady pace of growth and keep you out of trouble caused by inappropriate investment advice.*

The investment industry seeks to convince you that you are ignorant of basic investing guidelines, and it is often correct, although it neglects to add that you don't need an MBA to be able to comprehend the primary rules of good investing. As a result, you depend on "professional" guidance for decisions.

Whatever definition of the term "professional" you may harbour, it probably relates to a person performing a specialized function in an objective manner. Objectivity, or the lack of it, lies at the heart of many complaints about the actions of commission-paid "professional" financial advisors. If your advisor's investment recommendations influence both the growth of your RRSP and the income of the advisor, what happens when one conflicts with the other? How do you suppose the broker resolves that conflict? In your favour or his?

Or consider this analogy: The vast majority of us have no idea how a television set works beyond our use of basic controls such as the on-off switch and volume level. It doesn't matter. We don't need to understand digital comb filters, magnetic quadra poles, vertical aperture compensation, or other internal complexities. We just need to know that a clear picture and sound will arrive when we turn it on. This ignorance of internal operations would not prevent us from complaining if the TV set blew up after a few months of use and no one accepted responsibility for our loss. At the very least, we would demand a refund and avoid purchasing that brand of TV in the future. We might also shun the dealer who recommended the set to us.

During the tech market collapse of 2000 and the bear market that followed, most Canadians watched the value of their RRSP assets shrink like a TV image when power is lost. Few abandoned their brokers and financial advisors. Instead, most accepted without question the argument that investment losses are inevitable from time to time. This is not a necessarily true statement, nor did the losses need to be as deep and disturbing as they proved to be. RRSP and RRIF owners who silently accepted deep reductions in the value of their investments in common stocks, either directly or within mutual funds, were basically hoodwinked. How? By being convinced that they did not see the entire picture, by permitting their investments to include greater risk than necessary, and by having their trust exploited.

Read the promotion material provided by any full-service brokerage firm or mutual fund and ask yourself what the underlying message is. *The message is always trust*—trust us to know what is happening in the stock market, trust us to manage your money wisely, trust us to make decisions that you are unqualified to make, and trust the various self-regulatory organizations to look out for your interests. But can you? Too many Canadians have discovered their trust misplaced in everything from their financial advisor to the Canadian legal system. It's time to correct things.

Let's Hear It for Capitalism!

For all of its warts, capitalism, like democracy, remains the best of the available systems. By definition, investors believe in the system and reject, as do I, any treatise for controlled markets. Socialists we are not.

Committed capitalists preach the benefits of a free market, one that exists to make the pursuit of self-interest economically efficient.

They neglect to point out that free markets work best when both sides of a deal know the score, and this is where the bright and shiny armour of the investment industry grows rusty. To be blunt, much of the industry does not want you to possess more information than needed to make a sale to you. Remember the adage, "A little knowledge is a dangerous thing"? The investment industry seems to believe that substantial knowledge is even more dangerous—not to you, but to them. Wider knowledge provides wider choices. This may be helpful to you, but it is not generally helpful to much of the investment industry, which prefers to limit your choices.

You may choose to believe that the investment industry exists to make you wealthy. It does not. It exists to build its own wealth.

You may choose to believe that organizations established to monitor the capital markets are dedicated to serving the interests of the small investor. They are not. They are equally concerned about encouraging the entry of corporations into the capital markets and protecting the interests of the various members making up the organization.

You may choose to believe that enforcers of federal and provincial laws will respond to claims of larcenous behaviour such as forgery and the misstatement of personal information with the full weight of the law. They will not. Canada's investment terrain is strewn with the wreckage of accounts whose losses due to broker malfeasance were never totally replaced (nor were the brokers themselves punished beyond fines they could, in most cases, easily afford to pay).

Many questionable actions in Canada's investment industry have grown more outrageous and widespread in the years since 1980 as a result of the mounting value of RRSPs, which represent an unprecedented level of investment value in the hands of an extraordinary number of Canadians. The larger the RRSP pot grows, the greater the number of hands dipping into it.

About six million Canadians owned RRSPs or RRIFs in 2003, representing a total value well in excess of $400 billion.[3] In an asset base that large, mistakes are bound to happen. When the assets are entrusted to third parties whose income is dependent on where and how often the assets are directed, rather than how well they perform, the boundary between honest errors and conscious misdeeds grows murky.

"The fox knows many things," the Greek poet Archilochus taught long ago, "but the hedgehog knows one great thing." Archilochus describes the fox as a cunning creature, fleet of foot and mind. The hedgehog, in contrast, is slow and ambling, preferring to mind its own business. The fox knows many ways to ambush the hedgehog, and often tries. The hedgehog knows only how to roll itself into a ball with spikes protruding outward, protecting itself until the fox departs—and it knows how to do this perfectly.

In an industry populated with brilliant, sly, and ambitious investment advisor-foxes, it is essential that RRSP/RRIF owners know how to assemble a diversified portfolio of high-quality stocks, bonds, and mutual funds; why and when to trade them when necessary; and who might be claiming a portion of their investment assets, and by how much. With this much knowledge and a reasonable degree of awareness, you need not fear the foxes.

Without it you are unclothed and unprotected, lacking both the hedgehog's spikes and its talent for using them.

BROKERS AND ADVISORS:
WHOSE MONEY IS IT ANYWAY?

When Hillary Cornell[1] was 25 years old, her father persuaded her to begin investing her money, a policy she followed for the next 35 years. Her father was seeking to teach her financial independence, and he succeeded. Her experience with two brokerage firms produced another lesson.

In the afternoon light of her mid-Toronto living room, the 60-year-old divorcee tells her story with a shifting blend of outrage and humour. Having built an impressive portfolio from an inheritance and earnings during her career in real estate, Hillary relies on income generated by her investments to support herself and her son. She structured her portfolio to safeguard a sizeable share of her assets during economic downturns, generate cash to cover her living expenses, and provide some degree of growth to account for inflation. There is nothing complex about this recipe—it's Investment 101 stuff.

In 2000, on the cusp of a bear market, Hillary grew concerned about the private investment counsel she was receiving from the brokerage firm, associated with a large European bank, that was handling her account. "They didn't seem to have any focus to their strategy," she recalls. "At one point they suggested I start investing in German banks, which were doing terribly at the time. When they couldn't provide a rationale, I decided to move on."

A friend suggested she transfer her portfolio to a division of a major bank specializing in handling accounts for people with high net worth. This proved more complex and costly than she expected. "When I informed my previous broker that I was moving my account, they began applying all kinds of fees I had never heard of before, including a thousand-dollar 'closing of relationship' fee. In total they took about $5000 out of my account, just because I chose to move it to a better place."

Unfortunately, the brokerage proved not to be a better place after all.

Hillary Cornell's new financial advisor handed her a blank Know Your Client form to record her personal investment goals, level of investment knowledge, and other details. "I signed it on his assurance that he would complete it later," she says ruefully. "I told him I had good, but not sophisticated, investment knowledge. I had never dealt in futures or options, for example. I also stated that my investment goals were preservation of capital and income production, with some growth opportunities."

She grew comfortable with her advisor's warm assurances that he would be looking after her account according to her needs— so comfortable that it was several months before she realized the advisor had moved a substantial portion of her account into call options based on a short-selling strategy.[2] This was not only contrary to her directives but represented the opposite end of the preserve capital/generate income risk spectrum. "I had no experience in short selling," she points out. "It's not something I understand or that I want to be invested in."

Then disaster. "In October 2002, my advisor called to say that call options for 58 different stocks had expired a day or two earlier," Hillary says. "The stocks had rallied [risen in price], which meant that I had to buy them at a higher price. 'I didn't see the rally coming,' he told me, 'and I wasn't able to get all of my clients out of the market in time.' I said, 'You mean it wasn't physically possible for you to push all the buttons?' and he said, 'That's right, I couldn't do it.' He admitted that some buttons had been 'pushed,' but none of mine were. Then I learned that I could be responsible for covering all the potential losses in my account—and it came to $700,000. I went into shock!"

Hillary's first inclination was to move her account out of the brokerage as quickly as possible. "But what brokerage would accept my account with so many bad short positions and such a large potential shortfall? When the advisor tried to calm me down by saying the market would soon drop and the short positions could be covered then, I decided to stay. I didn't have much choice."

Stay she did, but soon after, when the brokerage made a trading error costing her $4000, she wrote instructions to the branch manager demanding that the company replace her loss and instructing the firm that no trades were to take place without her direct and explicit instructions. This was especially important because she would be on holiday in Mexico for all of February 2003 at a location without a telephone. "I mentioned that I would be visiting a nearby internet café every day," Hillary says, "and provided an email address where I could be reached if any problem arose."

No contact was made between her and the broker during her vacation, but when she returned in early March, a stack of envelopes bearing the brokerage's return address stood waiting for her. "My heart sank when I saw them because I knew what they were. They were receipts for transactions I had never requested—over 20 of them."

Hillary hoped for either an explanation or an apology for the trades made in direct contradiction to her instructions. "When I called to ask why they had done these trades after I instructed that none was to be made, the advisor almost shouted at me. 'I've been busting my ass to put money in your account, and you can't even understand what I'm doing for you!' I asked about the short positions I still had, and if I would have to cover them with my own money if the market didn't drop. He told me to forget about it because whatever we lost on one group of trades we would more than make up in another." She shakes her head. "He intimidated me until I finally gave in. I'm sure he wouldn't have spoken to a man that way."

Through several weeks of haggling, Hillary Cornell finally moved her account to a smaller brokerage, where a representative converted the balance of her account to income trusts and preferred shares in blue-chip stocks—"exactly where I should have been from the beginning."

She sought legal counsel to recover at least a portion of her losses and filed a complaint against the advisor with the Investment Dealers Association. An investigator reported that the advisor claimed Hillary had made several long-distance telephone calls to him while on vacation in Mexico, each instructing him to make the trades she was objecting to. This assertion was easy to prove, or refute, from telephone records, although nothing more was made of it.

Hillary's lawyer informed her that the bank brokerage indicated it would be willing to discuss a settlement without going to court. She is seeking about $400,000 in lost assets due to the broker's actions taken in direct contradiction to her instructions. She expects her legal fees to total between $50,000 and $150,000. By mid-2004 no arbitration date had yet been established.

Driving much of the changing attitudes of investors toward the brokerage industry is a growing awareness of the folly and unfairness of the industry's commission-based system of remuneration. Stockbrokers, whatever description they might hang on themselves (the industry prefers *registered representatives* or *RR*), delight in calling themselves professionals. The word suggests more than it defines (the Oxford dictionary identifies profession as "any calling or occupation by which a person habitually makes a living"). Those engaged in helping clients meet a goal or set an investment strategy want us to equate their activities with highly skilled activities such as those practised in the medical profession. But the analogy isn't a good one. How much trust would you place in a physician whose income was earned from commissions paid by pharmaceutical companies whose medication the physician prescribed? How confident would you be that the doctor's recommendations were directed toward your physical well-being rather than his or her own financial health? Yet this is how the brokerage system works.

Or what of another profession, such as real estate? Agents work on commission as well, although they are required to reveal and are permitted to negotiate the commissions earned through handling property sales. The commission-based brokerage industry does everything it can to conceal its means of making money, both during and for years after the transaction.

Search any full-service brokerage website and explore the library of promotion material it distributes, looking for information on the commission it will charge to purchase or sell securities on your behalf. There is none, although the commission you paid will appear on your statement *after* the fact. Nor is a full-service stockbroker likely to discuss competitive management expense ratios (MERs), the fees that mutual funds charge for handling your investment, much of which is returned to your broker for steering you into the fund. (I'll deal with that mess in the next chapter.)

Salespeople in other industries earn a living from commissions, brokers may mutter in defence. Buy a car, a refrigerator, or a stereo system and a portion of the purchase price will likely be kicked back to the person who sold it to you. Brokers, of course, don't like being compared with car salespeople, and it may be unfair—to the person selling the car. Cars come with warranties, and if the salesperson talks you into spending a few thousand bucks on a new Whizzmobile V8 with all-power equipment, you have some assurance that the thing will function at least until its warranty expires. Three weeks after a commissioned broker talks you into dropping a major portion of your RRSP into the *Standback & Duck* Emerging Markets Venture Fund, promising it will generate long-term growth for your retirement, and it sinks like an anchor, will you have the same opportunity to set things straight? You may think you have, through organizations such as the Investment Dealers Association, your provincial securities commission, or the civil courts. But plan on taking precious little hope with you if you go, as I'll examine later.

Simply put, the system works in favour of brokers and against unsophisticated investors. Here's how.

Imagine you're buying paint for your living room. You enter a paint dealer or hardware store and ask for semi-gloss white latex paint. Pretty specific. Assume that the paint salesperson turns to the shelf where the paints are displayed and finds two brands of paint that fit your description, both similarly priced. One, however, earns the store $10 in profit, the other, $15 in profit. Can you expect the salesperson to choose the $15-profit brand? Of course you can. Can you blame him? Hardly.

Brokers will claim that a good paint salesperson asks questions about the customer's needs before choosing the brand of paint, and that may be so. Substantial evidence exists, however, that brokers follow the biggest-margin rule in choosing investments for their clients. How else to explain that the largest mutual funds, in terms of assets, offer the largest returns for brokers who recommend and sell them, and rarely the best returns for the clients who buy them? Or to put it another way: *Why are the most effective mutual funds, as measured by long-term returns to their investors, often the smallest in total assets under management?*

Industry defenders will say that it's easier for a small fund to generate profits, which is not true at all—a lot of small funds are dogs. The truth ...at successful funds often pay no commissions to brokers, so the brokers never recommend them. Mutual funds managed by companies such as McLean Budden, Saxon, and Phillips, Hager & North consistently score above-average in long-term returns for investors, yet are rarely, if ever, recommended by brokers, *because these funds are focused on making the investor wealthier, rather than the advisor.*

Brokers also argue that they have a responsibility to assist clients in avoiding inappropriate high-risk investments. They have, and the best ones do. But within the industry, broker performance is measured less by the smiles on the faces of clients and more by the size of the sales commissions generated. Like it or not, full-service commissioned brokers are salespeople, and salespeople are pressured to meet ever-higher sales targets, generating more commissions for themselves and more income for the brokerage.

The problems with this approach multiply with every success. Once a broker or advisor achieves recognition as a Big Producer, she is cut a good deal of slack when it comes to discipline and supervision. You don't quickly fire a broker pulling in a million dollars in commissions each year, and too much wrist slapping for problems such as sloppy paperwork may drive her into the arms of another brokerage. In case after case, high-production brokers and advisors charged with malfeasance ranging from recommending inappropriate investments to out-and-out theft from a client's account were treated with such partiality by management that complaints and concerns regarding their actions were often deflected or minimized.

Losers Have No Friends in the Investment Industry

Michael Holoday, one of the most infamous of Canadian scam artists in the industry, rose to membership in the Chairman's Club of his large brokerage within three years of obtaining his trading licence and several years before his 30th birthday. Only the top 5 percent of all brokers at Midland Walwyn, Holoday's employer at the time, earned this recognition, yet no one seriously questioned how Holoday achieved so much so soon. When questions about his methods of building client assets and relationships were asked from time to time, at least one member of the company's board of directors shrugged his shoulders and admitted that he did not understand Holoday's system. No one chose to dig farther, because no one wanted to upset a million-dollar-a-year producer, and Holoday was permitted to continue dipping his fingers into his clients' assets. By the time the industry stumbled onto his tricks, over $20 million had passed through his hands and vanished.[3]

Brokers argue that Holoday and others are anomalies, exceptions that prove the rule about investors needing the wisdom and resources of honest brokers. Admittedly, the honest brokers easily outnumber Michael Holoday and his ilk. Unfortunately, the brokerage industry's definition of honesty is more dependent on what the broker fails to tell the client than on information provided to the client.

Should clients demand straight answers to tough questions when a broker makes an investment recommendation? The brokerage industry agrees they should. But this effectively negates the trust between broker and client. *If the broker's role is to assist in building the client's assets in a manner that reflects the client's objectives and tolerance for risk, why should it be necessary to grill the broker about suitability and alternatives?* Second opinions may be advisable where major surgery is proposed or a serious disease has been diagnosed, but rarely does the outcome affect the income of the physician or surgeon. Seeking a second opinion on a personal medical matter may be considered prudent, but any attempt to obtain an opinion of one advisor's recommendations from another broker is likely to infuriate the first broker and delight the source of the second opinion (who will almost always criticize the first broker's strategy).

The other factor at play here is the exasperated response of advisors to tough questions from clients, described in classic fashion by Hillary Cornell. Clients are often caught in a no-man's-land between being blamed for not digging far enough into broker actions when they fail to ask questions, and being accused of not appreciating the hard work of their broker when the same questions are posed. Too many advisors are guilty of bullying their clients whenever the advisor's recommendations are seriously questioned.

Do not expect the industry to provide satisfactory and timely support as a result of inappropriate investment advice provided by your licensed financial advisor/broker/registered representative. Investigations are slow, decisions are slower, penalties are light, and any replacement of the losses suffered will be both rare and stingy. The lesson is clear: The best way to protect your investment assets is to take charge of their care and assume limited reliance on the systems and measures provided by the industry.

At the brokerage level, several devices exist as evidence of the industry's concern for investor protection. They may be well meaning, but their effectiveness is determined more by the individual investor's diligence than by their mechanics. If your RRSP or RRIF is held at a brokerage, you may believe that various means, including those below, are in place to protect your investment. In reality, they offer more protection for the brokerage than for you.

The Know Your Client Form: Not Exactly Show and Tell All investments can be categorized as suitable or unsuitable, supplemented by some absolute dogs. The measure of each investment's suitability depends on the investor's economic status, long-term needs, expectations of return, and investment knowledge. A wealthy person with several thousand disposable dollars may choose to spend it on a weekend at a casino or on shares in a high-risk gold mine venture. Either action would be suitable. But the gold mine should never represent a major portion of the average Canadian's RRSP investment, especially if the plan's owner is 40 years of age or older.

Penny mining stocks are an obvious example of an unsuitable RRSP investment. Others are more difficult to determine for inexperienced investors but are readily apparent to licensed brokers—or should be. The Know Your Client (KYC) form is designed to establish your suitability for various investment options and confirm that the investments your broker recommends to you are in fact appropriate.

Investors may be required to complete and sign a KYC form provided by the broker or advisor. The form includes details about the client's approximate net worth, gross annual income, investment objectives, risk tolerance, investment knowledge, and estimated risk capital (ERC), which is the amount of money the investor can afford to lose. Brokerage staff can read KYCs like a road map, evaluating net worth, gross annual income, investment objectives, risk tolerance, and investment knowledge, which all function as guideposts toward suitable investments. In theory, this evaluation process is true. In practice, it is not always applied.

Opening a brokerage account involves signing a multitude of documents, most drafted in dense legalese. The KYC document may be portrayed as just another piece of paperwork, with the new client cajoled to sign a blank form, leaving the advisor to fill in the details. Since the KYC form does not commit the client to an obvious financial obligation, many clients add their signatures as instructed. In a legal sense, it is foolish to sign any document without reading and understanding it. Practically, it is a perfectly reasonable act, and thousands of KYCs in brokerage files contain information that bears little resemblance to the client's real situation. It's all a matter of trust, remember?

While fudged data on a KYC form does not represent a financial obligation by the client to the broker, it provides the broker with the investment equivalent of a get-out-of-jail-free card. Financial advisors with visions of Ferraris in their eyes may be tempted to insert a fictitious description on a blank KYC form bearing the investor's signature, indicating the investor claimed to be sophisticated, have substantial wealth, and other qualities justifying high-risk investments. If a client discovers her savings have been stripped almost bare through unsuitable investments justified by such claims on the form, cries of "I expected someone else to fill in the details" will not carry a great deal of weight or sympathy among regulators or judges.

In recent years, brokerages have instigated the practice of forwarding copies of KYC forms to investors after they were reviewed by someone in a position of responsibility, such as the branch manager or the brokerage's compliance officer. In this manner, investors have an opportunity to sound an alarm when the information bears little resemblance to their actual status. An investor receiving a copy of a KYC form in this manner owes it to herself to set aside the trust factor and review the information. Anything at odds with her situation, especially information relating to net worth, gross income, risk tolerance, and investment objectives, should be reported and corrected before investment decisions are made.

The Prospectus, Also Known as How I Cured My Insomnia Law dictates that you cannot purchase new securities without being provided with a prospectus (unless the securities are exempt from this requirement). Reading a prospectus means absorbing several pages of dense language printed in small type. If you don't have a background in financial law, the average prospectus has all the communication value of a bad translation from Sanskrit. About the only message you'll absorb from a prospectus is that investing is hopelessly complex and should be attempted only by a professional or in the presence of one—that is, a licensed broker or advisor.

You have 48 hours after receiving a prospectus to change your mind and ask for your money back. There are people in this world who have amputated their own limbs when necessary. There are also people without a law degree who can fathom the meaning of every phrase and intent in a mutual fund prospectus in one reading. I suspect the numbers of each are about equal.

From a practical standpoint, you need address only two key elements in any mutual fund prospectus.

What are the investment objectives of the fund? Is it to invest in Tibetan microbiological ventures when you agreed to purchase units in a conservative Canadian blue-chip value fund? Is it to generate income when you thought you were investing in long-term capital growth? If the description does not match the investment strategy you understood your advisor to have recommended, call within 48 hours of receiving the prospectus and ask for clarification.

What are the fund's charges and fees? Is a sales commission being paid to your advisor? If so, how much is it, and was it negotiable? Does the fund waive a front-end commission for a back-end deferred sales charge (DSC)? Were you aware of this? Do you agree to it? How much is the management expense ratio (MER), the amount of your investment that is withdrawn by the mutual fund management firm each year? Both DSCs and MERs represent money out of your RRSP, and are detailed in the next chapter.

Discretionary Trading: Close Your Eyes, Cover Your Ears, and Hang On   Never relinquish the right to approve decisions on buying and selling assets in your RRSP except under extraordinary circumstances. The decision should remain yours alone, and you should agree to transactions only after your advisor provides sufficient rationale and reveals any costs involved. Brokers and advisors who perform transactions without consultation or approval are engaging in discretionary trading, a practice that is illegal unless a signed agreement is provided by the client.

The opportunity for a broker or advisor to trade in a client's account without prior consultation opens the door to the possibility of churning an account—buying and selling common shares, mutual fund units, bonds, and other investments over and over for the sole purpose of generating income for the broker through the commissions earned from each transaction. Evidence that trades in your account have been conducted without consultation and approval should be presented to the branch manager of the firm handling your account, along with a demand that the practice cease and any losses incurred as a result of the trading be reimbursed. If the brokerage refuses to do so, seek legal counsel. Even if the brokerage replaces your losses, consider changing firms. Churning is theft, and why should you trust anyone who has stolen from you?

The Compliance Officer: He's Either With You or Against You (Hint: He's Not Always With You)
Every investment firm boasts a compliance officer or, if the firm is substantial enough, several of them, dedicated to ensuring that certain rules of investment policy are followed. This may be reassuring to investors who like the idea of someone watching over their accounts and the actions of their broker or advisor. It should not be. The primary role of compliance officers in a brokerage or securities trading firm is to protect the firm, not the assets of clients.

The Investment Dealers Association of Canada, the industry's self-regulating organization, defines the role of a compliance officer as "a support function, much like a legal department, and not a business line function. In the normal course, the Compliance Department does not have direct authority over line personnel such as those in Sales and Trading." And later: "Investigations which include a review of the supervision of business functions may not directly involve Compliance Officers, whose role is to advise and support the Executives responsible for those functions."[4] Nothing in the description addresses the need to protect individual investors.

Obviously, if a compliance officer is made aware of actions that appear to conflict with the client's needs or directions, he will—or should—investigate, applying cease-and-desist rules if necessary. On the knife-edge of decision making, however, the compliance officer's actions will be directed toward avoiding damage to the firm rather than damage to the client's interests. Often, of course, these amount to the same thing. But not always.

When clients of Michael Holoday called the compliance officer at Holoday's brokerage firm to complain about problems in their account statements, their queries were directed back to the broker. In retrospect, this was like complaining about a fox in the henhouse and being told the fox would fix things. The same compliance officer, once Holoday's actions became apparent, eventually alerted the police to his discoveries, and justice began its slow and agonizing process. Had the compliance officer acted on the clients' behalf rather than that of the brokerage firm when questions were first raised, Holoday's scams would have ended months earlier.

Things have changed since then, the industry assures us. Perhaps. But the principal role of the compliance officer remains to protect the firm's interests first.

Monthly Statements: They Are Not Junk Mail Think of each RRSP statement as a weather vane, revealing in which direction the wind is blowing, and how strongly. You are looking for confirmation of any transactions that occurred, evidence of transactions you do not recall approving, fees or charges against your account you do not understand, and the general status of your plan, indicating either reassuring growth or disturbing losses.

Losses should not necessarily trigger a call to your broker or advisor. During the extended bear market of 1999–2003, even clients of the brightest, most dedicated advisors suffered losses in equity-based mutual funds and individual stocks. In situations such as this, the key is not whether you lose but how much the losses stack up against your personal investment strategy and the general investment environment. A quick glance at the financial pages of a newspaper will provide a basic benchmark. Has the Toronto Stock Exchange dropped by 5 percent over the past month? If so, a 3 percent loss in your Canadian equities is not something to fret about.

You don't need to scan your statement like a beady-eyed tax collector studying a corporate balance sheet. You do need to take it seriously, check for any surprises, and file it away at least until your next review with your broker or advisor.

Comfort Letters: Do Not Take Comfort in Receiving One   Unsolicited communication from your broker should be welcomed from time to time, with the exception of a happiness, or comfort, letter. Such a letter may appear on the letterhead of your broker or advisor, the brokerage branch manager, or the compliance officer, and its wording will change according to the purpose of the person sending it. Somewhere in the body of the letter, however, you will discover one or more of these queries:

- Are you satisfied with the performance of your account and the service provided by your broker or advisor?
- Do you understand that risk is associated with all investing activities?
- Do you review your financial statements on a regular basis?
- If you had a question or comment about your account, would you contact your broker directly?
- Are you aware that certain charges may be applied to your account according to the trading activity, "etc."?

The letter may request you to acknowledge its contents, sign your name at the bottom, and return it to the brokerage as soon as possible. The brokerage will likely pay the postage.

Such a letter should bring neither comfort nor happiness to you. Instead, it should set red lights flashing and sirens screaming. Happiness/comfort letters might better be termed trouser letters, because they are designed to cover the advisor's ass. Their arrival is an almost certain indicator that something may be awry in your account, and your acknowledgement of the account's status, confirmed with your signature, could enable the firm and its staff to successfully defend itself against charges of malfeasance should the value of your RRSP drop through the floor.

What kinds of things might prompt a brokerage to issue such a letter? Any of the following:

- Excessive trading in your account, suggesting churning
- Substantial losses, beyond that suffered by the market in general
- The presence of unsuitable high-risk investments
- A dramatic change in investment strategy
- The opening of a margin account or other activities suggesting unprecedented levels of risk
- High commissions and fees withdrawn from your account balance

Your best response to a happiness/comfort letter is a refusal to sign it. Instead, telephone the sender and ask the following questions, noting their response:

- What prompted you to send me this letter?
- What is there about my account that is causing concern?
- Have I suffered unusual losses?
- Am I trading too much?
- Are the commissions too high for my account?
- Are either the brokerage or my broker/advisor being investigated?

- Did you send this letter to other clients?
- Is the activity in my account consistent with my investment objectives?
- By the way—what are my investment objectives according to your records?

Once again: *Never sign any document relating to your account without fully understanding its meaning and implications, because such a document is almost certainly designed to provide the brokerage with protection somewhere down the road.* In one of the most egregious examples of employing documents as weapons, Michael Holoday asked a client to sign a letter praising Holoday's performance, then used the letter to allay concerns at a brokerage where he sought employment. A year later, when Holoday's fraudulent activities were revealed, that brokerage sued the client for $10 million, arguing that the letter bearing the client's signature represented 50 percent of its decision to hire Holoday. Since the brokerage was claiming a potential $20 million loss, the brokerage claimed that its client owed the firm $10 million. Welcome to the investment industry.

The Gospel According to John De Goey

How can clients believe that their best interests are being addressed once they understand that the primary role of the compliance officer is to protect the brokerage, and a major goal of management is to motivate the advisors to generate income via commissions from trades within client accounts?

A solution may be at hand, encroaching into the industry with all the speed of a glacier and none of its power. It is led by an articulate financial advisor named John J. De Goey. De Goey boasts the familiar alphabet of professional qualifications behind his name, but that's where the similarity with the majority of brokers and advisors ends. For one thing, his resumé includes a stint with Consumer and

Corporate Affairs Canada rather than the banking or accounting background most advisors bring to the job. This experience undoubtedly influenced an even more remarkable difference between him and other financial advisors: He wants to see the commission-based system replaced with direct fees charged separately to clients, and the sooner the better.

"Financial advisors call themselves professionals," De Goey says in his enthusiastic and articulate manner, "but they are not. Most are commission-based sales agents masquerading as professionals. Name one true profession that depends entirely on commissions paid by the products or services they recommend. There is none, and the industry has to start admitting it."[5]

"The current system is inherently unfair to the investor," he explains. "Consider mutual funds. Some pay no commissions, but good luck getting a commission-based advisor to recommend one, no matter how well it fits your needs. Others pay varying rates of commissions and incentives. How can an advisor claim to be unbiased in his or her recommendations when their decision has a direct and substantial impact on their income?" In that situation, De Goey suggests, who can blame advisors and brokers for making recommendations that benefit them most?

The motivation for an advisor to recommend investments that suit the advisor's needs rather than the client's is strengthened by the lack of any legal recourse for the investor. An advisor who recommends high-risk investments, such as derivatives, risks being accused of providing inappropriate advice, and both the advisor and the firm management could be subjected to fines (but not always—see Chapters 9 and 10). An advisor who proposes a Canadian equity-based mutual fund that charges high management fees and kicks back a large proportion to the advisor, rather than another fund with superior performance but no kickbacks, risks nothing and gains substantially.

Moving from the current system to one free of embedded commissions will prove neither swift nor easy, but De Goey is convinced it is inevitable. "In the fullness of time, the industry must reinvent itself as a true profession," he claims. "At the beginning it may involve short-term pain for long-term gain, but we financial advisors are always preaching the idea of long-term benefits, so this should fit right in."

While De Goey hoped to stir up a hornet's nest of industry controversy with his 2003 book *The Professional Financial Advisor,* a year after his book's appearance there was still no stampede by advisors toward the new investment Jerusalem. Why not? "It's like Christianity," De Goey smiles, picking up on the analogy. "Everybody wants to go to heaven but nobody wants to die first."

Or perhaps the industry snubbed De Goey's book because it was more concerned with expressing hysteria over something less specific than his proposals, and less imminent as well. This was the so-called *Fair Dealing Model (FDM),* an elephantine document that took four years to be delivered in early 2004 by the Ontario Securities Commission (OSC), which expected another two years of debate before any of its proposals would be implemented. (As we shall see in Chapter 9, the OSC often makes the mills of the gods look like merry-go-rounds.)

In its 250-plus pages, the *FDM*'s major components are a proposal for three kinds of relationships, a single licensing requirement for brokers and advisors, and transparency where fees, commissions, and sales charges are concerned. Nothing in the document is newer or more revolutionary than canned soup. Models for the three relationships already exist as self-directed plans, full-service brokerages, and discretionary trading. Yet many industry members, led by Advocis, the country's largest association of financial advisors, protested as though the *FDM* incorporated threats to their first-born. While the industry has both a reason and a right to explore proposals requiring them to keep detailed records on the advice submitted to clients, many of the responses from its members were more hysterical than helpful. Advocis howled that the proposal was "an unjustified power grab that will further fragment the regulatory system in Canada," adding that the OSC model "would add significant new costs at a time when compliance expenses are already out of hand."[6] By mid-2004, a wide consensus within the investment industry suggested that the *FDM* was more than flawed.

Say, Just Where *Are* Those Customers' Yachts?

None of the industry's negative response to the *FDM* and its goals surprised anyone, since more than a year before the OSC released its missive the president of the Independent Financial Brokers of Canada (IFBC) called the document "very, very scary," adding that the OSC "can just act in the public interest to seize you and take you before the courts. We're seriously concerned about that—this is Big Brother gone wild!"[7]

Any legitimate concerns that Advocis and the IFBC might have made were buried in a frenzied negative response ignoring issues that spawned the OSC's efforts in the first place. One was the unfair nature of the commission-based compensation system for brokers and advisors who claim their function is to prescribe and employ investment policies in the sole interests of their clients. The other was the result of a survey among licensed brokers and advisors, many of them Advocis and IFBC members, stating that 75 percent of them agreed that the payments earned from mutual funds and other investment instruments affected their decisions in recommending one over the other.

Assuming the OSC *Fair Dealing Model* were implemented in anything like its original draft, the negative reaction of industry groups such as Advocis and the IFBC was more than inappropriate—it was foolish and counterproductive. By acting like 1950s-era politicians seeing Communists under every bed and howling at any change that might threaten their remuneration schedule, they refused to acknowledge the inequities of the current system and the growing public ire against their "profession."

It remains to be seen if De Goey succeeds in dragging his colleagues toward genuine professional status. As long as Eliot Spitzer grabs headlines with his crusade against Wall Street malefactors, and millions of Canadians grow aware of the manner in which the investment odds are stacked against them, the problem will not vanish beneath cries of anguish from some brokers and advisors that their financial future is being threatened.

More than 60 years ago, Fred Schwed authored a critical look at Wall Street in a book titled *Where Are the Customers' Yachts?* The book has remained in print since, and until the answer is provided by brokers and advisors whose dreams of financing their yacht purchases are driven by hidden fees and commissions paid for by their clients, neither the book nor skepticism about their "profession" is likely to vanish.

Mutual Funds:
You Win, They Win;
You Lose, They Still Win

For Kathleen Sinclair,[1] there was much to mourn and a little to be thankful for in 1999. She mourned the sudden death of her husband at age 55, but she was thankful that she had no mortgage on their house, almost $100,000 in her husband's RRSP (transferred to her as beneficiary), and about an equal amount in Canada Savings Bonds held outside the RRSP.

"Spence used to buy bonds every year, as a form of saving," she explains, seated near a window in a waterfront restaurant. She remains youthful and vibrant at 57, although her expression slips into one of sadness as her story unfolds. "Whenever they matured, he would buy more. Lately, they didn't pay much interest, but Spence just liked the idea of having an investment that was backed by the government and made more money than a bank savings account."

Unsure of what to do with the bonds maturing a year after her husband's death, Kathleen responded to a newspaper advertisement for a local brokerage firm. "When I called, they referred me to a man who said he had several years' experience dealing with people just like me—people with a fair bit of money who were unsure how to handle it," she recalls. "He kept telling me I needed to get 'more bang for my buck' and stuff like that, because the next 10 years would be critical in making the money I would need for retirement."

A week after their first meeting, the broker submitted his proposal: Kathleen should sell the bonds, purchase an equity-based mutual fund, and leverage her investment for maximum growth. "I had no idea what he meant by 'leverage,'" she says. "He told me it was a method of doubling my profits without doubling my investment. He said that's what smart people did, and that I was in a perfect position to take advantage of it. He really stressed that I needed to make as much money as possible over the next 5 to 10 years." She smiles briefly at her own words. "He was very convincing."

Kathleen's broker explained that the brokerage would loan her $100,000 using the equity in her home as security. Together with the cash from the savings bonds, this would generate $200,000 to be invested in a global mutual fund that the broker said had been averaging 15 percent growth each year for the past 10 years. "He showed me the charts and brochures," Kathleen says, "and he circled the average return. It was 15 percent, which he explained meant my money would double every seven years." The $100,000 would be loaned on a demand basis at 6 percent interest per year, reviewed and adjusted annually.

Soon Kathleen was signing documents and providing personal data on a Know Your Client form, a loan application, and other paperwork required to open an account at the brokerage. Although Kathleen described her investment knowledge and experience as limited, the broker suggested she write it down as average. "He assured me that everybody said their client was average, and 'some people upstairs at our place,' that's how he put it, got nervous if it was different." He increased the annual income of her part-time sales clerk's job from $24,000 to $30,000, and estimated the value of Kathleen's home at $325,000 instead of the $250,000 she had proposed.

Within a week, a statement arrived from the brokerage listing the transaction and showing that Kathleen owned 17,770 units of the mutual fund, priced at $11.25 per unit. "That's the only time it was even close to $200,000," Kathleen recalls. "Every month after that, my statement showed less and less money."

After six months, Kathleen's investment had dwindled to less than $180,000. "I called to tell him that I was worried," she says. "He told me that markets go up and down all the time and I should stay calm, I was well invested. He told me that he had lots of money in the same mutual fund. 'I'm not worrying,' he said, 'so why should you?' He treated me like I was a fool, a child, just some pest he needed to get rid of."

Two months later, the mutual fund was valued at less than $170,000 and Kathleen was reading news reports about a bear market. "I had no idea what that meant," she says, "until somebody told me that nobody would be making money on the stock market for a long time. 'But I don't have money in the stock market,' I told her. 'I own mutual funds.' That's how foolish I was. I thought there was a difference."

Almost one year after purchasing the mutual fund, her account had dwindled 20 percent to barely $160,000. She began calling her broker, seeking assurance that she was doing the right thing, but he rarely took her calls. "I began to believe he was avoiding me," she says. "When I did speak to him, he would get impatient, tell me that the markets could turn around tomorrow and that I'd be thanking him then. But nothing turned around. I spoke to my son, who lives in Montreal, and he was furious. 'Tell him you want out of [the mutual fund] now,' he said, 'and don't take No for an answer—they're ripping you off!' So that's what I did."

Kathleen called her broker the next day, insisting that she speak to him. "I want to sell that fund," she told him. "It's not right. I didn't expect to get rich, but I didn't want to lose money either. My husband worked and saved for years to get that money and I can't stand seeing it disappear like that."

This time the broker sent documents for her to sign. She did, noting they confirmed she was closing her account and instructing the brokerage to forward a cheque for the balance. The cheque and a summary statement arrived two weeks later.

"That was just about the worst day of my life," she says. Her eyes begin to blink and fill with tears. "I felt as close to being ..." She hesitates, looking for the word. "Assaulted as I ever want to feel."

The statement noted that her $200,000 investment had been redeemed for a gross amount of $156,910. From this, the brokerage claimed $100,000 from the loan used to leverage the purchase of the mutual fund units and another $6125 in interest and other charges for the $100,000 loan over one year. The mutual fund sponsor had already subtracted $12,000 for the deferred sales charge. "It just said 'DSC amount,' Kathleen says, shaking her head. "I had no idea what it meant, and when I called the broker, the one who had looked after my account, he snapped at me. 'It means deferred sales charge, which is 6 percent if you cash out in the first year,' he said. 'Didn't you read your prospectus?'"

Kathleen's venture into mutual funds as a way of preserving and increasing her husband's nest egg built over 25 years had shrunk from $100,000 to $38,785 in barely 12 months. Furious at the news, Kathleen's son wrote to the brokerage demanding that it replace at least a portion of her loss. The brokerage refused, citing the documents used to open her account. He hired a lawyer to make the same demands, and these were rejected as well. The lawyer billed Kathleen's son for his services and suggested his mother contact a firm specializing in investment lawsuits. This firm asked for a $5000 retainer, said it would bill Kathleen monthly for hours expended on her behalf, and suggested the odds of recovery were "about 50-50 based on experience with other cases such as this."

Kathleen decided not to take action.

For 60 years after their introduction, mutual funds were mysterious playthings of the investment-savvy and the idle rich. Most people understood that common stocks were shares in a public corporation; owning one share out of a million available meant you owned a similar portion of the actual company (or, more correctly, of the company's publicly available capitalization), as well as a portion of profits declared as dividends. Investing money in the right company at the right time promised better opportunities for real wealth in the long term than salting pennies away in a bank account. It still does. But for the sometime-investor focusing on her RRSP as the principal investment opportunity in her life, stocks in public companies carry the aura of roulette tables and shell games.

The challenge for small investors was deciding what companies' shares to buy, how much to pay for them, and when to sell them. Most people lack the time, inclination, and knowledge to perform these tasks effectively, and mutual funds solve the problem by pooling money from thousands of investors into one professionally managed operation. For a fee, known as the management expense ratio or MER, a fund manager makes these decisions and his success is measured by the growth or decline of the fund's value over time. The MER is applied to the total amount of all money invested in the fund and subtracted on a daily basis over the calendar year. A MER of 2.5 percent applied to a $100 million fund—a rather small fund today—yields $2.5 million to the fund manager annually.

When you invest in a mutual fund, you purchase a number of units at the current market price. A $10,000 investment in a fund whose units are valued at $10 buys you 1000 units. As the total value of the fund increases or decreases, the value of each individual unit rises and falls accordingly. At each year-end, funds distribute profits as extra units. The profits are generated by a rise in the market value of the companies that the fund has invested in, by the dividends paid to the shareholders (mutual funds that own stocks are shareholders), or both. Instead of increasing the value of individual units, distributions increase the number of units in the same proportion. Thus, should the mutual fund described above yield a 10 percent profit in one year, your $10,000 investment might now represent 1100 units valued at $10 each, not 1000 units valued at $11.[2]

Mutual funds remained exotic to traditionally conservative Canadians for years, in part because they were sold by the same brokers who traded stocks. Most Canadians, especially those with RRSPs, chose to save rather than invest, treating stocks and bonds as mysterious alien devices requiring special skills, inside information, and perhaps even a degree of larceny. The vaults of the chartered banks bulged with cash deposits in savings accounts that paid a fixed interest rate, were at least partially guaranteed, and could be accessed with the stroke of a pen on a withdrawal form, all because mutual funds made people uncomfortable.

Even with growing participation in RRSPs through the 1970s and into the 1980s, Canadians still preferred the dull certainty of daily interest savings accounts and guaranteed interest certificates (GICs) over the baffling vagueness of mutual funds. In 1987, barely $20 billion, less than $850 per capita, was invested in mutual funds by Canadians. Yet 13 years later, well over $400 billion was sitting in Canadian mutual funds, representing $15,525 for every man, woman, and child in the country.[3] What happened?

The original $20 billion grew as a result of an increase in the value of equity markets over the years, but this growth was nowhere near the 2000 percent increase represented by mutual fund values. Instead, four loosely connected occurrences in 1987 boosted the natural spirit of free enterprise to produce what some observers describe as a boon to retirement-bound Canadians, and what others consider an investment device worthy of a Frankenstein.

Four Horsemen of the Mutual Fund Invasion

The infamous stock market crash of October 19, 1987, represents a watershed point in the story. Black Monday, as it was tagged, marked history's largest single-day drop in North American stock market values, when prices fell 22 percent. The resulting chaos and paper-based carnage generated headlines and commentary that echoed long after market prices began recovering their previous levels. Canadians who had not invested in equities to that point grew aware that substantial money had been lost in one day, but they could not ignore that the same losers appeared to be recovering their losses rather quickly.

It was no great distance from there to the concept of earning similar levels of wealth while reducing the chance of losing it in a repeat of Black Monday. The idea gained strength when pundits began mouthing assurances that there would be no repeat of that event, blamed for the most part on preprogrammed computer trading. Changing the computer programs would reduce the chance of such catastrophic losses in the future without limiting opportunities for growth, an industry statement that novices heeded with great interest.

The year 1987 also marked the 40th birthday of the first wave of baby boomers. Many things happen to people when they turn 40, and not all of them are necessarily bad. The idea of retiring while retaining your health, both mental and physical, grows more appealing with every day beyond the age of 40. One of the most successful marketing campaigns in Canadian history, London Life's Freedom 55 theme, launched in the late 1980s, consisted of two messages to the early boomers: You are just 15 years away from early retirement, and, How are you going to accumulate the money to enjoy it? Not with GICs and savings accounts, that's for sure. There had to be a better way, and so the boomers began studying alternatives more closely.

Event number three in 1987 was marked by the deregulation in Canada of four interlinked services: banks, trust companies, insurance companies, and stockbrokers. Until then, each industry had been effectively isolated from the others, with the scope of the services they could offer restricted by regulations. Banks did not deal in equity investments; trust companies could not make personal loans; only licensed brokers could sell insurance; and stock brokers were the financial equivalent of the neighbourhood drugstore, trading investment products for cash. Deregulation of banking, insurance, and investments produced many changes to the face of the country, but in a dollars and cents measure none had a greater impact than the opportunity for chartered banks and trust companies to provide and promote equity investment opportunities, sold as mutual funds first through their own branches and later through their own brokerage companies.

Banking deregulation altered the public's perception of mutual funds almost overnight. One day they were considered mysterious playthings of the wealthy, the next day they were being discussed by the same smiling folks you met when you made a deposit in your chequing account, or paid your telephone bill, or shyly enquired about a loan to buy a new car. The structure of mutual funds hadn't changed, for the most part, but the method of marketing them had. By the late 1980s, every chartered bank in Canada was promoting its own family of funds, encouraging clients to move their money out of GICs and savings accounts and into the funds. It was tempting, promising, and painless.

Mutual funds were no longer intimidating. Were there any more solid, secure, and trustworthy institutions in the world than Canadian chartered banks, which retained at least a vestige of the same prudent and conservative philosophies of the dour Scots who founded most of them? If banks were offering mutual funds, could they be that risky? And since mutual funds are favoured by the rich, can there be any better way to retire at 55 and spend the winter walking a beach in Florida? Not bloody likely!

With the banks marketing their own house brands of funds, independent fund managers such as Trimark, Mackenzie, Templeton, AGF, and others stepped up their sales promotion programs, all aimed at RRSP owners. The banks might have the consumers' confidence, but the independent fund managers had the performance figures and the marketing savvy to grab the attention of investors. Banks not only were new to the mutual fund game, they were also conservative. This made consumers feel rather more comfortable with the bank funds, but comfort eventually was edged aside by greed. Where the banks were promoting annual returns of 10 to 12 percent, the stronger independent funds were boasting returns of 15 to 20 percent. Bigger returns meant faster RRSP growth, and faster growth meant edging closer to the beach walked by those smug and satisfied retirees in the Freedom 55 TV commercials.

The Marketing Gimmick That Spawned a Monster

One downside was apparent for mutual funds operated by independent managers. Novice Canadian investors had difficulty getting around it, and the independent funds looked on it as an anchor holding back a roaring speedboat.

Banks did not apply sales commissions to their mutual funds, promoting them as no load, which meant, in the promotion vernacular, *Every Penny of Your Investment Goes to Work from Day One*. The banks' funds were sold by salaried employees who, once licensed and qualified to carry out the transaction, handled mutual fund sales the same way they opened savings accounts, sold GICs, and accepted loan applications.

Independent mutual funds, however, were sold through financial advisors and brokers who earned their income from commissions on the stocks, bonds, and mutual funds traded on behalf of their clients. Sales commissions for mutual funds came off the top of the investor's nest egg and could reach as high as 9 percent. Unsophisticated investors naturally balked at this idea. If an RRSP investor had $10,000 to plunk into a savings account or a bank-sponsored mutual fund, all 10 grand began earning interest from the first day. Handing $10,000 to an independent mutual fund could mean that as little as $9100 made it into the fund. Practically, it made sense—somebody had to be paid for doing the work of connecting you with the mutual fund. Psychologically, it was a poke in the eye, and many Canadians investing in mutual funds chose the comfort and economies of bank-sponsored funds.

In truth, the upfront sales commissions were negotiable, although polite Canadians either chose to go along with whatever amount their advisor proposed or simply walked away. Some brokers and advisors used the high front-end load as leverage to close a deal by offering, without being asked, to reduce their "usual" 9 percent commission to half that amount. Even then, it hurt to see 4 or 5 percent of your hard-earned money go into someone else's pocket right off the top. The truly wealthy, who had been purchasing mutual funds for years, never paid anywhere near that level of sales commissions. With $1 million and more to invest in a fund, a tiny percentage of the total was more than adequate compensation to the salesperson. Half of 1 percent in a $1 million investment meant $5000 in the salesperson's pocket, an amount that could be recovered by the investor in one day. Only the little guys, who could least afford it, saw front-end commissions take a major bite out of their savings. Life was unfair.

And then Mackenzie changed everything.

Of all the independent mutual fund companies in Canada, none was more aggressive or savvy at marketing its products than Mackenzie Financial Corporation. Borrowing from industries as varied as beer and tobacco, Mackenzie literally roared ahead of the pack in the 1980s when it sponsored a Formula One racing car emblazoned with its logo. While enticing customers with racetrack glamour, they were rewarding brokerage salespeople in a similar jet-setting manner. The company's annual sales promotion programs for advisors and mutual fund salespeople grew infamous for the scope of the rewards offered. Place enough clients and, more importantly, enough clients' money with Mackenzie mutual funds and you were jetted off to a five-star hotel in Hawaii, Barbados, Las Vegas, and similar destinations at Mackenzie's expense. Well, not really—every penny in a mutual fund originates with clients, but who wants to dwell on that while sipping mai tais in Maui?

Mackenzie, and the advisors and salespeople who promoted its funds, was doing well in 1987, but Mackenzie introduced a way they could all do even better. That was the year Mackenzie launched the Industrial Horizon Fund, sold without a front-end load. When you put money into the Industrial Horizon Fund, not a dime was skimmed off for the salesperson or financial advisor who sold you the fund. Advisors loved pushing the Industrial Horizon Fund to whomever they might encounter because it was easy to seal the deal. Other independent funds took money off the top of your investment to pay your broker, but now, with the Industrial Horizon Fund, neither Mackenzie nor the broker took a penny. Was this evidence of unprecedented generosity? Not in the least. It was the effect of a deferred sales charge, or DSC. Brokers and advisors called it a gold mine, because they still earned about 5 percent commission up front, just as before. Small investors called it a godsend. Over the years, critics began calling it a monster. The DSC works like this.

While none of your initial investment is deducted to cover sales commissions when you purchase units in the fund, a sales ("redemption") charge is applied if you sell them within a fixed period. (DSC mutual funds are referred to as "back-end load" funds for this reason.) When first introduced, this period extended nine years, but it has since been cut to seven years for most funds. The amount of the redemption charge is reduced each year the fund is held. Hold the fund long enough and you pay no sales charge when you sell it. A typical redemption schedule looks like this:

REDEEM YOUR ASSETS DURING ...	AND YOU PAY
Year 1	5.5%
Year 2	5.0%
Year 3	4.5%
Year 4	4.0%
Year 5	3.5%
Year 6	2.5%
Year 7	1.5%
Year 8 and beyond	0%

Since equity-based mutual funds—funds that invest primarily in publicly traded shares of corporations—were touted as ideal for long-term investors, this feature sounded like a good fit. It became an even better fit when advisors actively encouraged clients to hold onto the fund even when the earnings were disappointing, a brilliant tactic that put a positive spin on a negative feature. If your mutual fund was losing money instead of making money, why dispose of it in the first few years and pay a DSC for the privilege, ensuring that you'll lose even more money?

Consider this scenario: You invest $10,000 in the *Standback &
Duck* funds and discover to your horror, two years later, that the
value of your investment has declined to $8000. Hey, markets go up
and markets go down, and nothing about mutual funds is guaranteed,
right? Still, you begin to question the financial acumen of the
people running the fund and decide to get your money out and cut
your losses—until your financial advisor points out that a 5 percent
redemption charge will be applied against the original investment in
the fund, representing another $500 loss to you. Wouldn't it be better
to hang on and wait for the fund to recover? Many people do.

The marketing appeal to investors who failed to foresee this
scenario was phenomenal, and within months of its introduction
virtually every mutual fund sponsor was beating the drum about its
own back-end load fund. Like other aspects of the mutual fund
industry created to attract and retain clients, the DSC was a song-
and-dance act produced by fund sponsors, directed by brokers and
advisors, and acted out by their trusting clients. It was also more
proof, if proof were still needed, that there is no free lunch.[4]

Return of the No Free Lunch Rule

Everyone in the investment industry bragged about the benefits of
back-end load funds to investors, but no one discussed costs and
incentives, except in the deepest, darkest paragraphs of the fund's
prospectus. Mutual fund salespeople—advisors, brokers, insurance
sales staff, and anyone else with a licence to trade securities—continued to earn fat upfront commissions from their sales, just as before.
The funds could afford to pay the sales commission up front *because
they skimmed a larger amount off the top of the client's investment year
after year* through a higher MER.

As noted earlier, the MER is drawn out of client assets to cover the
fund's operating expenses. For the majority of funds, the MER does

not cover the cost of trading shares held within the fund. Mutual fund managers buy and sell shares and bonds according to the fund's objectives. Just as you would pay a fee or commission when trading shares in the stock market, fund managers have to pay similar charges. Well, actually, they don't—as a fund unit holder, you pay for the trades, but you don't know it. Nor do you see it, because the cost is hidden from both you and the MER. If the fund manager decides to purchase 1000 shares of Acme Widgets, priced at $10 per share, to be included in the fund portfolio, and the trading commission to be paid is $100, the price per share will actually be $1.10 per share. Hey, you didn't expect the fund to dip into its MER, did you? So in addition to the MER deducted from the fund's performance, trading costs are subtracted as well. In many mutual funds, this can be considerable. Some funds actually buy and sell as much as 60 percent or more of their portfolio each year. Every trade costs you money in poorer performance.

In theory, the MER is related to the degree of effort and expertise needed to manage the fund on behalf of the investors, or unit holders. In practice, they tend to be determined by whatever the market will bear and, in Canada, the market bears too much.

Most Canadians pay little attention to the MER because they have no idea what it is, how it is paid, and how much it costs. The awareness is growing, but it remains appallingly low, and during the late 1980s it was essentially non-existent.

This made it easy to increase the MERs of DSC-based funds high enough to accommodate the now-hidden sales commissions. Once upfront and deducted from the original investment, the commissions were now concealed and paid for over time by the mutual fund investors through a higher MER. Clients were encouraged or induced to retain the DSC funds long enough for the commission to be recovered through the increased MER. No Las Vegas magic act made better use of smoke and mirrors.

Among the many pros and cons of investing your RRSP or RRIF in mutual funds, one fact is acknowledged by just about everyone outside the mutual fund industry (and perhaps surreptitiously by some within the industry): *Excessive mutual fund MERs represent a serious drain on the financial resources of people who purchase the fund units.* A superb illustration of this view is provided by Barclays Global Investors, a maverick fund company distributing exchange traded funds, or ETFs. (For more about ETFs, see Chapter 6).

In the spring of 2004, the cheeky folk at Barclays estimated that April 12 would be Fee Freedom Day for Canadian mutual fund investors. This was the point where mutual fund investors stopped paying their mutual fund managers, through the MER rates, and started paying themselves.[5] Mid-April was actually a substantial improvement over the previous year. In 2003, Fee Freedom Day arrived on July 28, meaning that more than half the earnings from mutual fund investments were paid to mutual fund managers and not to the investors.

Another illustration of the unfairness of the Canadian securities industry concerns U.S. mutual funds and their availability to Canadians. Or, more accurately, their unavailability. The North American Free Trade Agreement (NAFTA) was created to open the door for a flood of goods and services across The World's Longest Undefended Line on a Map. Originally, this was to include stocks and mutual funds. Today, you can purchase shares in American companies such as Microsoft, Exxon, and General Electric, but do not attempt to buy units in well-managed U.S. mutual funds with low MERs. In spite of NAFTA, they remain unavailable on this side of the border, and Bay Street has made no effort to remove the barrier. Why should it? The average Canadian mutual fund charges a MER of 2.62 percent, while the average U.S. fund applies half that amount. Would lower MERs help Canadians build their RRSPs and manage their RRIFs more effectively? Bet on it. Will our mutual fund mavens block the availability of low-MER U.S.-managed funds such as Vanguard, with its enviable track record of generating returns for investors, to be sold in Canada? Same bet.

Many mutual fund sponsors seem to view their MERs as an unlimited source of income to be tapped whenever they choose. How else to explain these statistics garnered by one of the leading research firms serving the Canadian investment industry?

1. The average MER of all mutual funds in Canada rose from 2.02 percent in 1995 to more than 2.6 percent as of April 30, 2004. No evidence of a correlation between these increased MERs and higher mutual fund expenses is apparent.
2. Almost 8 out of 10 mutual funds increased their MER levels between 1998 and 2002, a period when sharp drops in mutual fund returns were recorded virtually across the board.
3. Investors paid sponsors of Canadian mutual funds $2.8 billion via MERs in 1995. By 2002, this amount had quadrupled to more than $10 billion.[6]

Do not expect your financial advisor or mutual fund salesperson to discuss MERs unless challenged, at which point she will likely reply that the level of total return—the money you hope to make—is more important than the MER amount, which is the money the fund is certain to make. You might pause here for a moment to ponder who the winner might be in this business.

MER charges have been compared with the death of a thousand cuts, leaving you (or in this case, your RRSP portfolio) bleeding almost unnoticed. Prime examples: the original Trimark Fund, launched in 1981 and one of the most successful global equity funds (investing in companies around the world), and its DSC sibling, the Trimark Select Growth Fund, introduced in 1988, the year after Mackenzie shook up the industry with the DSC. Duplicating the front-end load Trimark Fund in every aspect but one, the Select

Growth Fund replaced the front-end load with a DSC, using the standard seven-year declining redemption charge. The original Trimark Fund boasted a MER of 1.62 percent, which was eminently reasonable for a fund of its scope and calibre. The Select Growth Fund applied a MER of 2.40, an increase of 50 percent. How much impact does the larger MER have on the fund's performance— or more specifically, on the money the fund generates for you and your RRSP? Compare the figures (as of January 31, 2004):

DSC VERSUS NO DSC – TRIMARK FUND RETURNS (%)				
FUND	3 YEARS	5 YEARS	10 YEARS	SINCE INCEPTION (MONTH/YEAR)
Trimark Fund	5.11	9.41	10.57	15.22 (9/81)
Select Growth Fund	4.52	8.79	9.45	11.57 (5/89)

SOURCE: GLOBEFUND.COM, FEBRUARY 10, 2004. REPRODUCED WITH PERMISSION.

Those are decent returns, especially over the long term, proving that Trimark's fund managers are earning their keep. (It also proves the point that mutual funds, carefully selected, continue to represent an essential element in any well-managed RRSP portfolio.) Apply the no free lunch rule, however, and the price becomes clear—a reduction of almost 3.5 percent annually over the life of each fund, *despite the fact that the investments in both funds are identical.*[7]

Higher MERs resulting from back-load funds are not the only price paid by investors who trust their advisors for guidance. The binding contractual agreement between the fund company and the investor in a DSC fund means a substantial penalty will be paid if the investor tries to act according to his or her own interests. If you were sold units in the AGF International Value Fund on a DSC basis sometime in 2000 or 2001, you learned this expensive lesson.

The International Value Fund was a star in AGF's stable through the late 1990s and into 2002. Its net sales of $1.6 billion in 2001—hardly a banner year for mutual funds—exceeded those of every other fund in Canada and, with total assets under management of over $7 billion, the fund was the second-largest of its kind in the country. Everyone acknowledged that the fund's success was the product of one man's genius. His name was Charles Brandes, and he managed over a third of all of AGF's mutual fund assets out of his San Diego–based company, Brandes Investment Partners. In the year 2000, Brandes managed to squeeze 27.78 percent return out of the fund for unit holders of the AGF fund, and even through the snarling bear market of 2001 he produced a profit while similar funds were sliding into a crevasse. Everyone was happy—unit holders who watched their RRSP values grow, financial advisors who were earning healthy sales commissions, and AGF, which boasted the largest, most successful foreign equity mutual fund in Canada. The only person unhappy, or at least not as happy as he might have been, was Brandes himself, and in early 2002 he announced that he was jumping ship from the Canadian mutual fund industry to launch his own line of funds.

The news shook the Canadian mutual fund industry, and while AGF management made reassuring noises to the folks who owned the $7 billion in fund assets, recent investors who purchased units on a DSC basis were faced with a difficult choice: remain with an unproven and probably inferior manager of their assets, or pay as much as 5.5 percent to jump ship and follow the guy whose performance they had sought in the first place. Most DSC funds permit you to switch within the family of funds—in this case, to another AGF fund—without paying a redemption charge. You can also redeem 10 percent of the value of your funds each year without incurring this charge. Neither option, of course, enables you to drop a fund without penalty if the fund proves either unsuccessful or unsuitable for your investment needs or, as in this case, when the attraction that drew you to the fund walks out the door.

Yet another invisible barrier to switching mutual funds exists. Like most ways that mutual funds get wealthy from your assets, it is invisible only to the people putting up the money. Everyone else in the industry knows about it. They just prefer not to discuss it.

Trailer Fees: You're Hitched and You Don't Know It

Much of the investment industry loves to trumpet the phrase "Buy, hold, and prosper!" like a mantra, suggesting that these three actions are all that's needed to ensure growth in your RRSP. In fact, mutual fund operator AIC Ltd. has trademarked the core expression as its corporate slogan: "Buy. Hold. And Prosper." The phrase originated with multi-billionaire investor Warren Buffet, who used it to summarize his investment philosophy of carefully choosing well-managed companies, buying shares in them at an attractive price, and building on that investment over time. This is far more complex and demanding than the three-verb inculcation employed to condense Buffet's strategy.[8]

"Buy, hold, and prosper," as created and practised by Buffet, has merit because it defers the taxes applicable when an investment is sold for a profit, enhancing long-term growth. It also works best for closed-end funds or corporations like Buffet's Berkshire Hathaway operation, and not nearly as well for open funds like the vast majority marketed to Canadians for RRSP purposes. Finally, it assumes that the "buy" portion of the recipe occurs only when the price of shares in a blue-chip corporation such as Petro-Canada or TD Bank are priced low enough to represent a bargain. Buying shares in companies when the price reflects or exceeds their true value rarely ensures prosperity. Overpay for any investment and you can "buy and hold" forever without making a penny.

In fact, "Buy, hold, and prosper" has greater meaning to the commission-based salespeople who foist DSC-based funds on their clients than to investors. Over the long term, fund salespeople prosper as long as their clients hold these funds, regardless of the fund's performance. *While the clients watch the value of their mutual fund (and RRSP investment) dribble away as a result of a bear market or substandard performance by the fund manager, the person who talked you into that turkey is growing wealthy from your original investment.*

How? With trailer fees, used by mutual fund companies to influence your financial advisor with your money. Trailer fees ensure prosperity for fund companies and advisors and, from time to time, even you. The difference is that your future prosperity is uncertain, while theirs is guaranteed.

A trailer fee is a sales commission paid to the person who sold you the mutual fund for as long as you own the units. Like every expense incurred by mutual funds, you get the bill. Once again, the bill is never presented to you, and mutual fund companies would prefer that, like Aunt Edith's drinking problem or Uncle Eddie's criminal past, you just not talk about it. (Why are they called trailer *fees* and not trailer *commissions*? Because you and I would balk at a commission paid where no transaction has been made to generate it. It's another example of mutual fund window dressing.)

As long as you retain ownership of the mutual fund units sold to you, the person who made the initial sale receives, every year, a portion of the assets you hold in that fund. The amount varies by fund company and fund type; it is as high as 1 percent for front-end load funds, and 0.5 percent for DSC funds.

Not every mutual fund pays trailer fees, nor does every fund carry a load, either front-end or back-end (DSC). Commission-based salespeople rarely if ever discuss no-load funds or acknowledge their existence. To commissioned-based advisors and brokers, no-load funds are like a drunk at a formal reception—everybody pretends he's not there.

If $100,000 of your RRSP is invested in *Standback & Duck* funds paying a trailer fee, as much as $1000 will be removed each year via the MER and forwarded to whoever sold you the fund, whether its value grows or not. Imagine if your advisor talked 100 clients into purchasing $10,000 worth of *Standback & Duck* funds each year. Who is really getting wealthy from these funds?

Trailer fees are a carry-over from the life insurance industry, where they were considered as nefarious as in the investment industry. The investment industry would prefer that you not know about them, and that people like me not talk about them. This was made clear in February 2004 when AIC, the "Buy. Hold. And Prosper" company, announced a new schedule of trailer fees payable to brokers and others selling high-MER/DSC funds managed by AIC. Here's how AIC promised to pay their commissioned "professionals" who sold the qualifying funds to their clients and encouraged the clients to Buy. Hold. And Prosper.

AIC FUNDS		
DSC YEAR	ANNUAL TRAILER FEE (%)	DSC REDEMPTION FEE (%)
1	0.500	6.0
2	0.525	5.5
3	0.550	5.0
4	0.575	4.5
5	0.600	4.0
6	0.625	3.5
7 and beyond	0.750	Nil

SOURCE: AIC FORM 03-1560-E (12/03).

Note that the trailer fee increases each year a client retains the AIC mutual fund in his or her portfolio. Imagine a client approaching the commissioned broker or advisor, three years after purchasing an AIC fund, to ask about the wisdom of selling the fund and transferring the investment to a different fund company in pursuit of better returns. Regardless of the fund's returns—and AIC funds by and large have not been stellar performers—the advisor must explain that it will cost the client 5 percent of her initial investment to withdraw from the fund as a result of the DSC, not a pleasant prospect if the fund's value has declined in the interim. In addition, moving out of an AIC fund will mean lost income to the advisor of as much as 0.75 percent of the client's investment every year. Do you honestly think all brokers and advisors will respond to the client's request for guidance with an unbiased opinion? Do you believe in the tooth fairy?

In the same February 2004 revised trailer fee schedule noted above, AIC made an extra effort to paint a rich and rosy future for advisors selling AIC funds, by converting the trailer fees from cold percentages to hot dollars (the Year 1 revenue includes the initial sales commission).

COMMISSIONS AND TRAILER FEES FOR SELECTED AIC FUNDS ($)								
CASH FLOW*	YEAR 1	YEAR 2	YEAR 3	YEAR 4	YEAR 5	YEAR 6	YEAR 7	TOTAL REVENUE
AIC Regular	5500	500	500	500	500	500	500	8500
AIC Pools	5750	750	750	750	750	750	750	10,250
AIC Funds	5500	525	550	575	600	625	750	9125

* Initial investment of $100,000; zero market appreciation

SOURCE: AIC FORM 03-1560-E (12/03).

Assuming no growth in the client's investment over seven years—a daunting thought, but not unheard of—the salesperson would have pocketed around $10,000 in sales commissions and trailer fees over that period, with the prospect of continuing future returns. Meanwhile, the client's investment hasn't shifted a penny. If the investment is worth less than the initial $100,000, the salesperson still collects, albeit not as much in actual dollars. If the client's investment increases, so does the annual trailer commission. If the client wins, the salesperson wins; if the client loses, the salesperson still wins. Just who is taking the risk here?

The iceberg of deception beneath this visible tip is revealed on the same AIC document listing these revised trailer commissions and DSC redemptions, for prominently displayed in the upper right-hand corner is the AIC admonition: *For Advisor Use Only—Not to be distributed to investors.*

AIC does not want current or potential investors to be aware of the amount of money withdrawn from their accounts to reward the "professional" commission-paid advisors. Indeed, it does not want investors to know of the very existence of trailers, or any other revelation illustrating how AIC drains money from the clients' asset base. This lack of transparency, and the intense effort of most mutual fund sponsors to keep their clients in the dark about such matters, drives people such as Glorianne Stromberg mad. Stromberg is the author of two scathing critiques of mutual fund sales and management policies. Referring to AIC's "not to be distributed to investors" chart and its "upwardly creeping trailer fee," Stromberg notes that "everything that comes out [of the clients' assets] is slightly more outrageous. We need to improve the disclosure system in the mutual fund industry, but every time a proposal is made to improve transparency, the industry either drags its feet or fights it directly."[9]

Nor was AIC the only fund sponsor eagerly looking for ways to fill its cash drawer at the expense of RRSP/RRIF owners. Investors Group, the country's largest mutual fund sponsor, jacked its DSC schedule up by as much as 200 percent in mid-2003, as the table below shows.

INVESTORS GROUP REDEMPTION FEES			
WHEN REDEEMED	OLD RATE	NEW RATE	INCREASE (%)
Years 1–2	3.0	5.5	83.3
Year 3	2.5	5.0	100.0
Year 4	2.0	4.5	125.0
Year 5	1.5	4.0	166.7
Year 6	1.0	3.0	200.0
Year 7	None	1.5!!!!	150.0
Year 8 and beyond	None	None	Unchanged

SOURCE: *GLOBE AND MAIL*, "HOW TO AVOID FEES," MAY 20, 2003. REPRODUCED WITH PERMISSION.

Did Investors Group raise its DSC schedule because the company needed more revenue to stave off financial disaster? Hardly. The previous year (2002), its parent company reported gross income from fees alone exceeding $1.8 billion, leaving a net income before interest, taxes, and dividends of almost $512 million, representing a 28 percent profit margin. Over the same year, Investors Group recorded sales of almost $5 billion and boasted total managed assets—the sum of all portfolios owned by its clients—of more than $37.5 billion.[10]

Was Investors Group planning to improve the quality of its service to clients, or perhaps reduce its MER, or add value to justify the higher DSC schedule? Apparently not. In fact, the company slipped in yet another squeeze play on its clients by adding to the new DSC schedule a note that it retained the right to apply redemption fees to clients who switched between Investors Group funds. By accepting your Investors Group advisor's recommendation to transfer your RRSP dollars into one of its DSC mutual funds, you agreed to pay a penalty to redeem the units even if the fund proved to be the biggest dog since Rin Tin Tin.

By the way, do not assume that shunning a fund with a DSC is one method of avoiding trailer fees. AGF, for example, offers both DSC and non-DSC options on many of its funds. With an AGF fund carrying a DSC, the advisor receives an upfront commission of 4.9 percent, reduced to 3 percent or less for a fund with no DSC. Why would an advisor propose purchasing a fund with no DSC? Would it be to free you from the penalty of selling the fund within a few years if you were unsatisfied with its performance? Perhaps. More likely, however, it is because most AGF equity funds pay an annual trailer fee on front-end loaded funds that is double that of DSC funds.

If you pay an upfront commission of 2.5 percent for a non-DSC fund from AGF, after five years your advisor has collected 7.5 percent of your original investment in commissions versus 7.4 percent (4.9 + [0.5 × 5]) with a DSC fund. For every year past the fifth, the front-end load sale puts your advisor ahead of the game. And if the fund increases in value year by year—hey, wasn't that the original idea?—the trailer fee grows accordingly, increasing the advisor's gain.

Brokers and advisors argue that trailer fees compensate them for services that do not involve trades and thus present no opportunity to earn commissions. There is undoubted value in the wise counsel of an advisor who recommends that you ignore transient hiccups in the market and economy and remain fixed to your established strategy, if this is indeed appropriate. Trusting that this advice is valid becomes a matter of faith on your part once you are aware of the trailer fees. The underlying concern here is not whether financial advisors deserve to be paid for their counsel. Of course they do, and fairly. The larger question addresses the lack of transparency and the effect of a commission-based system on advisor objectivity.

There is an old bar joke that straddles the gulf between crudeness and metaphysics. It goes like this: "Why does a dog lick its testicles?" Answer: "Because he can." (The joke has more male adherents than female fans.) Change the subject and venue, and it becomes this: "Why do mutual fund sponsors charge such high MERs, boost their DSC fees, and milk every available drop from the very people they are supposed to be enriching?"

Same punch line. Are you laughing?

F-Class Funds: A Stumble in the Right Direction

The mutual fund industry began responding to concerns about high MERs and trailer fees with a product known as F-class funds. The F stands for *fee,* indicating they are designed for use by fee-based advisors, and so pay no sales commission. F-class equity funds have a MER about one full percentage point lower than funds paying a sales commission. Investing $10,000 in an F-class fund and gaining an extra percentage point in returns will increase your benefit over five years by $510 and over 10 years by $1046, on average.

The catch was that you still needed an advisor to acquire an F-class fund, which meant you would be paying a fee of some kind. But if you felt more than capable to manage your own portfolio, why should you pay hefty commissions and trailer fees to an advisor who simply follows your instructions? Until mid-2004, Canadians couldn't buy F-class funds anywhere except through a full-service broker. Why not make them available directly from the fund companies?

Two reasons. First, most fund companies consider financial advisors as their true clients, not investors. Selling F-class funds directly to you might appear to be undercutting advisors, who could begin to discover reasons not to recommend the funds no matter how appropriate they may appear. Second, making F-class funds widely available would produce transparency for all investors who buy funds, and the history of the investment industry is to avoid transparency the way a nudist avoids poison ivy.

In April 2004, discount online brokers E*Trade Financial and ASL Direct announced they would be distributing, for the first time, F-class funds from AIM Trimark and Elliott & Page, whose Monthly High Income Fund is a favourite of retirees. The announcement represented an important step in permitting savvy investors to reduce the costs and increase the potential rewards of mutual funds in their portfolios. Both brokers declared they were negotiating with other fund companies to distribute their F-class funds in the same way.

If this was a breakthrough, it soon broke down.

Within a week, AIM Trimark repudiated the story, claiming it never agreed to the idea of selling F-class funds through online brokers, while Elliott & Page stuck with the deal to sell their F-class funds directly. Speculation suggests that AIM didn't want to annoy fee-based advisors who would prefer that they handle the F-class funds exclusively. If true, this represents a familiar defensive short-term posture that dominates the mutual fund industry. Do-it-yourself investors are poles apart from those relying on brokers and advisors, and the idea that an investor would end a positive relationship with an advisor simply because F-class funds were available directly from the company is nonsense. More likely, perceptive do-it-yourself investors who avoided AIM funds with their heavy MERs just might have been attracted to the company via the F-class funds.

How Do You Like Your Obfuscation?

It's unlikely that anyone in Canada is more tuned to the need for reform in the country's mutual fund industry than Glorianne Stromberg. Nor is anyone more outraged, in her quiet, measured manner, at the industry's antics. Stromberg practiced corporate and securities law for several years before being appointed to the Ontario Securities Commission in

1991. While filling this role in February 1994, Stromberg was directed to review the regulation of mutual funds in Canada. Her report, *Regulatory Strategies for the Mid-'90s: Recommendations for Regulating Investment Funds in Canada,* was issued in 1995. Three years later, she was asked by the federal government's Office of Consumer Affairs to conduct a similar study to outline how Canadians making mutual fund investments within their RRSPs might obtain reasonable protection when dealing with salespeople, advisors, and the industry generally. This produced *Investment Funds in Canada and Consumer Protection: Strategies for the Millennium* in January 1999.

Both reports and their recommendations were received with great enthusiasm by consumer watchdog groups, and with nods of approval by industry representatives (individual advisors tended to react with shrugs or sneers). Stromberg was feted and congratulated in much of the media. Her hard work and perception were evident in every aspect of the study, and her proposals were acknowledged in many quarters (but by few brokerages) as both practical and effective. So what happened?

Stromberg smiles and shakes her head. "Not much," she says. "We made some small steps forward, and I'm pleased about them. But the resistance to keeping investors informed continues as strong as ever. Look what the industry wants to do with the prospectus. They say they want to simplify it, but this just means they want to remove much of the relevant information. Now the CSA [Canadian Securities Administrators] is going further by suggesting that clients do not have to receive a prospectus before making an investment decision, and the advisor needn't supply one unless asked for it."[11]

Like bitter medicine, reading a prospectus is supposed to be good for you, but few people absorb it. The laws of every provincial and territorial securities commission in Canada state that a prospectus must be prepared whenever an issuer (company, limited partnership, trust, or mutual fund) promotes securities to the public. It must provide full, true, and plain disclosure of important facts relating to the securities being issued and be delivered to every person who invests in the securities. The prospectus includes details of fund performance, management guidelines, fees and commissions, and various other minutiae, buried in text that appears to be written by legal scholars for whom English is a second language and Chaucer is a near contemporary.

"Nobody ever reads a prospectus," many mutual fund sponsors mutter. Observers such as Glorianne Stromberg point out that a prospectus is rarely made to be read—it's made to fulfill a legal requirement. Many prospectus samples appear designed to reduce the likelihood of *anyone* reading it, and since most mutual fund sponsors agree with Stromberg on this point, suspicion remains that fund sponsors are ensuring a self-fulfilling prophecy. The prospectus does, however, establish ground rules for management of the fund and, in theory at least, provides assurance to the investor that her assets are managed according to her expectations.

In recent years, fund sponsors have begun proposing that the rule requiring them to distribute a prospectus with every purchase be waived in favour of simply telling the investor that a prospectus is available. If you want one, ask for it. Otherwise, who cares? Wary minds might suggest that fund sponsors would prefer a complete elimination of the prospectus lest investors begin discovering why so many people in the investment industry sail yachts and drive BMWs, while not enough clients do either.

From time to time, some enlightened fund company decides to make its operations more transparent, assuming that candour and clarity might generate greater trust and, ultimately, more investors in the fund. The most recent company to try this tact was Fidelity, who actually made an effort to simplify their prospectus, making it more accessible and easier to absorb. Nice idea, except that other mutual funds grew antsy about the idea of clients having an opportunity to learn all they should know about their fund's operations, and certain quarters of the industry reportedly applied pressure to maintain a standardized approach to prospectus design and content. The result has been wall-to-wall obfuscation. Score another one for the mutual fund industry.

Finally, when it comes to defending itself against charges of setting its priorities well ahead of investors, the mutual fund industry slips into a defensive mode that makes a cornered grizzly bear appear cuddly. This is not a business that takes criticism lightly. Ken Kivenko, an investment advocate who publishes *The Fund Observer* (formerly *The Fund Monitor*), a newsletter critical of industry practices, compiled some "marginalization" approaches to the industry's critics.

FUND INDUSTRY MARGINALIZATION APPROACHES TO CRITICS

CRITIC	APPROACH
Academia	Obscure professors just trying to get attention.
Newspapers/Media	They're just trying to sell more papers.
Investor advocates	A bunch of cynics with too much time on their hands.
Former regulatory commission staff	That's why they're called "former"!
Deposit insurance commissions	All they want to do is move fund assets to bank accounts.
Consumer groups and organizations	A perpetual bunch of gripers that don't understand the business.
Securities regulators	A bunch of do-gooders with a theoretical cost-insensitive approach to regulation.
Low-cost fund companies	They'll stay small.
Independent fund industry analysts	They're all on the take with hidden agendas.
Abused investors	People who should never have invested in mutual funds— a bunch of whining Canadian Savings Bonds/GIC refugees.
Attorneys General	They're seeking publicity as a route to the premier's office.
Authors of books such as this one	Stay tuned.

SOURCE: *THE FUND OBSERVER*. REPRODUCED WITH PERMISSION.

It Shouldn't Be Complex— It Should Be Open

Barbara Benson[1] prefers to meet in a midtown restaurant instead of her rental apartment. She should not even be living in an apartment, she believes; she should be living in a condominium.

At age 75, Barbara remains an exceptionally attractive woman. She arrives impeccably groomed, in a sleek black dress and wearing subtle silver jewellery, looking every bit the society doyenne. In fact, during the last 15 of her working years, she had been an office secretary. A single mother since her marriage dissolved when she was 40, Barbara managed to raise her two children without financial assistance and is proud of her daughter's obtaining a medical degree and her son's establishment of a successful contracting business in her native Winnipeg.

Those were reasons enough to take pride in her achievements, but there was more. "I worked full time until I was 68 years old," Barbara says in her gentle voice, which carries no hint of bitterness or resentment. "I was always determined never to be a burden to my children, especially when I retired. I scrimped and saved, and did without a lot of things. I never bought a home, but I contributed to my RRSP every year and invested outside my RRSP."

Thanks to her long-term contributions and some wise counsel, by 2000 Barbara managed to accumulate $440,000 in her RRSP (converted to a RRIF when she turned 69) and her non-registered portfolio. At age 70, with substantial assets in hand, her primary focus should have been on preserving capital—holding on to what she had, rather than seeking growth, which invites elevated risk.

"I paid attention to everything I heard and read about investing," she recalls with a wry smile, "caught up in the hype about where the market was going and how to take advantage of it." She attended seminars, including those featuring a local financial advisor who hosted a Saturday afternoon phone-in radio show dealing with financial and investment matters. The advisor promoted investments described by him as "fabulous mutual funds" and "fantastic opportunities."

"He was well known throughout the city." Barbara says. "A real promoter, and he invited listeners to call him on his cellphone after the show to discuss their portfolio. He kept emphasizing that there would be no charge or obligation for a consultation, and no charge for financial planning. So I thought, 'Why not?'"

The broker–cum–radio personality balanced his aggressive, sometimes haranguing attitude on the radio with impressive qualifications. Both a certified financial planner (CFP) and registered financial planner (RFP),[2] he was vice-president and regional manager of a national investment firm.

Barbara Benson stirs her soft drink with her straw as she recalls her decision to obtain a free opinion of her portfolio from the broker. "When I visited him at his office, he went to his computer and showed me the 'dogs,' as he put it, in my account. According to him, they were all dogs, and if I really wanted to ensure my financial security in the future, I should transfer both of my accounts to him. So I did."

It was April 2000, on the cusp of the collapse of the North American equity markets, led by the fall of tech stocks such as Nortel. Transferring her accounts required Barbara to sign a number of documents, and among them was one authorizing her new broker to sell her current investments and purchase other ones on her behalf.

"When I moved my accounts to him, he sold everything in both portfolios—everything!—including all the investments I had outside my RRIF," Barbara recalls, and her until now smiling exterior shows its first sign of crumbling. "It was disastrous!"

The first hint of calamity arrived in a letter from Canada Customs and Revenue, noting that the sale of mutual funds and stocks held outside her RRIF had produced a tax liability based on the capital gains generated when her portfolio assets were sold. She had never faced a capital gains tax in her life, and she had to cover the tax bill out of her savings.

If Barbara's advisor had set out to coordinate her new portfolio expressly to produce maximum losses, he could not have done a better job than the assortment of mutual funds assembled for her.

First, he spread her assets among 43 mutual funds, almost all in the technical growth sector that reached its zenith in mid-2000, around the time he purchased them. Tech funds (industries based on computer products and services, wireless and cellphone equipment manufacturers, biochemical developments, and so on) are risky investments that generate extreme price volatility and exceptionally high MERs and, coincidentally, large commissions for the salesperson. Barbara's lifetime investment was now in the worst place at the worst time. Incredibly, the celebrity broker–broadcaster found a third way to ensure that her investments shrank even further.

Of the 43 funds purchased for her accounts (all with DSCs), 22 were priced in U.S. dollars, a tactic explained by the advisor as a means of obtaining diversification. "He told me Canadian stocks made up only 2 percent of all the world's investment markets," she says. "'You must diversify your investments,' he kept saying, 'and get a lot of them out of the country,' Naturally, I went along with him."

In reality, Barbara's investments were more crucified than diversified. Geographical diversification represents a wise investment strategy, but truly effective diversification involves spreading your investments over a broad range of countries, economies, and industries, yet Barbara's mutual funds were valued in U.S. dollars exclusively. The downside of geographical diversity is a heightened risk of currency fluctuation. When the Canadian dollar falls against foreign currencies, investments in countries with a currency of a higher value will rise in proportion. That's the good news. Any rise in the loonie's value against another country's currency, however, decreases the value of investments priced in that currency.

From 2000 onward, Barbara's foreign-based mutual funds fell not only because they were in high-risk sectors but because they were priced in U.S. dollars, which began a long slide against the Canadian dollar. While anyone with Canadian-priced high-risk investments saw their portfolios erode by 30 to 40 percent, Barbara's dropped by a further 20 percent based on the decline in the U.S. dollar against the loonie.

Barbara's losses were beyond distressing and crippling—they were criminal.

Consider this sample list showing the changed value of each fund between April 2000 and March 2003.[3]

BARBARA'S RRSP – BEFORE AND AFTER			
FUND	APRIL 2000 ($)	MARCH 2003 ($)	GAIN/LOSS (%)
AGF American Growth	9370	2570	−72
AIM European Growth	14,630	5430	−63
AIM Global Health Sciences	2770	1585	−43
AIM Global Technology	5600	1400	−75
CI Global Tech Sector	5710	1420	−75
CI Global Telecom	8140	3550	−56
CI Global Telecom Sector	3950	720	−82
Fidelity Focus Technology	4930	1285	−74
Fidelity Global Asset Allocation	38,695	23,190	−40
Fidelity Growth America	9935	5015	−50

During the three years that Barbara entrusted her savings to the broker, only one of the 43 back-loaded funds purchased for her by the broker showed a profit. This was Fidelity Focus Financial Services, purchased at $1265 in April 2000 and valued at $1365 three years later, producing $100 in profit for annual earnings of less than 3 percent, about the same as a bank's daily interest savings account.

"I had so many tearful meetings with [the advisor] about these losses," Barbara explains. "He would tell me to be patient, to trust him. If I suggested selling some of the bad mutual funds, he said it would cost too much money to sell them because they had a deferred sales charge, and the only way to get my money back was to hold on to them. But they kept falling and falling, and by the spring of 2003 I had lost over $200,000. I was devastated and terrified. I had to do something!"

In early 2003, Barbara took her statement, showing the myriad mutual funds and steep losses, to another advisor in the same brokerage firm, who was appalled. The second advisor, convinced that Barbara's portfolio had been designed to make her advisor wealthy rather than Barbara, raised the matter with the company's compliance officer and pointed out how her accounts had been mishandled. In response, the compliance officer shrugged and noted that Barbara's accounts dated before [the compliance officer's] arrival at the brokerage and claimed he therefore could do nothing.

The advisor who directed Barbara's money into this disastrous mix continues to maintain his reputation as an investment genius with a phone-in show on a local radio station, imploring listeners to contact him for an assessment and restructuring of their portfolios. How many of his clients have suffered the same devastation as Barbara, but are too embarrassed or too intimidated to express their concerns publicly?

While investment "professionals" may construct a portfolio that appears designed to enrich themselves through sales commissions, trailing fees, and hidden incentives, rarely are they called to account for their misdeeds. Whenever they are, their defence is consistent and widely accepted by regulators: Equities by nature rise and fall over an extended period, and clients must assume that the long-term trend will be upward while accepting the downside risk. If challenged, Barbara's advisor would no doubt use this defence, bolstered by claims that Barbara was an experienced investor and by assurances that the market would likely recover, eventually allowing Barbara to recoup her losses.

Nothing in any investment guideline would justify creating a portfolio for a 70-year-old woman consisting almost exclusively of high-risk, back-loaded mutual funds, with a majority of them set in U.S. currency. The concept defies every tenet of astute investing. Barbara Benson's highly regarded financial planner likely reaped about $20,000 in upfront sales commissions plus perhaps $5000 in trailer fees over the three years that her portfolio was under his management. The firm's compliance officer fulfilled his role as sentry on behalf of the brokerage—not the clients—by noting that he had assumed his position after the account had been opened and thus could do nothing. Should the client have launched action to recover her losses on the basis of mismanagement of her account? Perhaps. A number of regulatory bodies exist to address this kind of malfeasance, but the record of their effectiveness in cases such as this one is abysmally low, as you shall see.

Nor is the legal system sufficiently equipped or dedicated to deal with the matter. The civil courts are crowded, banks and brokerages insist on closed-door arbitration, and lawyers are expensive. A plaintiff may be required to pay a retainer of several thousand dollars at the outset of legal action, plus monthly charges for a year or more, with little assurance that legal costs will be recovered. Meanwhile, the defendants boast an almost impregnable defence.

Bolstered by the alphabet of degrees and certificates trailing their name, advisors and brokers will claim that their investment guidance was appropriate at the time it was given. Every financial advisor with a calendar and calculator might concur that stocks listed on the Toronto Stock Exchange will rise by 10 percent next month, but this is no guarantee that they will not fall by a similar amount instead. Every investment involves risk, and clients should know this going in. Why blame the advisor for unforeseen events beyond his or her control? The basis of the industry's defence can be summed up in this manner: When a broker's prescience is accurate, his actions are justified; when it is faulty, the client must accept the risk.

Investors who manage to pursue their claims to arbitration may encounter a skeptical, unsympathetic response. One client at an arbitration session explained to the judge that she had sought only relatively secure investments, had never expected more than a 10 percent annual return, and had insisted on minimizing any risk to her capital, accumulated over several years of patient growth. Yet within a year of a new advisor restructuring her account after her previous advisor retired, she saw an erosion of over 30 percent in her RRSP account, all of it based on the new advisor's guidance. Wasn't this evidence of account mismanagement?

The judge simply shrugged. "Not necessarily," he said. "I lose money in the stock market myself from time to time." A decision was handed down in favour of the advisor, leaving the client to dip into the remainder of her savings to cover her legal fees.

Age Must Be a Factor in Determining Strategy

The investment industry tries to shrug off complaints about undue losses, especially in RRSP/RRIF accounts owned by members of the over-60 crowd, by noting that clients must accept the risk of loss when investing, and much of the regulatory and legal apparatus appears to support this argument. The claim is so much hogwash.

Once again: *There is a difference between risk and uncertainty.* Risk can be assessed and accounted for. Uncertainty cannot be. Risk is interest rates rising and the stock market dropping. Uncertainty is September 11, 2001. It is the duty of every financial advisor to address the question of risk in each client portfolio, and it need not be the client's duty to help in determining this factor, because *when it comes to RRSP and RRIF accounts, the overriding determination of risk is the client's age.* The calculation is, or should be, automatic.

Working from the client's age, the path toward prudent account design becomes open and accessible. The submitted strategy may (and perhaps should) vary according to aspects of a client's knowledge and lifestyle, but age is the primary determinant. The most common method of applying this reasoning is to match the percentage of guaranteed investments—GICs, government bonds, and cash—to the client's age. At 35, you need only have about one-third of the value of your RRSP in guaranteed investments; at age 75, guaranteed investments should represent three-quarters of the total. (For more details on this formula, see Chapter 12.)

Guaranteed instruments do not totally eliminate risk but, as with other risks, this one can be managed. Long-term bonds and GICs carry the risk that rising interest rates and inflation will reduce their value over time. A five-year GIC paying 4 percent annual interest may look reasonable today, but if the same investment is paying 7 or 8 percent next year and you're locked into the lower rate, you lose ground. The risk can be managed by laddering fixed-interest instruments such as GICs and bonds. An investment of $10,000, for example, can be divided into fifths, with one-fifth maturing in one year, another fifth maturing in two years, and so on. Each year the maturing investment is rolled over—reinvested at the current interest rate—for five years. In this manner, when interest rates rise you take advantage of the higher interest paid by investing a portion of your fixed-interest assets in the new rate, and when they fall you already have a majority of the investment growing at the old rate.

Once the age-percentage rule for fixed-interest investments is understood, it may be manipulated according to individual needs and expectations, but the rule still holds. I know of one 70-year-old man, for example, who has flipped the rule—he holds 70 percent of his RRIF portfolio in equity and resource-based mutual funds, primarily gold and precious metals in mid-2004, and only 30 percent in fixed interest vehicles. He is also an experienced, astute, and gifted investor with no dependent children, no mortgage on his luxury home, and an in-home business that generates a substantial annual income. He understands and preaches the rule. But he also qualifies as an ideal exception to it.

The Fiction of "Inevitable Losses"

Advisors, planners, and brokers tend to discuss risk only after the fact. In this sense, they are like the elevator mechanic who points out, as you plummet down the open shaft, that you can't expect the elevator to be there all the time. "Be prepared to take losses," they admonish.

It is not unrealistic to expect that losses can be avoided with your RRSP/RRIF investments. This expectation may be difficult to realize, but isn't that why you rely on a professional advisor in the first place—to achieve goals and levels of growth that you are unable to accomplish yourself? As investors, we have to start discarding the notion of accepting periodic losses from mutual funds even while the fund managers and commissioned salespeople reap profits from them. There is a precedent for such thinking. His name is Warren Buffet.

Over 39 calendar years stretching from 1965 to 2003, Buffet's company lost money for investors only once, in 2001, when the value of shares in his Berkshire Hathaway firm dropped 6.2 percent. For the record, the S&P 500, a standard index of stock performance, fell almost twice as far that year and slipped a further 22 percent in 2002, yet Buffet regained his 2001 loss plus an additional 4 percent. Perhaps losses are inevitable only if you expect them to be.

There are few Warren Buffets in the world, and even fewer of them are advising Canadians on their RRSP/RRIF portfolios. Yet Buffet can teach us some things that provide enlightenment, if not enormous wealth. As both an investor and a realist, his success was built by following two cardinal rules:

RULE NO. 1:   Never lose money.
RULE NO. 2:   Never forget Rule No. 1.

Buffet managed to fulfill Rule No. 1 for 38 out of 39 consecutive years by applying diligence, focus, and hard work to the project— hardly a unique recipe, but one unfamiliar to many commission-based brokers and financial advisors. I anticipate their objection to this comment will be based on practicalities. Buffet has just one account to manage—his own, on behalf of shareholders in Berkshire Hathaway. Brokers and advisors may deal with hundreds of portfolios, with each client expecting individual attention to his or her special needs. That's a valid point, but it falls apart under close examination.

Putting it simply, too many advisors are handling too many accounts. Seeking to maximize one's income is understandable, but going beyond the point where service quality slips below an acceptable standard is inexcusable. One of the most common complaints made by RRSP investors is that they hear from their advisor once a year, usually just before the deadline for RRSP contributions. If advisors can find time in February to make blanket calls to everyone on their client lists, they should be able to schedule quarterly or at least semi-annual portfolio reviews of every portfolio whose assets exceed six figures in dollar value. Dedicated advisors will provide consultation as required at a level well below this figure, helping to build the client's assets even when the assets barely justify the advisor's time, with the expectation of future benefits when the client prospers. This is a form of investing, after all.

The alternative pursued by some advisors is to rely on computer programs when making investment decisions for clients. This has the benefit of producing reams of peripheral information in order to impress clients with enough data to divert their attention from the fact that their goals are not being met.

Year by year these reports, based on off-the-rack computer programs, expand in content and shrink in relevance. Along with a year-end statement revealing that Barbara Benson had seen 40 percent of the value of her investments vanish after three years with her radio-celebrity broker, she received a 16-page personal financial plan, the substance of which was primarily boilerplate and the value worthless. No full-colour pie chart or graphs could conceal the fact that little if any of the investments were appropriate for her age and status.

Among the report was a page titled Goals and Priorities, noting that at age 73 (in 2002), her life expectancy was 85. Yet the asset mix assembled for her (including both RRIF and non-registered accounts) by the advisor consisted of—

Cash	0%
Income	20%
Growth and income	20%
Canadian growth	10%
Global growth	33%
Aggressive growth	17%

Equity-based mutual funds are generally categorized according to two measures: value and growth. Value-based funds invest in established companies that are underpriced at the time of purchase; growth-based funds purchase shares on the promise of what they might become, rather than on actual profits. As a result, growth-based funds tend to be far more speculative than value-based funds and harbour much higher MERs. So why were none of Barbara Benson's funds based on value? She sought income and security. What she received was speculation and risk. (For more details on value versus growth funds, see Chapter 12.)

Whenever advisors scramble for quick answers to meet an expanding client list, they follow a herd mentality. Instead of pondering the full range of investment alternatives, they note the general direction of thinking in the marketplace and follow the crowd. Are other advisors recommending a particular mutual fund or fund sector this month? There must be something to it, so why not propose it? There is safety in numbers—if the investment tanks, an advisor's defence can be that scores of others were making the same decision, so there must have been some perceived benefit. The herd mentality remains as prevalent among financial advisors as it does among investors, and when the herd breaks into a stampede, only the wise advisors suggest you step aside and let it pass. *When everybody thinks the same, nobody is thinking at all.*

The prospect of advisors reducing their client list to a manageable size is unlikely to occur as long as their income remains commission-based. Call it greed, call it business acumen, call it human nature, but while advisors rely on the steady receipt of commission cheques and trailer fees—in other words, as long as they function primarily as salespeople and only incidentally as investment counsellors—the financial disaster suffered by Barbara Benson and thousands of other Canadians whose trust exceeds their comprehension will continue unabated, unchallenged, and uncontrolled.

The Seduction Factor: Do We Become Angry or Chagrined?

Canadians with RRSP and RRIF portfolios pay MER rates considered excessive in other markets, especially the United States. We do it for two reasons: lack of knowledge on our part, and lack of transparency on the part of the industry and its marketers.

Consider money market funds, which are suitable as a place to park your RRSP contribution while you decide on a long-term investment strategy, or as the cash portion of your RRSP. Money market funds invest in government treasury bills, which means they are about as difficult to manage as a sidewalk lemonade stand. Check the financial pages of your local newspaper for the interest that federal and provincial governments are paying on 90-day T-bills. You buy the T-bills, sell them after 90 days to earn accrued interest, use the cash to buy more, wait another 90 days, and so on. That's how to manage a money market fund. It's not only a no-brainer, it's risk-free.

MERs for money market funds are admittedly much lower than any other type of mutual fund, but many have excessively high MERs in relation to the returns they generate. The difference in *gross* earnings between mutual funds is essentially infinitesimal. After all, every fund dips into the same pool. But the difference in *your* earnings is phenomenal.

For a true evaluation of money market fund costs, add the MER to the latest total annual return, divide the sum by the latest annual return the fund generated, and multiply by 100. This represents the percentage return of money earned from your dollars and retained by the fund manager. A reasonable figure might be 30 percent; the average is 40 percent, and many are higher—far higher.[4] Here's a sampling of the amount of money various Canadian money market funds pocketed, based on the above formula.

SELECTED MONEY MARKET FUNDS: % RETURNS AND PROFITS RETAINED BY FUND				
FUND	MER	RETURN*	TOTAL	RETAINED
Acuity Money Market	2.13	0.53	2.66	80
AGF Canadian Money Market	1.54	1.34	2.88	54
AIM Short-Term Income B	2.37	0.47	2.84	84
Investors Money Market	1.13	1.79	2.92	38
Maritime Life Money Market C	2.14	0.91	3.05	70
TD Premium Money Market	0.32	2.71	3.03	11
Altamira T-Bill	0.38	2.63	3.01	11

* As of March 31, 2004

The AIM fund paid itself 84 percent of the profit earned by its unit holders' money for performing the same function as the other funds. Why? Because it can. If you like the TD Premium Money Market fund with its relatively healthy return and low 11 percent retention of earnings ... feggitaboutit—unless you have $250,000 to invest. That's the ante needed to join this fund's party, and it's one reason for the rock-bottom MER. File this under The Rich Get Richer. The Altamira fund is just as good and requires a much lower ante, but lots of luck having a commission-based advisor recommend it to you—it's no-load, like all Altamira funds, and pays no commissions or trailer fees.

Since the cash portion of most RRSPs and RRIFs should not exceed 15 or 20 percent of the portfolio's total, these low yields won't seriously depress your portfolio's performance in the long run. In essence, the low returns are the price you pay for liquidity and security. But why pay one fund manager eight times as much to hold your money as another, since both are investing in identical instruments?

If you would drive several blocks to save a nickel a litre on the gasoline you put in your car—and most people will—why wouldn't you make a decision to pay one-eighth as much in management fees for several thousand dollars of your RRSP investment? *Because you were not aware of the alternative.* Gas stations post their prices prominently. Mutual fund companies do not.

Where Is Eliot Spitzer When You Need Him?

Legal and borderline-legal activities of mutual fund sponsors in the United States were highlighted in 2003 through the headline-grabbing efforts of New York State Attorney General Eliot Spitzer. The most prominent self-aggrandizement promoter since former New York mayor Rudy Giuliani, Spitzer managed to highlight a number of abuses that had gone unnoticed and uncorrected for years and which lined the pockets of mutual fund executives at the expense of investors.

Among the activities identified by Spitzer and his crew was late trading, which is similar to placing a bet on a horse race after the winner has been declared. Late traders use the six-hour time difference between the closing of European stock markets and the closing of markets in New York to make profits unavailable to retail investors. When the London market closes, the gain or loss for that day is fixed, but North American mutual funds investing in European stocks are still priced according to the previous day's close. A sharp rise in European stock markets would trigger a late trader to purchase units that day in a mutual fund holding these stocks. The fund's unit value would rise overnight and be sold for a certain profit the following day when new valuations were posted.

It sounds like a sure way to make money, except for a couple of obstacles. One is a question of law—late trading is illegal in both the

United States and Canada. The other is a question of practicality—
no one except mutual fund insiders could even attempt to get away
with it, because investors like you and me cannot buy and sell mutual
fund units that way, thanks to high penalties for trading funds within
60 days of purchase. Yet several dozen people in the United States
managed to practice late trading and make a bundle of money in the
process. Spitzer's investigation proved that top management in many
mutual fund companies knew or should have known that late trading
was being conducted by their own people, yet they declined to take
action until threatened with criminal charges.

Late trading is not strictly a victimless crime that enables a small
group of people to enjoy opportunities the rest of us envy. Late
traders earn a profit without actually spending money on the investments within the fund—the ones that people like you and me make
possible. And the profits they take home come directly out of our
pockets, one way or another. Money rushing in and out of a fund
means the fund manager must keep substantial cash on hand, perhaps
more than she wants, to handle the late trades. This is cash that
cannot be invested the way you and I expect it to be; one qualified
source estimates late trading can cost legitimate fund investors
between 1 and 2 percent annually in lost earnings.[5]

Responding to a spate of revelations regarding late trading among
U.S. funds, in November 2003 the Ontario Securities Commission
leapt into action in defence of Canadian mutual fund investors.

It wrote a letter.

The letter, sent by OSC chairman David Brown to all publicly
traded mutual funds under OSC jurisdiction, politely requested fund
managers to provide evidence the managers had of late trading in
their funds, along with the results of any investigations launched. The
matter was of questionable urgency, since it gave the fund managers
almost six weeks to respond. Here is what the OSC promised to do
with its findings:

Your responses will be kept confidential to the extent permitted by law. Note however that it is our intention to summarize the feedback we receive on an overall basis and to report back to you on those results at a later date.

And the letter concludes:

As is our normal practice, we ask that you provide a copy of this letter to your funds' auditors and to your funds' and/or the manager's Board of Directors, or to the funds' trustees, as the case may be.

We look forward to working with you to reaffirm investors' confidence in the mutual fund industry. Thank you in advance for your cooperation.[6]

If the OSC were seeking to "reaffirm investors' confidence in the mutual fund industry," why does it promise to report its results only to the mutual fund managers? Who is looking after the interests of the retail investors, whose $400-plus billions are funding the industry?

Well, perhaps the media. Six months later, the *Globe and Mail's* Report on Business section ran a series of articles on the Canadian mutual fund industry, kicking off with a detailed examination of the churn rate for more than 100 international and global funds. The churn rate measured how often units within the fund changed hands over the four-year period from 2000 to 2003; a churn rate of 100 percent was the equivalent of every unit in the fund being bought and sold within one year. The results, in many cases, did not require an affable letter from the OSC to generate some suspicions.

SELECTED CANADIAN MUTUAL FUNDS, 2000–2003				
CHURN RATE (%)				
FUND	2000	2001	2002	2003
AGF Asian Growth Class	383	1185	599	364
AIC Global Advantage	908	1627	1046	431
AIC Global Diversified	898	1619	900	270
CI International Balanced	292	–	1300	764
Clarington Global Equity	286	400	457	292
RBC Asian Equity	246	325	522	115

SOURCE: *GLOBE AND MAIL*, JUNE 21, 2004. REPRODUCED WITH PERMISSION.

Note that units in AIC's Global Advantage fund—managed by the "Buy. Hold. And Prosper" company—changed hands more than 10 times annually in two consecutive years. During 2001, the equivalent of each unit in both AIC funds was bought and sold about every three weeks. If we assume that a substantial number of fund holders held their units, the rest must have been traded far more often than every three weeks to produce this figure.

Admittedly, these are not gigantic funds in terms of asset value. The CI International Balanced is the largest, with assets just under $500 million, and the AIC Global Diversified is the smallest, at less than $40 million. Even so, how could units valued at almost half a billion dollars change hands 13 times in 12 months, as the CI fund appears to have done during 2002? There may be a logical explanation for this phenomenon, but if the OSC discovers it, we may have to wait a very long time for its mandarins to share the data with investors.

Canada not only lacks an Eliot Spitzer to chase down evidence of this activity and lay charges where appropriate, it lacks both the structure and determination needed to aggressively root out abuses throughout the financial and investment industry. Nothing like the U.S. Securities and Exchange Commission, with all its powers to protect the small investor, exists in Canada. Nor can we expect one in the foreseeable future. (For details on this lack of investor protection, see Chapter 9.)

No one likes to be reminded of his or her ignorance, but most people who invest in mutual funds must face the reality that *they don't know what they don't know.* They trust "professionals" whose obligation toward their own well-being often dominates any comparable concern for the clients' well-being. In investment, as in romance, trust and ignorance produce a willingness to be seduced, and Canadians have been seduced by the mutual fund industry specifically, and the investment industry generally, for decades.

Soft Dollars—They're Paid for with Your Hard Cash

Little by little, the blackout material is being peeled from windows in the mutual fund industry to reveal how it manages to skim money out of the hundreds of billions held in trust. One of the more arcane methods relates to soft dollars.

Soft dollars do not refer to rubber loonies. It's a backdoor method used by mutual funds to retain a larger portion of the MER charged against the funds in your portfolio—or maybe pay for a junket or two to Phoenix in February. Here's how it works.

Mutual funds buy and sell shares in the companies making up the funds in the same way everyone else does—through brokers. A fund trading $100 million in stocks every year represents a major account to brokerages that charge a commission on every trade. Persuading fund managers to place trades with their brokerage takes more than a smile and a shoeshine on the part of the broker. One of the things it may take is a rebate on commissions. This is neither new nor exclusive to the investment industry. But it's the manner in which these rebates are handled that raises concerns.

Suppose the brokerage charges the mutual fund five cents for every trade handled—a nickel for every share purchased and every share sold. The hard-dollar cost to the mutual fund might be just two cents per share; the remaining three cents becomes either a cash rebate (which should go directly into the fund assets and thus into the hands of investors—an unlikely event) or a credit to be exchanged for specialized services. The credits are labelled soft dollars.

Is it worth getting excited about a lousy three-cent rebate? Yes it is, because of the scale of things. Trade enough shares and those three-cent rebates start adding up to real money—like $100 million annually, or about 20 percent of the industry's total trading commissions, according to one source.[7] The total may be even higher, because one qualified critic of soft dollars suggests the rebate portion could represent as much as 80 percent of the transaction commissions paid from fund assets.[8]

Soft dollar rebates can be spent by mutual funds on a variety of items, such as research reports, financial analysis software and the computers to run it, trips for fund managers and staff to attend investment conferences in Switzerland or seminars in Arizona, and rent on VIP boxes in arenas and stadiums where advisors and brokers, not fund investors, can nibble smoked salmon and sip Chardonnay high above the ice or turf. Some of these perks can be justified in terms of assisting fund managers and staff to do their jobs, but that's what the MER is for—management expense ratio, remember? Spending the hidden commissions on these items means the fund gets to retain a larger portion of the MER for itself.

Canadian regulators are several steps behind those in the home of laissez-faire capitalism when it comes to protecting retail investors from this contrivance. In 1998, the U.S. Securities and Exchange Commission discovered that soft dollars were used to purchase fund-management "necessities" such as Broadway theatre tickets, limousine rides, and interior design services. The SEC brought its hammer down on a number of investment industry giants, including Massachusetts

Financial Services, Morgan Stanley, Janus Capital Group, and Bank One, persuading them to abolish the use of soft dollars.

When this news broke, the supposed pacesetter among Canadian securities watchdogs, the Ontario Securities Commission, claimed it would take action. The subject, said a spokesperson for the OSC, "is definitely on our radar screen ... and we are definitely keeping abreast of all the developments in the U.S. and the U.K."[9] As we shall see, statements like this suggest we should "definitely" not expect anything of substance to emerge from the OSC for some time.

Meanwhile, people with more clout than individual investors and more perspicacity than the OSC, such as those managing the Ontario Teachers' Pension Plan Board (total 2004 assets: $76 billion), refuse to use soft dollars offered by brokerage firms, claiming, "They are so rife with conflict of interest [they] shouldn't be touched with a ten-foot pole."[10]

Soft dollars are yet another symptom of the way your RRSP assets, if invested in a mutual fund, become accessible in various ways to those we entrust with our money. Unjustifiable high MERs, punitive DSCs, hidden trailer fees, soft dollars, and a prevailing lack of transparency all warrant serious investigation by appropriate regulatory bodies.

Perhaps because we are Canadians and typically unresponsive to rabble-rousers, or simply because it's more soothing to be chagrined at our innocence than angry at our persecutors, we have done little or nothing in response to the misdeeds of people we entrust to help us build a secure financial future. It's time we defended ourselves with knowledge and armed ourselves with a determination to trust ourselves first. In this manner, we can remind the investment industry just who is working for whom.

The mutual fund industry will claim that investors never comment on MER levels and DSCs as long as the funds are producing 15 percent or more interest, as many (but certainly not all) achieved during the later 1990s. That's like saying that everyone has a reliable car when it's running well. The test of quality arises when conditions are less than ideal, for both driving and investing. (Nor is the industry's self-serving claim necessarily true. From 1996 to 1999, the Toronto Stock Exchange 300 composite index delivered outstanding returns—more than 17 percent annually—yet the number of complaints rose more than 150 percent.)[11]

The industry's comment avoids the issue of transparency. It is not far-fetched to suggest that a clearer vision of its operations might provide Canadian investors with more realistic expectations and greater confidence in the abilities of their advisors.

On a wider scale, Canadians need to understand how the mutual fund industry earns income from the assets of its unit holders and how its structure invites abuses that would be intolerable in any other business. Consider Power Corporation of Canada, controlled by the Desmarais family. Among its holdings are five companies, each promoting its own lineup of mutual funds. In mid-2004, these tallied as follows.

THE INFLUENCE OF POWER CORPORATION AND ITS SUBSIDIARIES	
POWER CORPORATION DIVISION	MUTUAL FUNDS MARKETED
Canada Life Assurance	70
Great-West Lifeco	116
Investors Group	345
London Life	56
Mackenzie Financial Corporation	226
Total	813

On that basis, about one of every four mutual funds marketed to Canadians is controlled by one company which, in turn, is controlled by one family: the Desmarais family. This kind of concentration of power is not unusual in Canada—the print and broadcast media industry is similar—but this does not make it any less intolerable or dangerous.

The problem is compounded by the influence these funds have on the companies in which they invest. Ownership of common shares provides mutual fund managers with enormous clout in determining and approving corporate policies through boards of director elections and other means. The influence exerted by large funds is massive. In mid-2004, of the 30 Mackenzie funds investing in Canadian corporations and revealing their Top 10 holdings via the Globefund website, these are the number that identified ownership in major Canadian corporations:

TOP 10 HOLDINGS IN 30 SELECTED MACKENZIE FUNDS	
COMPANY	NUMBER OF FUNDS LISTING COMPANY IN TOP 10 HOLDINGS
Bank of Montreal	14
Bank of Nova Scotia	18
BCE	21
Brascan	13
CIBC	10
Loblaw Co. Ltd.	12
Manulife Financial	26
Onex	10
Royal Bank	12
Shoppers Drug Mart	20
TD Bank of Canada	13

SOURCE: GLOBEFUND.COM, MARCH 31, 2004. REPRODUCED WITH PERMISSION.

These are companies listed in the Top 10 holdings of each fund that posted its holdings (not all funds did). With larger funds, these represent enormous quantities of money representing massive numbers of outstanding shares for each company.

In the Mackenzie Ivy Canadian fund, for example, its Top 10 holdings represented almost half of its total assets, which in April 2004 were valued at $5.47 billion. The table below shows how much, in dollars, the fund controlled of each of its Top 10 companies.

MACKENZIE IVY CANADIAN FUND – ASSETS OWNED (TOP 10 HOLDINGS) APRIL 2004		
COMPANY	% OF FUND	VALUE ($)
George Weston Ltd.	6.78	370,866,000
Omnicon Group	6.66	364,302,000
Shoppers Drug Mart	6.42	351,174,000
Danaher Corp.	4.84	264,748,000
Loblaw Co. Ltd.	4.58	250,525,000
Canadian National Railway	4.02	219,894,000
Berkshire Hathaway	3.51	191,997,000
Bank of Nova Scotia	3.23	176,681,000
Suncor Energy	3.23	176,681,000
Royal Bank of Canada	3.19	174,493,000

SOURCE: GLOBEFUND.COM, APRIL 30, 2004. REPRODUCED WITH PERMISSION.

Even a company as massive as George Weston Ltd., whose assets in mid-2004 totalled $16 billion, must respect and pay attention to anyone who controls over $370 million in its common stock. The funds do not actually own the shares in George Weston; they merely manage them. The shares are owned by each unit holder in the Mackenzie Ivy Canadian Fund. Since Weston shares were also controlled by several other funds in the Mackenzie family, Mackenzie's total influence was actually much larger. Extend this across all of the 800-plus mutual funds held under the Power Corporation umbrella and the influence of these investments becomes significant.

Advocates such as Joe Killoran have long called for greater transparency in all dealings between mutual fund sponsors and corporations, with little success. Such disclosures could be easily implemented in the various communications distributed by the fund companies to their unit holders, but none seems interested—primarily because the unit holders are not aware of the situation and thus are themselves uninterested. But given exposure to illegal activities uncovered by Eliot Spitzer and his attack dogs in the United States, and the much weaker enforcement machinery and atmosphere in Canada, are we to assume that the Canadian industry is substantially more trustworthy? Only at our peril.

Where Is the Quid Pro Quo for Investors?

Anyone who doubts the power of the country's mutual fund industry and the strength of its resistance to greater oversight should reflect on periodic attempts by securities administrators to monitor its actions.

In early 2002 the Canadian Securities Administrators (CSA), the closest entity Canada has to a national securities commission, began examining ways to ensure that the mutual fund industry in this country is behaving itself. Among the goals addressed by the CSA were avoidance of conflicts of interest and assurance that the industry is acting according to the welfare of investors. Mutual fund companies owe more than a fiduciary obligation to the people who entrust the firms with their assets; they owe a wider responsibility to act according to the same general guidelines applied to other industries.

The CSA chewed over recommendations from mutual fund representatives and, after almost two years, it burped up a Pablum-like formula that had everyone criticizing its blandness—everyone, that is, except the mutual fund industry.

The proposal unveiled by the CSA in January 2004 suggested, rather innocuously, that mutual fund companies be required to set up independent review committees (IRCs) to monitor potential conflicts of interest that arise. In most industries, a board of directors is assigned the role of overseeing operations, but guess what? Canadian mutual funds are not required to have boards. So the idea of each fund employing an IRC (some already do) sounded both wise and tenuous. The industry was being asked, in effect, to once again regulate itself—hardly a draconian proposition. In fact, the proposed rule permitted a fund company to ignore the proposals of its own IRC, if it chose to do so.

Even this restrained idea was too much for the industry to accept, and it responded to the idea of compulsory IRCs by demanding a quid pro quo. If mutual fund companies were to be required to establish IRCs to monitor potential conflicts of interest, they insisted on the right to free managers from previously restricted transactions, even if these transactions might conflict with investor interests. And they got it.[12]

Among the transactions that the industry wanted more freedom to conduct was self-dealing, which occurs when the parent company of a mutual fund instructs the fund to purchase shares in a third company to benefit the parent corporation. The practice is strictly prohibited in the United States and the United Kingdom; in Canada, the industry wants flexibility to engage in it.

The IRCs, by the way, will have the right to publish their findings in the funds' annual reports. But guess what? The industry also wants to repeal the need to issue annual reports to every unit holder. First it fights the establishment of IRCs, then it proposes a method of keeping IRC findings from investors.

Investor groups were outraged at the gutting of the original plan. Managers of mutual fund companies simply nodded and smiled. One commentator noted that Canada and the United States were moving in opposite directions when it came to protecting investor interests. "We see ... the continued divergence of the paths taken being taken [by the SEC] in trying to bolster its already extensive mutual fund governance regime," said industry critic Stephen Erlichman, "and by the CSA's made-in-Canada solution proposing a more narrow independent review committee model without any requirement for mandatory compliance plans."[13] Erlichman is referring to a U.S. mutual fund governance system, in place since 1940, which calls for mutual fund companies to maintain a board of directors, among other directives. When scandals of mismanagement and self-serving policies began brewing in the fund industry, the SEC tightened its control by demanding stricter compliance procedures and dictating that at least three-quarters of all mutual fund directors must be independent of management.

Glorianne Stromberg, whose qualifications for commenting on industry practices are as stalwart as her reputation for speaking her mind, was furious at the proposals. She declared them "outrageous," adding, "They fly in the face of common sense" and are "are akin to revoking the rules of the road and leaving it to individual users of the road to set their own rules. The resulting chaos and injuries could be catastrophic." In case anyone doubted her emotional state of mind, Stromberg declared: "The CSA's stated expectation that fund managers and their independent review committees [RICs] will start with the existing rules and build on them is pathetic in its naïveté."[14]

The mutual fund industry remained smugly silent—"except for the sound of champagne corks popping," commented one wag.

INVESTMENT PORNOGRAPHY
AND RED SUITS

Mara Bonduro,[1] a 78-year-old widow, is functionally blind, speaks English poorly, and has a grade-school education. Her life, following the death of her husband, was made more pleasant thanks to her son, who welcomed her to his Florida condominium each winter, and about $350,000 in her RRIF, accumulated by her and her husband during their working years. Withdrawals from her RRIF, most of it invested in strip bonds and conservative mutual funds, provided money for rent, food, and clothing.

When a new advisor was appointed by the brokerage handling Mrs. Bonduro's RRIF upon the previous broker's retirement, he persuaded her to transfer 88 percent of her portfolio to higher yielding (and much riskier) growth funds, all purchased on a DSC basis with high MERs and lucrative trailer fees for the broker.

Mrs. Bonduro could no longer comprehend the statements, and wrote several letters explaining that she could never understand if she was making or losing money. None was answered to her satisfaction.

In fact, she was losing money. Within two years, half of the RRIF value had vanished, along with her confidence of enjoying a financially secure future. With the assistance of her son, Mrs. Bonduro sought legal assistance, and her lawyer drafted a letter to the brokerage seeking an admission that the investments recommended by the new financial advisor were totally inappropriate to the client's needs. The letter requested the brokerage to admit that its representative had assembled unsuitable investments and to replace the lost assets. In response, the brokerage replied:

> As you know, [Brokerage] mails account statements to its clients on a quarterly basis, as well as for months in which trading activity occurs, wherein the current value of investments is reflected. Trade confirmations are also issued shortly after each trade that occurs in an account.
>
> If at any time Mrs. Bonduro's intentions were not followed as you have suggested, we believe the seriousness of such a situation would have prompted notice to Branch Management for timely resolution. We have no record of any expressed dissatisfaction until we received [your] letter of complaint and claim.
>
> We suggest that investment advice is intended to provide a client with the guidance necessary to make a reasoned and informed decision, but it is not intended to substitute for the client's own decision-making.

The brokerage's defence is based on the lack of an objection to the appropriateness of the investments by its own internal watchdog—the compliance officer, perhaps—suggesting that there was nothing untoward in its advisor's actions. And even if the portfolio was improper, the 78-year-old blind woman with minimal education and English-speaking skills had at least tacitly approved things, so why blame the advisor?

The brokerage indicated it would defend its actions in civil court if necessary, launching legal action that will likely take years to resolve, return only a portion of Mrs. Bonduro's losses if her suit is successful, and incorporate a gag order preventing her from discussing any aspect of the case through to settlement and beyond.

In cases such as Mara Bonduro's, the response of the brokerage or advisor is often, "She had an opportunity to complain about the proposals or the performance of her investments, and she did not. Her expectations were unreasonable, and she now suffers from her own imprudence. She is, in effect, the author of her own misfortune."

This is not the argument made by brokers and advisors when soliciting funds from RRSP investors. At that point in the exercise, their position is reversed precisely 180 degrees. "You are not qualified to make wise investment decisions," they lecture. "This is a dark, dangerous, and complex industry, and we are here to help you grow wealthy by employing certain strategies that are beyond your comprehension."[2] But how much darker and dangerous is it to follow the advice of a commission-based salesperson who manoeuvres you from a conservative bond-based portfolio (which, of course, generates no commissions or trailer fees for the advisor) into a truckload of volatile DSC-based mutual funds?

Remember that mutual funds are not bought; they are sold. And the selling of inappropriate mutual funds, selected by salespeople *whose interest is at least compromised by the direct commissions to be earned from their recommended funds,* is one of the most disgraceful aspects of the investment industry.

Sheep and Tuna: Buying High and Selling Low

We are sheep. That's how unsophisticated investors are viewed by many financial advisors and brokers. Sheep are passive, dutiful animals to be shorn of their wool, generating income for shepherds while leaving themselves naked. Sheep are easily intimidated and can be herded by an animal no more clever than a border collie. (Joe Killoran's often-employed description of Canadian investors as "sheeple" fits rather nicely.) The biggest difference between sheep and most people who invest their RRSP and RRIF money in mutual funds is that the farmer feeds the sheep. When it comes to mutual funds, the sheeple feed the shepherd.

Almost every observer of the mutual fund industry notes that investors are irrational. Unfortunately, the claim is often true. What are the roots of this irrationality? Financial advisors, brokers, mutual fund salespeople, and mutual fund sponsors claim that they are genetic, like a predisposition of some people to gamble, take drugs, or smoke cigarettes. Investor advocates suggest the more likely causes of irrationality are misplaced trust, fear, and manipulation.

Here's a classic example of investment irrationality. Suppose, during your weekly grocery shopping, you discover your favourite canned tuna on sale. Last week it cost $2 a can. This week it's only $1 a can. That's a deal, so you sweep a dozen cans into your shopping cart and stack them in your pantry. You have made a rational buying decision.

If the price had doubled, and instead of $2 per can it was selling for $4 per can, would you stock up in the same manner? Of course not. That would be irrational. Yet this is the same way most people choose mutual funds. When the price of mutual funds and stocks shoot skyward, we allow ourselves to be convinced that it's time to board the bandwagon. We pay inflated prices for mutual fund units and stocks that others bought at half the price not long ago. When the funds and stock prices topple from the high price we paid for them, we grow even more irrational and sell the devils to … well, usually to the clever (and wealthy) folks we bought them from when the price was high.

Everyone who absorbed the lessons of grade two arithmetic can comprehend the wisdom of "Buy low, sell high." Why do so many

Canadians, intent on maximizing the earnings from their RRSPs and RRIFs, insist on buying high and, when the price inevitably collapses, selling low? Are we that irrational? Are we that genetically disposed to failure? Are we truly sheeple?

To a degree, our actions are a result of the manner in which mutual funds are sold and the way the salespeople are rewarded.

Investment markets, including stocks, bonds, mutual funds, resources, and commodities are priced according to two emotions: fear and greed. Or, if you prefer, depression and euphoria. Nightmares and dreams.

Fear drives people to sell in the face of threats ranging from terrorism to an oversupply of pork bellies. Greed persuades them that everyone else is getting rich, so they should join in.

Marketers of mutual funds know this axiom and have become expert at exploiting it to a remarkable degree. When things are going well, they feed our greed. When times get tough, they nurture our fears. There's nothing personal about it. It's strictly business.

Purveyors of Investment Pornography

During the last half of the 1990s, when mutual funds everywhere began generating substantial earnings in a market driven by abnormally low interest rates and a hyped tech market, mutual fund marketers engaged in investment pornography. The pornography description applies, financial advisor John J. De Goey explains, because "it gets you all hot and excited, but ultimately doesn't lead to anything productive." Mutual fund returns, trumpeted in newspaper advertisements with the same large type once reserved for declarations of war, qualify for the most egregious class of investment pornography when blasted from financial sections of our newspapers and financial commentators on radio and TV. The statistics and opinions must be important, or else why are they receiving so much attention?

But to those with a time horizon extending 10 years and beyond—which includes anyone under 70 years of age with an RRSP—investment pornography is, or should be, as insubstantial as tomorrow's weather forecast. It will be hot or cold, sunny or cloudy, calm or windy, wet or dry. And the next day, it will be different. Same with financial news. "In the short run," De Goey advises, "returns are unknowable. In the long run, they are inevitable."

In the late 1990s, when almost every mutual fund was crowing over annual returns of 15, 20, 25 percent and more while bonds were paying barely 5 or 6 percent, it was not irrational to ignore the entreaties. So millions of Canadians slid billions of RRSP dollars into funds at the top of the earnings curve. The higher the curve went, the more people clambered aboard, as though bandwagons roll on forever. They do not.

The ride was paralleled by the Bre-X phenomenon, which gave mutual fund companies an opportunity to create a new and exciting investment opportunity—or at least the illusion of it.

Bre-X Minerals Ltd. proved to be one of the great scams of all time, but while its worthless stock was rising ever upward, mutual fund companies saw an opportunity rising with it. Bre-X was the product of exploration for gold. So why not create a mutual fund based on exploration stocks, connected to natural resource funds? Well, why not bet the bundle on today's daily double while you are at it? Many exploration stocks are as likely to pay off as nags at a racetrack. This became a classic example of *funds du jour*.

When Bre-X and its resource cousins collapsed, telecom and internet companies took their place as new daily specials. Soon their high double- and even triple-digit returns made up much of the investment pornography. Encouraged by commissioned advisors, RRSP owners clambered aboard at the top of a new roller-coaster ride.

One of the most colourful guys in Canadian investment history was a stock promoter named Murray Pezim. One month he might be pushing a gold mine in Peru, the next month a textile company in Sudan. Pezim didn't promote stocks according to their value. He promoted what sold best. "If they want red suits," Pezim would say, "give 'em red suits." Murray Pezim died several years ago, and little has changed since.

Mutual Funds Bury Their Dead

Remember those hot exploration and resource mutual funds launched during the Bre-X furor, and the internet-based funds that followed? You'll find few of them around today, because the mutual fund industry keeps itself busy during bear markets by burying its dead, claiming the funds have been resurrected as winners. Perhaps no other industry in the world has the gall, the ability, and the dedication to conceal its failures by dressing them in the garb of success.

When every chicken shack operator could score a success by launching a mutual fund based on tech and internet stocks, AIM Trimark followed Murray Pezim's red suit rule and introduced several new funds investing in the tech bubble. They included the AIM Global Telecommunications Class, AIM Canadian Leaders, and, in June 2000, AIM RSP Dent Demographics Fund, all marketed with much fanfare and healthy MERs.

None of these new funds had any rationale for their existence beyond an attempt to take advantage of a marketing opportunity. In the bull market that dominated the late 1990s, fund companies expanded their lineup as a means of multiplying the potential number of funds that might prove winners. In effect, this was using someone else's money to bet more numbers at the roulette table—it increases your odds of winning and, if you lose, it's money out of someone else's pocket.

In a bear market, when few funds are able to post advances, the marketing strategy dictates that poor performers be hidden behind the skirts of more successful products.

The AIM RSP Dent Demographics Fund was a classic marketing example. The "Dent" had nothing to do with the risks of leaving your car in supermarket parking lots. It referred to the fund's inspiration, a man named Harry S. Dent, whose qualifications include a Harvard MBA, a degree in economics, and a book he authored in 2000 declaring North American stock markets would climb inexorably through to 2008, thrusting the Dow Jones Index to 40,000 or more, fuelled by baby boomer wealth and acquisitions. In mid-2000, the bandwagon was moving. Huzzah! Hop aboard and ride with us to wealth, or be left behind to wallow in poverty and squalor! That's as a good a reason as any to launch a mutual fund, right?

When its U.S. parent created a fund carrying Dent's name and based on his fearless predictions, AIM Trimark followed the lead in Canada, dressing Dent in a red suit. Perhaps it should have been a hair shirt, because here's how the fund performed over the next three years.

AIM DENT DEMOGRAPHIC TRENDS FUND	
2000	−32.68%
2001	−32.06%
2002	−17.22%

SOURCE: CONTRATHEHEARD.COM, JANUARY 2003. REPRODUCED WITH PERMISSION.

Anyone who bought $10,000 of Dent's red suit at the beginning of 2000 had a mere $3790 in his or her account three years later. The bandwagon hadn't just broken down—it had rolled backward into a ditch. AIM eventually buried the wreck in its Global Theme Fund. While at it, the company disposed of two other former stars, now ailing dogs, tucking its Global Telecommunications Class into the AIM Global Technology Class, and dumping its AIM

Canadian Leaders fund down the gullet of the Trimark Canadian Endeavour fund.

Glorianne Stromberg calls this technique "survivorship bias," designed to mislead investors into believing the fund sponsor is more successful than it appears. "It's a marvellously effective and efficient way," she suggests, "to fool most of the people all of the time."

"Buy and Hold." But When, and for How Long?

In fairness to mutual fund sponsors (and recalling the joke about the dog and its testicles), their marketing efforts are questionable and outrageous because they are permitted to be. Permission is granted from two groups: investors, who buy canned tuna/mutual funds with confidence when the price is high and sell with panic when the price is low; and regulators, who are unequipped or unwilling to demand more responsible actions. *The tactics of mutual fund marketers are used because they work, and they work because investors enable them to work*—through fear, through greed, and, unfortunately, through ignorance.

Consider the marketing program favoured by AIC, the "Buy. Hold. And Prosper" company, in the spring of 2003. In its publication titled *History Rewards Excellence,* AIC employed a variation on the device known in mutual fund marketing circles as a mountain chart, so called because, in tracing a fund's growth value over several years, the line appears like the north slope of Mount Everest— constantly rising past crevasses here and there on its way to an apparently infinite summit. With the bear market in 2000, mountain charts grew unfavourable because they were now showing the other side of the mountain, leaving the peak high above and far behind.

AIC's adaptation of a mountain chart is brilliant in its concept and doubtful in its credibility. Instead of using a line graph, it measured the growth in value of five sample companies over a 15-year period, thus justifying the firm's theme of "Buy, Hold," and so on. Here's what the chart showed (prepare to be impressed).

AIC'S FIVE EXAMPLES OF SPECTACULAR RETURNS	
COMPANY	GROWTH IN VALUE (%)*
American Express	+429
Johnson & Johnson Inc.	+1048
Loblaw Co. Ltd.	+1359
Nike Inc.	+1724
Pfizer Inc.	+1474
* December 1987 to December 2002	

SOURCE: AIC LTD. PRESENTATION: "HISTORY TENDS TO REWARD EXCELLENCE"/*TORONTO STAR*, MARCH 30, 2003.

Are you reaching for your wallet yet? Wait for some key facts.

First, only five companies are listed. It is not difficult to search out five companies at any point in time that have delivered impressive, even spectacular, returns. The trick is to identify them *before* growth is achieved, not after. It is also important to note that an equity-based mutual fund may hold shares in 100 or more companies; again, it is not surprising that a handful might deliver extraordinary results.

Next, note that four of the five companies are U.S. based. Three of these—Johnson & Johnson, American Express, and Nike—were held in AIC's Value Fund but only two—American Express and Johnson & Johnson—were among the fund's Top 10 holdings. Taken together, all five represented less than 10 percent of the fund's total holdings. How well did the other 90 percent fare?

Finally, and most importantly, consider the time frame being analyzed. In the investment game, 1987 is remembered as the year of the October Black Monday crash, when stocks tumbled through the biggest single-day collapse in history. Had you purchased American Express in early October 1987, before Black Monday's collapse, it would have taken seven long years to recover the pre–Black Monday price. In December 1987, American Express was a once-in-a-lifetime bargain. Were you wise enough to purchase it then? Were AIC's fund managers? Who knows? Nor did AIC identify the recent performance of these Big Five stocks, perhaps because after October 1999, American Express, Pfizer, and Nike all dropped in value—Nike by 20 percent.

What, in the end, did AIC's figures reveal? Only that the primary marketing tactic employed by mutual fund sponsors is the same one used by people fishing for trout: Dangle something fleshy on a sharp hook, yank at the right moment, and keep the net handy.

The fleshy bait in this case is a past history of impressive returns, the hook is the whispered legally required escape-clause/mantra "Past performance is no indication of future earnings," and the net consists of DSCs and sage advice about buying, holding, and prospering. Guess who the fish is.

Choosing Funds Strictly on Past Performance Is a Mug's Game

Fund performance over 1, 3, 5, and 10 years (if applicable) represents the core of investment pornography. The figures are used by RRSP/RRIF investors, as well as by advisors, brokers, and salespeople, as the basis for choosing a mutual fund. But how much can you rely on them?

Suppose it is 1999 and you are faced with choosing between two funds—the *Standback & Duck (S&D)* Canadian Equity Fund, and the *Fear & Greed (F&G)* Canadian Growth Fund. Both invest primarily in Canadian companies and both sport similar MERs. You start by examining the returns each has generated for its unit holders over the past five years, and they look like this:

S&D vs. F&G AVERAGE ANNUAL RETURNS (%)*					
FUND	1 YEAR	2 YEARS	3 YEARS	4 YEARS	5 YEARS
S&D	5.7	11.5	15.9	16.2	13.6
F&G	11.4	9.9	12.6	12.5	8.7
* January 1994 to January 1999					

Over the previous five years, the *S&D* fund produced average earnings each year of 13.6 percent for its unit holders. The *F&G* fund, while respectable at 8.7 percent earnings each year, looks weak in comparison. Which do you trust to make the most of your RRSP assets over the next five years? Most would choose the *S&D* fund, which explains the strong correlation between the best-performing mutual funds of last year and the bestselling funds of this year.

Small problem: *It doesn't work.* Buying last year's winners on the basis of that measure alone is as foolish as using last year's calendar. Here's proof.

Standback & Duck and *Fear & Greed* are pseudonyms for two Canadian equity-based mutual funds. If you had plunked 10 Big Ones down on the *S&D* fund back in 1999, see how you would have done five years later.

S&D vs. F&G AVERAGE ANNUAL RETURNS (%)*					
FUND	1 YEAR	2 YEARS	3 YEARS	4 YEARS	5 YEARS
S&D	20.4	15.2	10.3	14.1	14.3
F&G	81.4	57.7	31.9	28.2	25.5
* January 1999 to January 2004					

Your $10,000 investment in the *S&D* fund back in 1999 grew to $17,150 over the five-year period (14.3 annualized average × 5 years = 71.5 percent growth of $10,000). Hey, not bad. Had you chosen the *F&G* fund, investing the same amount of money over the same period, you would have $22,750 (25.5 × 5 = 127.5 percent growth) or $5600 more in your RRSP than with the *S&D* fund. This does not necessarily mean you have the better fund for the next five years. Research indicates that only about 38 percent of funds delivering better-than-average performance in any given year will manage to deliver the same level of performance, relative to other funds in their class, in the following year.

At first glance, it may look as though choosing the best mutual fund is a mug's game. It is, *as long as you base your choice on past performance figures exclusively, supported by the unchallenged recommendations of your commission-based advisor or broker.*

Fortunately, there is a brighter side. More than a handful of mutual funds beat the odds by delivering above-average performance on a relatively consistent basis. The trick is to identify them, which requires research and the honest assistance of a good financial advisor. Looking beyond average annual performance returns, you should favour funds with low volatility (the way in which the fund's returns and losses vary over an extended period compared with similar funds), especially when you are age 50 or older; low fees (reasonable MERs and no loads of any kind); the fund's mandate (what does the fund invest in—steady blue-chip companies? Volatile smaller companies? Special sectors such as mining or communications? Geographical areas such as Asia, emerging economies, Europe?); and qualified managers (Is he or she new? Highly regarded?).

Chapter 12 includes a checklist for identifying mutual funds that suit your needs and are most likely to enrich your portfolio. Meanwhile, here's yet another way that investment industry marketing skews things in favour of commission-based advisors.

Wrap Accounts: The Devil Persuades You He Doesn't Exist

One of the best movies of recent years was 1995's *The Usual Suspects*. Gritty and mesmerizing, it featured superb acting, great cinematography, and outstanding writing. The plot hinges on a statement made by the lead character, played by actor Kevin Spacey (who won an Academy Award for his portrayal). "The Devil's biggest achievement," Spacey's character says, "was in persuading the world that he doesn't exist."

The existence of wrap accounts suggests that someone in the investment industry was familiar with Spacey's line when the industry developed and marketed this product. How else to explain a service that enables a "professional" to earn more money by doing less work? If the investment industry can convince you that wrap accounts are a good idea because you pay a higher price for less service, maybe Satan pulled off his scam after all.

Wrap accounts are derived from a basic idea gone bad, like that casserole you tucked at the back of the refrigerator last month and forgot about.

The basic idea is asset allocation, the practice of shifting components in your RRSP/RRIF according to changing economic conditions and strategies. It's somewhat like piloting a ship across the ocean—you correct your course to adjust for tides and winds, and steer clear of shoals or storms, keeping your eye on your destination. Brokers and financial advisors might call it rebalancing, preferring the term to an analogy associated with shipwrecks and icebergs.

Banks and mutual fund companies promote wrap accounts as a means of constantly rebalancing your investment. Consign your money to one of their wrap accounts and they'll adjust the investment mix as needed, according to your investor profile. These profiles are usually assigned one of three descriptions: aggressive, moderate and conservative, based on your age, investment knowledge, and risk comfort level. Want to make as much money in as short a time as possible? You're aggressive. Want to preserve your capital and sleep well at night? You're conservative. If you don't feel totally comfortable with either extreme, you're moderate, which is where most people end up anyway.

While wrap account adherents make it sound as though the investment mix in your RRSP/RRIF is being tailored like a custom-fitted suit, you usually buy off the rack. Most wraps consist of mixes prepackaged according to the three profiles. Rather than being fitted for a wardrobe, it's more like choosing an airline meal—do you want the chicken, the beef, or the pasta? Forget about à la carte.

Pooled wraps are basic wrap plans dressed to go out on the town, which means they're aimed at a more affluent market. The packages are more elegantly wrapped and carry a name that suggests exclusivity. Two of the most prominent pooled wraps are AGF Harmony and Russell Sovereign, the latter a U.S.-based package marketed in Canada through RBC Investments, ScotiaMcLeod, TD Waterhouse, and other brokerages. Instead of everyday mutual funds, pooled wraps may hold funds not available to the great unwashed, although both types of funds may be directed by the same fund managers.

The advantages of pooled wraps, claims the promotion material, include research, consulting, monitoring, reporting, and perhaps custodial services. Plus prestige and exclusivity.

Here's where the Devil comes in.

First, wrap accounts do the same thing that your financial advisor or broker is supposed to be doing to earn his fee or commission. The basic premise of every financial advisor's pitch involves making decisions that you, you ignorant and uneducated slob, are not equipped to make. Advisors boast that they are in tune with investment policies and strategies, enabling them to guide you in buying, selling, adjusting, and otherwise rebalancing investments in your account. If your broker or advisor does this effectively, congratulations. But if he is being paid for this chore through sales commissions and trailer fees, why is he advising you to hire someone else to do the job?

Next, fees or commissions paid in exchange for the privilege of placing your RRSP/RRIF in a wrap account are in addition to charges already being levied by mutual funds held in the account. If the wrap account contains five mutual funds, each with an average MER of 2.5, for example, the wrap account fee might add an additional 2.5 percent, which means you're paying 5 percent for something that should be costing you half that much if your advisor were earning his commission and trailer fees. *But he is not*—that's being left to the wrap account people, remember? This is a good deal for advisors pushing wrap accounts—more money for less work. It is not a good deal for most wrap account clients, however. And it gets worse.

Wrap accounts cost you more than an extra level of commissions or service fees. They also limit the choice of funds available for your portfolio, which means if the mutual funds in your wrap account begin barking and chasing cats up trees, too bad—you lack the opportunity to ditch those dogs for another choice. Many wrap accounts also fail to provide opportunities for investing in sectors such as gold and precious metals. True, sector investing should represent only a minority portion of most RRSPs/RRIFs, but you have given up flexibility and opportunity in return for putting your portfolio on automatic pilot and paying a premium to do it.

Finally, it comes down to performance. A Porsche costs more than a Toyota because it goes faster and turns more tightly. Does it make sense to pay extra for RRSP/RRIF management that produces similar results with your investments? The simple answer is no. Every Porsche might perform the same, but not every wrap account does. In fact, some of the most popular wrap accounts *underperform* the market, charging extra for the privilege of watching your investments lag.

Consider Sovereign Portfolio, the most heavily promoted wrap account in the country, managing over $100 billion in client assets.

"Because each Sovereign Portfolio is customized to reflect individual investor needs and goals," boasts its website, "there is an infinite number of Sovereign portfolios." Perhaps. But the number of ways to assess Sovereign's bottom line is limited, and none is encouraging.

Here, from the promotional material for Sovereign, are average annual returns for RRSP portfolios in the three investor-style categories. Compare them with the average Canadian balanced mutual fund over the same period. Balanced funds invest both in equities—company shares traded on the Toronto Stock Exchange (TSX), for the most part—and guaranteed income sources such as government bonds and T-bills. Many advisors dislike balanced funds for portfolios $100,000 and up, believing better returns are available from a combination of equity-based mutual funds plus bonds. In this instance, balanced funds replicate the promoted benefit of wrap accounts by offering both growth and security.

RRSP PORTFOLIOS – ANNUALIZED TO JUNE 30, 2004, NET OF FEES, CLASS A UNITS			
PORTFOLIO	3 YEARS	5 YEARS	10 YEARS
Conservative	2.30	2.23	6.43
Moderate	1.62	2.07	6.86
Aggressive	0.57	0.85	6.72
Average Cdn. Balanced Fund	3.4	4.2	8.0
S&P/TSX Canadian Equity Index	−1.0	6.5	8.6

SOURCES: SOVEREIGN WEBSITE, JULY 31, 2004; GLOBEFUND.COM, JULY 31, 2004.
REPRODUCED WITH PERMISSION.

By running your fingers down the list of 500-plus RRSP-eligible balanced mutual funds and choosing one at random, you were likely to choose a fund that easily outperformed an equivalent wrap account assembled by the vaunted Sovereign investment experts. Selecting a low-MER Canadian Equity Index fund would have placed you substantially ahead of the Sovereign wrap account within five years. If I were a Sovereign client—especially one categorized as aggressive— I would ask what I was getting for my money besides exclusivity and prestige which, the last I heard, rarely adds to the bottom line of anyone's investment.

If the performance of wrap accounts is open to question, their ability to enfold you in a fog of jargon and hype is indisputable. Consider this edifying passage from a published interview with a Sovereign investment manager attempting to explain the difference between a Growth and a Premium Growth portfolio: "'Core growth' exposed the investor to growth companies while reducing risk by diversifying the investors' portfolio across 40 to 50 stocks. 'Premium growth' on the other hand is designed to provide investors with an increased focus on growth stocks via a highly concentrated portfolio consisting of 30 to 40 large to mid-cap growth-oriented stocks through a predominantly bottom-up stock selection process. There is a focus on higher alpha and more emphasis on earnings momentum, estimate revisions, earnings surprise, and an ability to generate strong performance in a more immediate time horizon."[3]

For the record, the last sentence means they'll accept higher risk to generate more money. (And when was the last time you encountered the phrase "earnings surprise" in an apparently positive context?) The paragraph tells you nothing except that the manager would benefit from a course in effective communication. It also suggests that the company is unfamiliar with the widely acknowledged precept that you should never invest in anything you do not understand.

Are wrap accounts ever beneficial? They are to the advisor or broker who successfully promotes them. To typical RRSP/RRIF owners, they appear one more way of being stroked while their pockets are picked.[4]

Exchange Traded Funds and Index Funds: Never Heard of Them? Guess Why

Evidence of the investment industry's dependence on commission-based sales and mutual fund marketing techniques can be found in two types of mutual funds whose descriptions are difficult for commissioned advisors to speak aloud. If your advisor, broker, or mutual fund salesperson has ever uttered the words *index funds* or *exchange traded funds* (ETFs) without tagging them with a negative description, you have a winner.

Few Canadian RRSP/RRIF owners know about either, despite the fact that many portfolios could profit from them. The difference? Marketing, of course.

Index funds, as noted earlier, mirror a chosen index designed to reflect the overall market or a defined sector of the market. The S&P/TSX Composite, consisting of companies that the brain trusts of the Toronto Stock Exchange believe represent the state of the Canadian stock market, is considered a broad index. The S&P/TSX 60 narrows the field to include only the 60 largest companies making up the overall index, while S&P/TSX Small Cap Index includes companies whose capitalization—the total value of all company shares available—is under $500 million. The famous Dow Jones Index and the S&P 500 track U.S. companies, while dozens of other lesser-known indices represent various economies according to geographical description (Europe, Asia, Pacific Rim, India) and business sector (transportation, energy, gold, and so on).

Index funds are passively managed, since the fund manager need only consult the chosen index to determine which equities to buy and sell. Other funds are labelled *actively managed,* describing the research, evaluation, monitoring, and perhaps even dart-throwing used by managers in their attempt to outperform markets.

If market indices are already assembled to provide a relatively broad view of a market or sector, and if most mutual fund managers fail to beat the market year after year (held back by both the impact of the MER and their own inability to forecast the future), why shouldn't a mutual fund simply mirror the chosen index? Management costs would (or should) be negligible, stock-trading expenses would be reduced, and the savings would (or should) be passed along to investors.

For the majority of mutual funds, this is true. The MER for most Canadian index funds is less than 1 percent, compared with an average MER of 2.82 percent for actively managed funds.[5] This gives you some idea why index funds are rarely recommended by people who earn their income from commissions. Those low MERs do not leave much room for trailer fees and other kickbacks—unless, of course, the recommended index fund has an outrageously high MER, such as the Great-West Life Equity Index, which taps its investors with a 2.37 MER despite that it seeks to track the S&P/TSX 300 within 25 basis points (0.25 percent). Unfortunately, it consistently trails the index performance by 2.5 percent, which, coincidentally, is close to its MER.

Index funds also have their risks. The folks managing the index march to their own drummer when they choose the companies composing the fund. In the summer of 2000, a single Canadian company represented almost one-third of the value of the TSX 300 Index, which meant that every mutual fund mirroring the index had one-third of its investment in that one company. No fund manager with an IQ higher than his waist measurement would invest such a large proportion of the fund in a single stock, but index fund sponsors had little choice except follow the TSX's lead. The company was Nortel. When it tumbled from $125 per share to less than a buck, the effect was like tying an anvil to your leg and tossing it out of your boat and into the ocean. Everything sank along with Nortel, a fate that most actively managed funds tended to escape to the same extent because they were able to rebalance the funds and place less emphasis on this single company.

In spite of this drawback (and most people consider the Nortel experience an anomaly), if you have more than two or three mutual funds in your RRSP/RRIF, one should be a broadly based index fund with a MER of less than 1 percent. Keep in mind, however, that an extended bear market in which stock prices fall for several years means your indexed fund will tumble to the same degree—index funds have no life preservers, in the form of an astute fund manager buying and selling to lessen the impact.

Some investors swear by index funds; others swear at them. In reality, most advisors fail to recommend an index fund, and most Canadians fail to ask about them because mutual fund sponsors fail to market them. See the connection?

An even better example of the industry's neglected stepchildren are exchange traded funds (ETFs). Like index funds, ETFs track a specific stock index according to company size, geographic location, industry, or some other established parameter. Unlike mutual funds, however, ETFs can be bought and sold like common shares of companies such as Petro-Canada, Hudson's Bay, and Dofasco. The value of each ETF unit fluctuates with the current market, and the cost to unit holders, meaning you and me, is minimal. No matter how you measure them, ETFs deserve a place in every RRSP/RRIF portfolio you can name. So why aren't they in yours ... or anyone else's, for that matter? Because of marketing, or the lack of it. And because of trailer fees, or the lack of them.

ETFs have not made anything near the impact they should have made, despite their many advantages and benefits. In 2004, following Eliot Spitzer's exposures of excesses and outright illegalities among mutual fund operators, ETFs held barely 2 percent of the U.S. market, and the figure was similarly low in Canada.

ETF sponsors are direct sellers, with no in-house sales staff to beat the drums on their behalf, and no trailer fee incentive to encourage commissioned advisors to do it for them. If yet another example were needed to prove the injustice of trailer fees and the manner in which they conflict with the advisor's purported role of acting as professional counsel for clients, it's this. In effect, trailer fees pay the advisor for doing nothing; their express purpose is to encourage the advisor to persuade clients not to sell, and certainly not to consider alternate investment vehicles.

All this confirms that RRSP/RRIF owners who invest with the prospect of long-term rewards need an understanding of the available alternatives. They should also, if dealing with an advisor, insist that she explain the options in detail. Any advisor or broker who refuses to discuss these alternatives or who clearly has made investment recommendations beneficial to the advisor or broker and detrimental to the client should be summarily fired and replaced. This, of course, is more easily advised than accomplished, as we shall see in the next chapter.

A Guide to Investment Divorce

Carol MacKinnon smiles in the sunlight that floods the deck of her cottage. Set above an inlet of Bowen Island, in British Columbia, the home represents a fulfillment of sorts for the 52-year-old leadership trainer and musician. Inside are her piano, her cello, and the various accoutrements of a varied and interesting life. Her dog naps at her feet and birds flutter around her feeder. Life is good—certainly better than three years earlier.

"I worked all of my life," she reflects. "I never wanted to work past 65 if I could help it, so I put everything I could afford into my RRSP." A single woman with ailing parents, Carol was determined to achieve financial independence and recognized the importance of obtaining independent advice. "I was a financial illiterate," she laughs. "I didn't understand mutual funds. I just knew I didn't want to be in the stock market because I figured that was a place for gamblers, and I didn't want to gamble with my money—I'd worked too darn hard for it! Of course, I didn't know that I was already in the stock market with the mutual funds I owned."

In the 1990s, Carol was employed in Toronto, where she struck a close friendship with a co-worker whose husband was a sales agent for a large insurance company. "She was a chartered accountant, he had a lot of experience; they lived in a large home in an exclusive Toronto neighbourhood, and both drove expensive sports cars," Carol recalls. "They were the picture of success. After a while, the husband suggested I transfer my account to him. I knew people in the investment community were paid by commission, but these were my friends. I trusted them. So I moved my account to him and kept maximizing my RRSP contributions every year. I was working long hard hours, and I knew this was the time, in my 40s, when I should be putting away every penny I could afford. So I did."

In 2000, Carol moved to Vancouver to be closer to her ailing parents on Bowen Island, keeping her account with her Toronto insurance agent friend and his wife. When the media began reporting news of falling stock prices in tech and internet shares, and the losses began to be reflected in her account statements, Carol grew concerned.

"I called my friends two or three times," she says, "asking if I was still okay, if my account was in the right mix, and I visited them as a friend and to discuss my account. Each time, I was told everything was fine, that my account was still around $400,000 in value, and I could retire any time I wanted."

Not likely. Within a year Carol's RRSP had dropped by more than $100,000, with no end of the slide in sight. "I watched my savings slipping away, all the money I had worked so hard to make," she says. "I didn't need to see it grow as much as stay where it was, or close to it. But everything I owned just kept going down, down ..."

Carol began to question the suitability of the investments chosen for her. Many of them appeared based on the same kinds of investments that seemed to be the hardest-hit. "You're panicking," she was informed by the insurance agent during one telephone conversation. "Do you really think that Nortel will not recover?" By this time, Carol's RRSP had lost $200,000, about half its value, and her retirement dreams were sinking with it.

When Carol found herself being intimidated by empty, often angry, responses to her queries, she began sending email requests for explanation. These produced accusations that she did not understand either the market or the investing strategy being used, and was not appreciative of the work being done on her behalf. One of these messages arrived in the winter of 2001 from the financial advisor and his wife at their winter home in Florida. "You're being foolish, you're losing your nerve," she was told. "We're the experts, so trust us!"

"That's when the penny dropped," Carol remembers with a rueful smile. "That's when I asked myself, 'Is this friendship really worth it?' I was at the point of real despair. I had never asked for handouts, never looked for special treatment. I had done everything to provide for my security. I understood there could be risks with investments, but losing this much money in such a short period of time just didn't make sense. Half my life savings had vanished in two years. I had hoped to be at least semi-retired, but instead I was back to working 80 hours a week, trying to make up the losses in my RRSP, which was supposed to be growing but was shrinking faster than I could replace the money."

One of Carol's pleasures is music, both vocal and instrumental. In pursuit of this, she joined a church choir on Bowen Island, travelling there by ferry two or three times a week to rehearse and perform. Singing was a way to avoid thinking about her RRSP losses. After choir practice one night in March 2001, her anxieties surfaced and without thinking she blurted out to one of the choir members standing near her, "I'm just so worried about my RRSP. I've lost over half my money in less than two years and nobody seems to care about it!"

"I had no idea who I was saying this to," Carol laughs now. "I had never spoken to this man before, although I had seen him at choir practice many times. He was just a nice older man, and I was surprised when he told me he happened to be a financial advisor living on Bowen Island and working from his home, although he kept an office in Vancouver. When he offered to review my account and give his opinion, I went along with the idea. I just wanted someone to give me an honest answer."

The answer that the financial advisor, a tall, soft-spoken Dutchman named Hans Merkelbach, gave her was, "Appalling!" Carol's account had been invested in life insurance–owned back-end-loaded segregated mutual funds investing in Canadian, U.S., Japanese, and European equities, each fund carrying MERs as high as 4 percent or more, and each with abysmal performance. Then things got worse. To transfer her investments from these DSC funds would cost Carol about $13,000 since the DSC would be applied not to the current value of her investments but to the original investment, which was twice as high as the funds were worth.

"When Hans explained this to me, I was shocked," Carol says. "But he wasn't. He told me he had seen many accounts like mine, designed to make money for the advisor first. I was flabbergasted that I was going to have to pay $13,000 of my money to correct a mistake somebody else had made." Now Carol understood what her friends had meant when they kept telling her she couldn't afford to get out of the money-losing funds; the high deferred service charges would take another major bite out of her RRSP assets. "That produced a new level of disgust in me. I wasn't sure what to do with my RRSP, but I knew I couldn't leave it in the hands of my 'friends' anymore. I sent them a letter informing them that I was moving my account to Hans Merkelbach, and I frankly never wanted to talk to them again."

And her friends' response?

A cool smile. "They asked if I really believed someone on Bowen Island could know more about investing than they could, located as they were in Toronto."

Her move proved fortuitous. By early 2004 her account, newly structured by Merkelbach, had recovered much of its value, reaching a balance of about $320,000 and climbing. Had she kept her portfolio unchanged from the way it had been assembled by her Toronto advisors, the balance would have drifted to about $130,000 (from about $400,000) on that same date, even after the market recovery of 2003.

"The effective word here is capitulation," Carol says, sipping her tea and scratching her dog's ear. The ferry from Vancouver sounds its horn as it rounds the corner of the inlet, approaching the island dock. The sun's early spring warmth is like a blessing. "There comes a point where you just have to surrender, where you have to let go because the evidence tells you to accept what has happened. It is a real spiritual moment of darkness. I was giving up on a friendship and giving up on dreams of the retirement lifestyle I thought I had worked for. I just had to move on."

Like all salespeople, financial advisors appreciate the value of nurturing personal relationships with clients. Unlike most relationships, however, this one is asymmetric, and the investment industry tries to keep it that way. Over and over, Canadian RRSP/RRIF investors are told they are not sufficiently knowledgeable to make good investment decisions and, to the extent that most Canadians lack awareness of basic investment strategies and instruments, this is correct. Unfortunately, as in Carol MacKinnon's case, the asymmetry of knowledge is used as a club to deflect concerns that clients may express about their own money.

If clients cannot understand and appreciate the investment strategy being proposed by financial advisors, the fault lies not with the clients who are rightly concerned that the strategy meets their goals, but with the financial advisors' ability to communicate. And when clients are honestly confused or distressed about the efficacy of the investment program, they deserve more than a response limited to "Trust us—we're the experts." They do not deserve bullying and disdain over their concerns. Yet this is precisely the way many financial advisors, brokers, and mutual fund salespeople have been treating Canadians for years. And no one seems to care about it.

Segregated Funds: They Are a Good Deal for Somebody, But Probably Not You

Some of Carol MacKinnon's RRSP was invested in segregated funds, a mutual fund hybrid that blends aspects of two industries—the investment industry and the insurance industry—into one product that assures substantial gains for the salesperson.

Over most of the 1990s, every major mutual fund and insurance company in Canada trumpeted its version of segregated (or "seg") funds, claiming they delivered the best of both worlds: the growth potential of equity-based mutual funds, and the guaranteed principle of GICs. It was like the travel industry promising the comfort of a sea cruise and the speed of a transatlantic flight at the same time. Who could resist?

Seg funds appeared to be the Holy Grail of investment faith. If the value of the fund rose substantially before the end of the 10-year term, you could lock in your profits at that point for another 10 years. And if the fund lost money over a 10-year locked-in period, your segregated investment didn't lose at all because the original investment would be there to be redeemed.

In reality, seg funds were old vinegar in new bottles, poured in because Canadians had grown wary of the benefits of whole life insurance peddled to them since Sir John A. was a pup. Whole life insurance was a package that promised both a life insurance premium to your beneficiary while you worked, and a pot of gold, or at least loonies, at the end of the rainbow when you retired. Eventually people realized they would be further ahead by purchasing cheaper term insurance and investing the difference in their RRSP, getting control over their future and a tax break at the same time. Insurance companies retaliated with seg funds, hooking them onto familiar mutual funds from reassuring names such as Trimark and CI Management.

Here is how the seg fund promoters explained things.

REGULAR FUND vs. SEGREGATED FUND PERFORMANCE		
	MUTUAL FUND ($)	SEG MUTUAL FUND ($)
Initial Investment	10,000	10,000
10-year/10% average return	20,000	20,000
10-year/2% average loss	8000	10,000
After Five Years		
10% average gain	15,000	15,000 (locked in)
After Another Five Years		
8% average loss	9000	15,000

Ten thousand dollars in both a regular mutual fund and a seg version of the same fund would grow in value at the same rate (for the purpose of this illustration), so an average 10-percent annual return would double the value of both in 10 years. If both funds lost money over that 10-year period, the regular mutual fund would have a lower value than the original investment—you would be out of pocket. If both funds gained, you could lock in the seg fund's gain and extend the term for another 10 years, ensuring you would not lose the gain you already earned, while committing yourself to maintaining the investment for the next 10 years.

Seg funds grew popular enough for insurance firms to tighten the rules in their favour. Most seg funds now guarantee only 75 percent of your original investment and require a 15-year lock-in period (as Carol MacKinnon's did), sucking much of the bloom from this particular rose.

It might be said that Carol MacKinnon's life insurance friend placed a substantial portion of her RRSP assets in seg funds as a form of guarantee for several years. It might even be argued that this constituted a conservative strategy intent on preserving her capital. But it would be a weak argument at best. Here's why:

- It is difficult to lose a portion of your principal over 10 years of investing in quality funds. In only one 10-year period between 1925 and 2000 did any North American index lose money (1929 to 1938, when Canadian stocks declined a total of 0.02 percent over the entire span). So why bother paying extra to protect yourself against a loss that will likely not occur?
- That seg funds originate with insurance companies and not investment specialists should tell you something about their true value. They are essentially insurance products, not investment vehicles.
- Like all insurance products, seg funds come with a premium, paid by the investor (who else?). In this case, the premium is buried in much higher MERs for the same kind of fund sold without the seg/insurance factor.
- The elevated MERs make it difficult to achieve the same returns as non-seg versions of the same fund.
- The biggest benefit of a seg fund is creditor protection (they may not be available for seizure in the event of a lawsuit and might be shielded from bankruptcy) and estate creation (you can name a beneficiary to receive a seg fund when you die).

"There was no hope that Carol would make money from those funds," Hans Merkelbach says.[1] "The kinds of losses suffered by Carol can shatter people's lives. If you are 50 or 60 years old or older, you will not be able to recover these losses, and it is foolish, maybe even criminal, for advisors to say in effect, "Stop your whining!"

Among a small group of investors, Merkelbach has become something of a legend for his contrarian views on the role of a financial advisor. He issues annual report cards to each of his clients, revealing the performance, positive or negative, resulting from his counsel over the previous year. Serving about 120 clients—"And I really don't want any more, thank you"—Hans and his wife live an idyllic life in a spectacular custom-built home on the shore of Howe Sound, B.C., where eagles nest in the tall pines, cruise ships pass by on the water, and snow-capped Mount Garibaldi shimmers in the distance. Although he maintains an office in Vancouver, Merkelbach prefers to work from an office on the second floor of his home, overlooking the water and the mountains.

"All Money Is Serious Money"

Merkelbach lacks a university degree, placing greater value on the experience he gathered as a bond trader and investment manager for insurance companies and mutual funds before obtaining his securities trading licence. "Degrees don't help an advisor do a better job for clients," Merkelbach suggests. "For some advisors it limits their ability because they become accustomed to doing things by the book. They're textbook-taught, so they make decisions according to whatever the textbook says, instead of what the market situation and the clients' needs tell them to do. Figuring things out for yourself takes hard work, and that's not something that many advisors take the time to do."

Merkelbach is especially dismissive of advisors who belittle investor concerns about losses. "All money is serious money," he states, "and should be treated seriously."

In Merkelbach's view, the majority of financial advisors sell products instead of investment advice. "As long as we have people in this business who cannot make a decent income from fees paid to them by their clients, we will have the commission system," he observes. "And as long as we have the commission system, we will never have full transparency. Embedded compensation ensures that real power in the industry is in the hands of the mutual fund sponsors and financial advisors, not the investor. Clients, especially those with RRSPs and RRIFs, must grasp this idea."

No critic of the DSC is more bitter than Merkelbach. "The DSC has hurt clients more than anything else in this business. It has been a bonanza for the mutual fund industry and a disaster for investors." He does not, however, retain as much distaste for high MER levels. "Sometimes a relatively high MER is not only acceptable, it is necessary, based on the amount of work needed by the manager to run the fund," he explains. "It's one factor in choosing a fund. You have to look at others as well."

Merkelbach's approach to making investment decisions on behalf of clients, in addition to accounting for each client's individual needs and expectations, rejects broad applications of the buy-and-hold system. "It works relatively well when equities and bonds rise in tandem, but works poorly during bear markets," he points out. Nor is he a great fan of asset allocation: "It's a 'popular mechanics' kind of diversification, a simplistic approach that can be compared to throwing darts at a board." Hope, Merkelbach suggests, plays a role in successful asset allocation. "Any time you find yourself hoping in this business," he says, "the odds are that you are on the wrong path, or that you did something stupid that needs correcting. During a bear market, the idea of moving investments such as mutual funds back and forth according to their performance levels will likely prove futile."

In mid-2004, with the prospect of rising interest rates, the return of inflation, and global uncertainty, Merkelbach favoured Canadian federal and provincial bond funds noting that these had outperformed every market sector over the 20 years between 1984 and 2004. He was also advising clients to move into resource sectors such as gold and precious metals, commodities, energy, and inflation-indexed government bond mutual funds.

Most of Merkelbach's clients were prepared to take his advice, and why not? In 2003, the accounts of all of Merkelbach's clients grew in value by an average of 34 percent. Those who had retained him as their advisor on or before November 1, 1999, when Merkelbach began plotting and issuing his annual report card, watched in glee as their portfolios produced a total return over the next 50 months— to December 31, 2003—of 110 percent, achieved through the worst period of a serious bear market.

Start by Asking Questions and Seeking Answers

Merkelbach's performance on behalf of clients proves that Warren Buffet's maxim—First, never lose money—is attainable. There are other Merkelbachs in the Canadian investment industry, to be sure. Identifying them is a serious matter. Here are some dos and don'ts, based on observations from many people on both sides of the investor-advisor fence, that are worth following when dealing with advisors:

- Don't feel you owe loyalty to a financial advisor or broker who a) does not appear as concerned as you about losses suffered in your RRSP/RRIF, b) chooses not to explain rationales for decisions or recommendations, c) contacts you only within 60 days of the deadline for RRSP contributions, d) appears uncomfortable or dismissive when answering questions about MERs, DSCs, and similar matters, e) proposes only funds with DSCs, or f) responds to questions or concerns in a dismissive manner.
- Don't choose a new advisor or planner based on a pitch made at financial seminars or forums. You are a fish, the seminars are

barrels, and the advisors, brokers, and planners are armed. Get the picture?

- Don't respond beyond a polite "No, thank you" to an unsolicited telephone call from an advisor or broker offering assistance. As a lad I visited racetracks, where colourful characters offered to pick winners for me. Advisors making cold calls are their progeny.

- Don't be impressed with a financial advisor's education level or status within his or her company. Formal education is less important in an investment advisor than intelligence, long experience, empathy for client concerns, personal integrity, and a willingness to work hard. Membership in a brokerage's President's Club, Chairman's Club, Gold Key Club, or similar group means the member sold more products than most others in the organization. You're not looking for an outstanding salesperson; you're looking for an outstanding advisor, and the two do not always coincide.

- Don't accept a financial advisor's boasts about gains in a bull market. From 1995 to 2000, a dart-throwing chimpanzee could have produced a winning portfolio.

- Don't permit yourself to be bullied or intimidated. If a financial advisor suggests that the proposed strategy, or any element of it, is too difficult for you to understand, ask for a simpler strategy—or a better advisor.

- Don't forget whose money it is, and who should profit most from it.

- Do start by asking friends, relatives, business associates, and others how they feel about their advisor. How much attention do they get? How comfortable are they recommending him or her?

- Do note if the advisor begins by asking a number of key questions before proposing a plan or revamping your existing portfolio. These should be questions about your income, assets, financial goals, health, marital status, pension program, and investment knowledge and experience. Answer directly and honestly. If your investment knowledge is low, don't try to impress the advisor by suggesting you're practically Warren Buffet's guru.

- Do ask about the advisor's success on behalf of clients during the bear market of 2000 to 2003. Did the advisor break even or gain? If not, how much did she lose on average? What was the advisor's strategy? How would she change it? Once you pass 50 years of age, a main criterion in choosing an advisor you can rely on is that she has a risk-averse investment strategy, also known as capital preservation.

- Do ask to see a sample statement from the advisor's firm. Don't worry about the figures—just decide if you can make sense of it. Are the assets clearly indicated? Can you understand key elements such as gain/loss, book value, and foreign content?

- Do note the advisor's familiarity with, and ability to discuss and recommend, a wide range of products. Which mutual fund companies, and funds within them, does he favour and why? Would he recommend no-load funds that pay no commission or trailer fees, if the funds fit your needs? If so, how would he charge for his services? How does he feel about bonds? Some mutual fund salespeople are very good at selling mutual funds (surprise!) but not so good at understanding and responding to individual investor goals and concerns.

- Do favour someone who listens more than he talks, rather than vice versa.

- Do note the advisor or broker's general appearance and carriage. You don't need a Ben Affleck or Belinda Stronach handling your portfolio, but you should favour someone who is well groomed, confident, respectful of your concerns, and open in his or her responses.

• Do ask how the advisor is compensated for her services. If by commissions, are those commissions negotiable under some circumstances? Would she consider switching to a fee system at some point?

Some of these questions may seem intrusive and so may be difficult to ask. If you feel this way, or if you sense any antagonism or resistance on the part of the advisor, keep asking yourself, Whose money is it, and who deserves to profit from it?

CELEBRITY BINGO

Of all the events planned for Teachers' Professional Development Day in February 1990, none interested Jean King more than the session on retirement planning organized by Moynes Securities Ltd. and featuring Brian Costello as keynote speaker.

"I had heard Mr. Costello on the radio," Jean King recalls in her north Toronto home, seated next to her husband Lindsay, a retired United Church minister. "He described the investments available through Moynes and spoke of them favourably. Later, I understood that Moynes Securities had paid Costello $2000 for his little talk to us."

Costello's "little talk" discussed the benefits of limited partnerships (LPs) as a way of maximizing capital to build a retirement nest egg outside an RRSP. The idea of investing in that manner held a good deal of appeal for Mrs. King, and as she listened to Costello describe potential tax benefits, she grew more than intrigued—she was practically pre-sold. After Costello finished earning his two grand for a 30-minute spiel, up to the microphone stepped an executive from Moynes to promote—surprise!—a limited partnership in a Kitchener, Ontario, condominium managed by Track Investments.

"The appeal [of the LP] was the increase in value of the condominium units, plus tax write-offs," Jean King explains. "We were promised between $73,000 and $86,000 in tax write-offs over five years."

Jean King bought two units in a deal that required her to pay $75,000 in borrowed cash and extended payments of $2400 every three months. It was a stretch for the couple's modest income, but it was also a commitment toward financial independence and a comfortable retirement. Besides, Brian Costello spoke highly of such an investment, and he appeared to be almost everywhere back in 1990—on a national call-in radio program similar to the one that enticed Barbara Benson (every major city in the country seems to sprout phone-in gurus who often employ their show as an extension of their marketing efforts), in newspaper columns and newsletters, and as a face and voice recommending various investment vehicles. Surely this was a prudent investment.

In reality, it was a disastrous decision. Limited partnerships based on real estate are high-risk ventures suitable for investors with the risk tolerance of nearsighted lion tamers. A limited partnership is simply a means of obtaining other people's money to finance an investment. Shares are sold through brokers, who skim as much as 10 percent off the top before management fees and expenses are deducted over the course of the investment, which may range from 7 to 10 years. During that period, investors are locked into the deal, meaning they can't vote with their feet and exit from a bad operation. They can only sit and watch their original outlay shrink day by day, hoping that something will remain when the term is up.

Even solidly based, well-managed LPs are not the kind of vehicle a prudent financial advisor would recommend to people like the Kings, and this one was neither. As events transpired, Track Investments was little more than a shell game, and its principals ultimately were convicted of 32 counts of fraud after the $2 million handed to them by hopeful investors vanished. The Kings lost the $75,000 cash borrowed to get into the venture, plus about another $25,000 in quarterly payments. Then things got worse.

"Revenue Canada changed their minds about the tax deductions they had been allowing us for several years," Mrs. King sighs, "saying we had gone into the deal with no expectation of profit. They wanted all of our deferred taxes back, which amounted to about $50,000. They kept applying interest to the balance while we argued against it, and eventually the amount they demanded came to $100,000."

The case reached the Supreme Court of Canada, which ruled against such clawbacks, forcing Revenue Canada, by this time renamed as Canada Customs and Revenue, to abandon efforts to recover the money. But to two retired people, the years of threats of property seizure and even jail terms exacted its own price, paid with frayed nerves and sleepless nights.

To this day, Lindsay King insists that the critical elements in this disaster were the persuasive presence at the seminar of Brian Costello and his celebrity status as a fount of investment wisdom. "Costello is good looking and an effective speaker," the reverend says. "As far as I'm concerned, Brian Costello was as much a part of the sales pitch as the phoney charts and graphs used by the salespeople from the brokerage firm."

Thousands of Canadians, many seeking assistance in managing their RRSP or RRIF, gather at financial seminars or near radios to absorb investment strategies from financial commentators who are famous … well, for being famous. There is little evidence that the fans of these investment celebrities grow wealthy from the advice being dispensed, and many indications that they pay substantially for bad counsel dispensed by unlicensed and unregulated advisors.

"These guys may be there [at a financial seminar] to give a perfectly credible story on the merits of investing in a certain fashion," says lawyer Neil Gross, who specializes in representing clients against brokerages and financial institutions, "and the next person to speak may be someone who is hawking a particular product that uses the same strategy. In some people's minds, this juxtaposition amounts to an endorsement."[1]

When the guru leaves the stage, he is usually followed by licensed salespeople, who build on the guru's "unbiased" comments. If both the guru and the brokers refer to the investment's higher risk aspect, concerns are neutralized by inserting a fear factor—the fear of failing to accumulate enough capital for retirement, leaving RRSP owners living in tarpaper shacks and dining on roadkill.

"The people I am most concerned about," Gross continues, "are the ones who wind up in the hands of somebody who tells them, 'Our computer-generated data say this is the amount of money you're going to need to retire.' And of course the number is stratospheric. Then they say, 'The only way we can get you to that number is by leveraging, and creating some tax-effective structure that involves borrowing.' They're told, 'You can retire, but only if you take some tremendous risks in the latter stages of your life,' and that's pretty scary."

It's more than scary to financial planners such as William Sloper of Burlington, Ontario. "It's unfortunate that the people who need investment advice the most are the ones attracted to celebrity gurus," Sloper says.[2] Part of his concern is rooted in a comparison between his own credentials and the standards of financial commentators whose primary qualifications are a radio appearance or a newspaper column. As a fee-based certified financial planner (CFP) providing assessments of client financial positions, Sloper's credentials are monitored by the Financial Planners Standards Council, which requires annual proof that he meets updated education standards.

While most financial commentators have regional bases, defined by the signal range of the radio stations whose time they may purchase to reach listeners and solicit business, a handful have national status. Most prominent among these are Brian Costello, Garth Turner, Jerry White, and Gordon Pape.

Pape achieved his fame over several years of publishing books and newsletters, most relating to mutual fund selection. Of the four, he is the only one with a valid licence to provide investment advice and speak favourably of specific securities. He has also, in recent years, ceased appearances at seminars and forums, preferring to limit his activities to periodic endorsements of products such as reverse mortgages, which he pointedly warns "are not for everyone."[3] To many in the investment industry, Pape is considered Mr. Clean. The remaining members of this group, however, have encountered various smudges on their reputations as unbiased sources of investment wisdom.

The unlicensed gurus are accountable to no one until they cross a legal line, something that rankles Sloper. "They rely exclusively on their credibility," he notes, "which can be high if they enjoy extensive media exposure. Unfortunately, a lot of bad advice can be dispensed before their credibility suffers."

Sometimes it suffers from bad publicity, in the case of Brian Costello. A native of Hamilton, Ontario, Costello began his career in 1971 with Richardson Securities, slipping out of the licensed securities salesman role to establish himself as a local commentator on financial and investment matters. By the 1980s, he had achieved national exposure via appearances on CBC radio, as well as through his newspaper columns and books, often employing his signature line, "Taking care of yooooouuuur money!"

Taking Care of Whose Money?

Taking care of Costello's money seems to have involved strategies he never mentioned on his radio shows or in his newsletters. In June 1982, Costello was convicted of walking out of a Sears store in Burlington, Ontario, with two radios and a cassette recorder stuffed in his trench coat. Found guilty, he was fined $500 and placed on probation for a year.[4] Later, he published a book titled *How to Beat the Tax-Man All Year Round,* which proved both prescient and flawed when he pleaded guilty to the charge of failing to provide Revenue Canada with requested documents on time.

None of this appeared to weaken Costello's appeal to Canadians hungry for his purported wisdom, or to sponsors who saw investors as nails and Costello as a magnet. In early 2001, he was heard from coast to coast on radio commercials promoting the Retrocom Growth Fund Inc., a labour-sponsored mutual fund. "If low volatility is what you are looking for in your RRSP this year," Costello's baritone intoned, "I recommend you look at Retrocom Growth Fund."

Low volatility indeed. The fund proved as active as Monty Python's dead parrot. From 2001, when Costello was trumpeting its qualities, to August 31, 2004, the fund lost money every year. While it's true that Costello advised listeners to obtain a prospectus and read it carefully before making any investment, akin to the "how to fasten your safety belt" demonstration given airline passengers before takeoff, many Canadians purchased units in the Retrocom fund because—well, because Brian Costello said it was a good idea.

Unfortunately for Costello, other people besides investors were tuning into Costello's pitch, including investigators at the Ontario Securities Commission. His paid promotion for Retrocom smacked of providing product-specific securities advice, which Costello was not licensed to offer, and when investigators began digging deeper, they came up with a raft of charges against him for activities going back several years. Most egregious, in the OSC's eyes, was an agreement between him and the Financial Planning Group (FPG) and DPM Securities Inc. Both companies were registered with the OSC to sell securities. Their profits flowed into a third company, called The Height of Excellence Financial Group Inc., which was not licensed by the OSC but whose chairman and 47.5 percent shareholder was Brian Costello.

FPG and DPM held free financial seminars, promoted as investor education events, and paid Costello $5000 plus expenses to appear as a keynote speaker. According to OSC documents, Costello would begin by making general comments about the state of the economy, eventually leading into investment strategies and investment vehicles to match those strategies. These frequently involved limited partnerships managed by companies such as EverVest Resource Management and Synlan Securities Corporation, which Costello would describe as "the best I've ever seen!" The latter operation was managed by Richard John Smith, one of the men involved in the disastrous Kitchener, Ontario, condominium development that had cost the Kings so dearly several years earlier.

Costello was also being investigated by both the Alberta and Saskatchewan securities commissions for similar violations, but it was the OSC that wielded the big stick, which they used to pummel him to the extent of banning him from any securities-related trading for five years, and imposing a fine of $300,000.

Ignoring laws requiring advisors and traders to be licensed and approved is bad enough, but observers such as Neil Gross, William Sloper, and former investment columnist Duff Young are more concerned about the pressure placed on attendees at financial seminars to leverage their investments through a personal loan or borrowing against the equity in their house. Duff Young spoke from time to time at these events, although he makes a point of noting that he was licensed as a securities specialist, that he avoided making specific investment recommendations, and that he never proposed leveraged investing.

Financial seminars, Young notes, can be an excellent opportunity for financial advisors to make money. "If the advisor gets a hundred people to attend," Young explains, "and just 10 go along with the idea, each borrowing $100,000 to invest, that's $1 million in mutual fund sales or $50,000 in commissions for the advisor. Not bad for a night's work."

Promoters of leverage-oriented seminars rarely suggest making equal monthly payments to benefit from dollar-cost averaging,[5] and Young claims to know why. "With a lump sum investment, [the salespeople] make all their commissions up front. Ask about dollar-cost averaging and they say, 'Listen, the client might chicken out if he puts 20 grand into it this month and then the market drops.' But if the client has invested 20 grand already and you can't convince him to buy more, now that the price is lower, I want to ask, 'What the fuck are you getting paid for, anyway?!'"

Young's concern was honed one evening while he was still making presentations at investment seminars. "The advisor who hired me had previously used Garth Turner," Young recalls. "He [the advisor] said he'd had excellent results, which meant he'd made a ton of commissions. Turner had proposed leveraged investments of mutual funds using home equity as security to borrow the money."

About an hour before his presentation was to begin, Young was horrified to see a mortgage lender set up a booth at the back of the meeting area, then walk through the room dropping a mortgage application on each chair. "I went up to the guy running the seminar and asked if he was recommending real estate–backed leveraging for everybody," Young recalls. "And he says, 'No, of course not. That wouldn't be appropriate. I only recommend leveraging for homeowners!'"

Be Careful What You Say about Garth Turner

Lacking Costello's baritone voice and mellifluous delivery, Garth Turner tries making up for it with an interesting substitute: haranguing. He harangues people at his seminars, in his newsletters, and on the pages of his several books. He is especially adept at haranguing journalists and writers who dare to draft a discouraging word about him and his activities. On two occasions, writings by me have generated letters of outrage and threats of legal action from Turner and his lawyer for commenting negatively on the quality of the advice he dispenses. The most recent arrived from one of Canada's heaviest-weighted law firms, ordering me to "desist from ever writing anything derogatory about Mr. Turner in the future," which seems to suggest that I could not even criticize his wardrobe, and appears to deny at least one precept in the Canada Bill of Rights.

During our meeting in Turner's office–cum–TV studio on Toronto's Bay Street, Turner bristles at the idea of anyone questioning the value of financial seminars like those he hosts, especially if they happen to be journalists, a profession he practised many years ago. "Ninety-nine percent of people making up opinions and levelling criticism at seminars like mine have never been to one," he grumbles. "It's the shoddiest piece of bullshit journalism I've ever seen in my life." According to Turner, he covers about 35 investment strategies during a seminar. "The idea is to get the juices flowing," he explains, "so they think, 'I'm not a victim, goddammit. I'm not going to be a victim of this economy or this stock market or my bank. I'm going to be proactive and seek solutions.'"[6]

While Turner may start the juices flowing, his logic encounters barriers in the form of legal concerns and practical performance.

On the legal front, Turner took something of a pratfall in his 1997 book *The Strategy: A Homeowner's Guide to Wealth Creation,* a comprehensive summary of his antipathy toward the concept that your home represents a wise investment. "Are you kidding?" he rasps. "You buy an asset with 90 percent leverage and you think it's a safe investment? We've got to get out of this mindset!" The Strategy is an extended tome on his anti–real estate sermon. If you have generated equity in your home—the difference between its current market value and the value of any remaining mortgage on it—put that money to use, Turner advises, by borrowing from a bank, using the equity portion of your home's value as collateral, and investing the cash in stocks or mutual funds.

This involves some degree of risk, to be sure, especially if both your investments and the market value of your home drop below the amount of money the bank has loaned you. Is this a dilemma? Not according to Turner. "If your real estate falls in value to the point where the home equity loan is greater than the worth of your home," he suggests coolly, "you can always take a walk. Then it's the bank's problem."[7]

But it's not the bank's problem. In Ontario and most other provinces in Canada, you remain liable for the mortgage debt, as any real estate lawyer or banker will confirm.

If Turner's legal prudence is questionable, his investment counsel is at best consistent and at worst flawed. To put it bluntly, Turner is an unrepentant bull about investing, which may explain why he is popular with brokers and financial advisors who sponsor seminars. Bulls say, "Buy," not "Hold," and buying makes money for seminar sponsors.

Turner is no fairweather bull. He has been unswerving in his advice through recent years, whatever direction the market may be moving. Because of his high profile, or his penchant for instructing his lawyers to dispatch threatening letters to critics, his prophecies are rarely questioned and assessed. Until now.

In a Canoe "Money" chat room back on September 27, 2000, Turner assured participants that the stock market was undergoing a mere mini-correction, the Dow would hit 30,000 by 2006, and "Nortel [then trading at $96.60] is a wonderful company and, given the recent decline in price, I think it is a strong 'buy.'" The TSE (now TSX) closed at 10,250 that day.

Two months later, the TSE had slipped to 8945 and Nortel had slid to $56.35, but Turner's enthusiasm continued to rise. "Will ... the TSE attain 11,000?" Turner asked in his column. "Will it be warmer again in April? How about clipping this column and taping it to the fridge?"[8]

Fridge tapers who groped their way to their morning orange juice in March the following year would have noticed that the TSE closed below 7700 and Nortel, at around $25, was well on its way to penny-stock status. But you can't keep a good guru down. "By the time the flowers bloom in Saskatoon," Turner wrote in his March 26, 2001, column, "the back of the bear market will have been broken. We will see sustained gains in Toronto and New York, and those who fled from stocks and equity funds into cash and money-market funds, taking a loss in the process, will be sorry indeed."[9] The daffodils bloomed. The market did not.

Turner was not the only prognosticator to poo-poo the idea of a bear market in early 2001, although he was among the most persistent and prominent.[10] Nor could all of his suggestions be faulted, for he frequently advised investors to diversify their assets among various sectors. The complaint against him and others of his ilk is that they tap the fear of baby boomer RRSP owners about not having sufficient assets for retirement. The virtually unrepentant bullishness of Turner's advice provides only one dimension and may, as people such as lawyer Neil Gross and financial planner William Sloper point out, persuade them to pay insufficient attention to preserving capital. The result may be that they assume greater risk than necessary or prudent.

While leveraging assets such as equity in the family home can afford greater investment opportunity for Turner's audience, the strategy definitely provides greater profit opportunity for the brokers and financial advisors who sponsor his seminars. Someone is surely getting wealthy here; the question remains, who?

Finally, a little humility wouldn't hurt where gurus such as Turner are concerned. You can plan for the future and you can prepare for the future, but you cannot predict the future, and equating claims that markets will rise with the certainty of flowers blooming in the spring is risky at best—too risky for RRSP investors age 50 and older.

Jerry White: Professor, Doctor, Whatever ...

Humility is not a quality easily attached to Jerry White, who has spent much of his professional life acquiring qualifications such as "professor" and "doctor." He has also earned substantial amounts of money by presenting himself to investors as something of a financial whiz, a mountaintop source of knowledge and advice earned from a lifetime of academic achievements and business success. The real story is somewhat different.

Over several years and on various biographical sites, White has claimed to be professor of entrepreneurial studies at the University of Toronto (1988–92), a professor at the International Management Centre, and professor of management at the College for Human Services in New York City (1992). On the business side, White was president of Mother's Restaurants Ltd., vice-president and director of book publisher Macmillan of Canada, and most recently spokesman for two failed investment and tax-benefit operations, UltimateWealth.biz and Canadian Gift Initiatives. He also claims to have authored more than 50 books, which may be news to the National Library, Chapters, and Indigo, which list only a handful.

White's reputation as a fount of investment and business knowledge has taken several hits in recent years, beginning with a scathing examination of his career by journalist Rod McQueen in 1996.[11] McQueen, a highly regarded business commentator, wrote that White earned his Doctor of Letters from the above-mentioned International Management Centre, a U.K.-based distance-learning school geared to on-the-job training. And that "professor" designation? White was an adjunct, not full, professor at University of Toronto, and for some time now the university has been instructing White to discard the flawed "professor" designation and stop suggesting that he obtained his doctorate there. As for the College of Human Services in New York City, White lectured there for one semester.

The quality of his advice gained through business experience is even less certain. His tenure as vice-president of Macmillan Publishing in the mid-1970s was marred by discoveries of questionable resumé claims, plagiarism, and the practice of negotiating and signing book contracts between himself as publisher and himself as author. He was fired in 1978.

White was indeed president of Mother's Restaurants, a once-thriving chain of pizzerias in southern Ontario, but not for long—only until it declared bankruptcy in 1988. If going bankrupt is caused by a virus, White might have caught it, because four years later he declared personal bankruptcy himself. His creditors, including Canadian Imperial Bank of Commerce and Revenue Canada, claimed that White owed them about $1.4 million. White filed for bankruptcy and moved to the United States, returning to Canada after things settled down.

Despite questionable academic credentials and a shaky personal financial record, White continued to host national radio broadcasts, dispensing investment advice and commanding a reported $3000 per night to appear at financial seminars. Then, in 2002, White popped up as spokesman for something called UltimateWealth.biz, an operation aimed at providing investors in Canada and the United States with, the website claimed, "the best new ideas, research, concepts and strategies available nowhere else on earth, totally exclusive to our subscriber base."

The main attraction of UltimateWealth.biz was the prospect of participants signing up friends as new members for as much as $1999 annually, generating cash commissions from these membership fees, multiplying profits when the people you sign up hustle more members and ... wait a minute. Doesn't this sound like a pyramid scheme? It did to me when I attended a meeting of UltimateWealth.biz prospects and salespeople in the fall of 2002. Within two weeks both the RCMP and the federal Competition

Bureau began investigating the operation and its elaborate promises—including the opportunity to earn a "CELEBRATION
BONUS—At Least $1,000,001 U.S. in addition to your Commissions
and Lifestyle Overrides!"—and soon UltimateWealth.biz vanished
from sight.

Like Old Man River, however, Jerry White kept rolling along.
The following year he appeared as yet another spokesman, this
time for something called Canadian Gift Initiatives (CGI), "a team
of highly skilled professionals dedicated to offering tax relief
opportunities to Canadian donors in partnership with Canadian
charities and international relief organizations. We accomplish this
through innovative fundraising and by providing quality humanitarian products that are urgently needed by people in impoverished
countries throughout the world."[12]

Propelled by commercials featuring White's sharp-edged voice,
CGI proposed a too-good-to-be-true tax benefit. Using cash donations from generous Canadians, the operation would purchase
"humanitarian products" at wholesale prices, deliver the products to
a charity selected by the donor, and issue a tax receipt priced at retail.
Thus, a $5000 cash donation might purchase items with a $15,000
retail value, which was the amount the donor could claim against
that year's taxable income. In a 50 percent tax bracket, a $15,000
deduction would generate a $7500 tax rebate, not to mention a warm
feeling. Worthy charities received much needed support, overtaxed
Canadians received fat tax rebates, and CGI principals—including
its estimated 300 commissioned salespeople[13]—received a few bucks
for their time and trouble. Was this a good deal or what?

Well, it wasn't, regardless of the wishy-washy legal and accounting
opinions posted on the website, and especially not because of the
endorsement attributed to noted tax consultant and columnist Tim
Cestnick. Cestnick publicly declared: "There is currently a donation
tax scheme out there called Canadian Gift Initiatives (CGI) which is

being promoted by Jerry White. Evidently, Jerry has been using my name to lend credibility to the scheme. I want to formally announce that I have very little knowledge of the scheme, and what I do know does leave me with some concerns, so I DO NOT endorse this tax shelter. I have not spoken with Jerry about the scheme, nor have I spoken with the people at CGI who have created it."[14]

A small misunderstanding, no doubt. In any case, neither Cestnick nor White nor generous Canadians looking for a tax break could do much about it a few months later when CGI announced it would no longer accept donations.

When You Question the Source, Question the Advice

The idea of anyone with knowledge and experience providing information to investors—especially those with substantial assets in their RRSP or RRIF and limited confidence in their ability to manage them—is a good one. That's why you're reading this book, right? The danger arises when critical investment decisions are made according to advice provided by a single source, and when the motives of that source are themselves questionable.

In legal circles you may hear the query *Cui bono?* loosely translated as Who benefits? Another, less elegant, way of saying the same thing is, "Follow the money." Who is certain to profit from the advice being dispensed? Whose money is being accessed? And who is taking a risk that may not be fully explained, understood, or appreciated?

Before agreeing to any investment proposal or, heaven forbid, signing an agreement to mortgage your home and make a lump-sum purchase of a mutual fund or other security, pause to ask who benefits. At financial seminars there will always be two prime candidates: the person making the pitch on investment ideas, offered as though it were a free public service (but who will receive a few thousand dollars for his appearance), and the sponsor of the event, usually a broker or financial advisor, who will receive, as a sales commission, a portion of the money you hand over.

Those are certain beneficiaries. Less certain is the prospect that the advice you receive and the investment vehicles offered by the sponsors are suitable for your needs.

Finally, anyone who provides investment advice on the basis of his ability to predict the future, and the manner in which it will affect your RRSP/RRIF and your ability to enjoy a comfortable retirement, should be linked more with Nostrudamus than with Warren Buffet.

SRO or SOL? The Failure of Self-Regulated Organizations to Protect Investors

She is not someone you'd expect to play the role of stubborn crusader, laying siege to monuments of stone and gold-tinted glass. But as Patricia Cosgrove relates her experience on behalf of her mother Norah, and their treatment at the hands of various organizations claiming to protect investors, her voice grows steely with resolve and barely restrained outrage.

"Things in my mother's account were wrong from the beginning," she says. "The Know Your Client form, which she never saw, claimed she had previous experience investing in stocks, and that her investment objectives were to be 50 percent income and 50 percent growth equity. That is simply not true. Many of the investments chosen for my mother were high-risk, including Nortel, Celestica, Laidlaw, Mitel, and a CI Pacific sector mutual fund. Most of the mutual funds carried seven-year deferred service charges, sold to my mother when she was in her mid-80s. Does that make sense?"

Cosgrove's mother Norah, 92 and more alert than some people 50 years younger, sits to one side, absorbing her daughter's words. We are in her west-end Toronto condominium. Norah's voice retains her British accent, and she carries herself with the dignity and gentle nature of a proper Englishwoman born in Edwardian times.

Patricia Cosgrove's litany of complaints against the Ottawa office of a bank-owned brokerage includes familiar criticisms— incorrect information posted on KYC forms; churning the account to generate commissions; resistance by the broker to discuss concerns about losses; and investments that defy age-appropriate guidelines for someone of Norah Cosgrove's age. "How can you justify changing a Know Your Client form to say that an 85-year-old woman has increased the risk exposure of her portfolio to 75 percent, and claim that her fixed assets had increased by $200,000 when no such change occurred?" Patricia Cosgrove asks. "You can't." Yet this is what Norah Cosgrove's file at the brokerage states, motivating Patricia Cosgrove's charge that the information was altered.

According to Patricia Cosgrove, the broker pressured her mother to move a substantial portion of her portfolio into the Sovereign wrap account, selling a number of Norah's Government of Canada bonds paying 9 percent interest to pay for the Sovereign units. "I understand the broker made 2 percent commission on the sale of the securities to go into Sovereign," Cosgrove says, keeping her voice soft and steady. "For her part, my mother suffered a total capital loss of over $60,000."

Concerned about her losses, Norah insisted on moving her account and shortly afterward purchased a condo in Toronto to be near her daughter. Demanding that the broker be punished and the losses suffered by her mother restored, Patricia began a process of complaint extending more than three years, achieving little beyond elevating her outrage and revealing unsettling attitudes on the part of the Ontario Securities Commission, the Investment Dealers Association (IDA), the Ombudsman for Banking Services and Investments (OBSI), and the regulatory process in general.

"The response of the IDA was incredible," she recalls. "The most disturbing comment was their claim that they found insufficient evidence to move the file to a formal investigation. 'Your mother is 90,' one senior IDA official said. 'What kind of a witness would she make? And after all, she could be dead within a year. You have to realize that our resources are limited and we have to get the best bang for our buck.' Is this IDA policy, to ignore broker misbehaviour if the client is old?" The IDA's response was to send "a letter of caution" to the advisor, but it refused to do anything regarding the advisor's right to hold a licence.[1]

When appeals to the IDA went nowhere, Patricia turned to the OSC, which, on reviewing the extensive documentation Patricia provided, noted that there was nothing on the incorrect KYC form or any of the records to indicate that Norah disagreed with the form's directive increasing her portfolio to 75 percent equities. "She never saw the form," Patricia almost screams in frustration, "so how could she disagree with it? [The broker] told me there is no regulatory requirement that new account application forms must be signed or reviewed by the client—yet these are the same forms used by the brokers to justify their investment strategies. It's insane!"

A meeting with the OBSI in October 2003 proved equally fruitless, except in its ability to raise Patricia's blood pressure still further. "[The ombudsman] told me that my mother didn't really need the money she lost. Seniors like my mother didn't need much money after they pay their rent or condo fees and buy groceries, there really aren't that many expenses for them to cover. When I asked about the wisdom of putting such a large portion of a 90-year-old woman's portfolio into equities, he shrugged and said his own late father had maintained a significant amount of his investments in equities. Well, his father had been a stockbroker, which is an entirely different matter. When I sent a letter challenging him on his attitude toward seniors, he refused to respond."

With none of the regulatory agencies prepared to acknowledge her assertion that her mother's portfolio had been mishandled—

"by this time I had honestly given up on the chance of recovering the lost money and just wanted someone to agree that things had been done wrong"—Patrica turned to small claims court as a means of making her point. A pre-trial hearing was set for March 23, 2004, in Ottawa.

"I went there from Toronto with all my files and a power of attorney permitting me to represent my mother," Patricia says. "I know something about small claims court. It's supposed to be a court of equity, an opportunity for individuals like my mother and me to be heard. But I couldn't believe what I encountered when I arrived."

The first thing she encountered was the co-chairperson of litigation, from one of the largest and most prestigious law firms in the country, who had travelled from Toronto to spend the day if necessary defending the brokerage against the claims of 92-year-old Norah Cosgrove. "I was stunned to see so much money being spent on such a small matter," Patricia says. "I mean, how much does it cost to have a lawyer of this stature travel to Ottawa for the day? Maybe $1000 an hour? Maybe more?"

Patricia was not intimidated by the presence of the heavy-duty lawyer, who remained pleasant and cordial. The attitude of the pre-trial judge, however, was in sharp contrast to that of the lawyer. "He was rude to the point of insulting, telling me that the power of attorney for my mother was deficient, and waving off my description of the case by saying he had no idea what a KYC form was, didn't know a thing about investments, and didn't understand what 75 percent in equities meant. All of his comments indicated that he thought I had nothing to complain about. Needless to say, it got nowhere."

Patricia gave up seeking a resolution about the broker's treatment of her mother, but she filed a complaint with the Human Rights Commission over the IDA's refusal to proceed based on the assertion that Norah might not be alive by the time its investigation was completed. In June 2004 the dispute was mediated and an agreement reached, the terms of which remain confidential (instructions from the Human Rights Commission) between both parties.

F ew investors are as fervent in their search for answers and accountability as Patricia Cosgrove. At the core of her case is the claim that details on her mother's KYC form were altered. These changes would have permitted the broker to increase the proportion of high-risk equity investments and DSC mutual funds to an inappropriate level. Changing information as entered on a legal document without the knowledge or approval of the signatory smacks of forgery, especially if the altered information benefits the person who changed it. How often has a financial advisor or broker been charged with forgery under these circumstances? Rarely, if at all.

This fact alone is convincing evidence that investors face a less-than-equitable environment when launching challenges against the investment industry. The problem grows more ominous when investors seek legal counsel to pursue their cases. Do not expect your family lawyer, the one who crafted your will and handled the purchase of your home, to fill this role.

Some law firms specialize in representing plaintiffs against brokerages and financial advisors. If you choose to follow the legal route, be prepared to pay a hefty retainer, followed by monthly charges extending over perhaps a year or more, with no prospect of having your day in court and limited chances of recovering anything beyond a portion of your claim. As Patricia Cosgrove discovered, the battlefield of legal challenge to the investment industry is strewn with client casualties, and all the heavy artillery is on the other side. Small claims court? If Patricia Cosgrove's experience fails to dissuade you, remember that the maximum you can recover there is $10,000. Which leaves little choice but to venture into the dark and confusing Valley of the SROs. Good luck, pilgrim.

SRO stands for self-regulated organization. To investment industry leaders, the term indicates that they are conscientious enough to look after themselves without government interference, thank you very much. To cynics, self-regulation means no regulation at all. The truth meanders somewhere in between.

The Investment Dealers Association: When the Going Gets Tough, the Advisors Get Out

The Investment Dealers Association of Canada, or IDA, remains the most prominent of the SROs claiming to act on behalf of investors. Its promotional material boasts that the IDA is "the national self-regulatory organization for the Canadian securities industry. We regulate the solvency, educational proficiency, and sales and business practices of Canadian investment dealers and their registered employees."

Sounds like the kind of guys you want in your corner when you feel wronged by the investment industry, doesn't it? It gets better—on paper, that is.

"The IDA provides front-line regulation of day-to-day activities involving clients and their investment dealer firms. Recommending unsuitable investments, performing transactions without client approval, or encouraging an excessive number of transactions are all examples of improper practices that can warrant a complaint to the IDA."

Be warned that the IDA's powers are limited to investigating complaints and imposing penalties only on member firms and their employees found guilty of violations. If you deal with a firm that is not a member of IDA (most are), you're SOL. And no matter how strong your argument may be about losing assets because of broker or advisor malfeasance, the IDA will not refund any money to you. It's not a bank; it's a police force. Well, sort of.

"The primary mission of the organization is to protect investors," Paul Bourke states.[2] Bourke is IDA's senior vice-president of Member Regulation and a former crown attorney, first in Ontario and later in Alberta, where he dealt with white-collar crime. After stints with the B.C. and Ontario securities commissions, he returned to Alberta to serve as deputy minister of Justice, moving into his current post in 2001. This is the kind of person you want standing up for your rights as a small investor. But, is the IDA the kind of organization to do the job?

The IDA's role as a guardian of investor rights is questioned among critics of the investment industry. Since the association's mission includes enhancing efficient capital markets in Canada in addition to protecting investor interests, this raises conflict-of-interest concerns. A task force established in 2001 by the Ontario Securities Commission—itself an organization subject to charges of divided loyalty—concluded that the IDA's dual role of serving as both lobbyist and regulator for the investment industry was faulty. The OSC's concern, echoed by a government-appointed committee charged with investigating the IDA, centred on the perception that the IDA is not impartial in its policing of the industry, and that penalties imposed on member firms and their employees are too lenient. One solution: The IDA should either protect investors or lobby on behalf of its members, but not play both roles. IDA president Joe Oliver dismissed the OSC's charges of impartiality and practically bragged that he had persuaded the government committee to back off, "because such a move [to separate the duties] was not justified."[3] When an SRO sways a government-linked organization to its view so easily, you have to question just whose interests the SRO is pursuing.

Bourke stresses that 80 percent of the IDA's budget and personnel are dedicated to its policing role, and notes that the association maintains complaint bureaus in Toronto and Calgary. According to Bourke, about 20 percent of calls received by the bureaus are investigated. But why do 80 percent never make it past the initial inquiry?

"Most are service complaints," Bourke responds. He is a tall, elegantly dressed man who carries himself with the quiet assurance of someone familiar with the environment of both boardrooms and courtrooms, grappling with the complexities of civil law and the personalities of aggrieved plaintiffs. "Perhaps the broker hasn't called them in a year, which we categorize as a simple service issue. Other complaints are out of our jurisdiction, or deal with criminal matters." Where evidence of criminal activity is evident, such as fraud or embezzlement, the matter is referred to local law enforcement officials. Whatever the basis of their complaint, investors cannot count on compensation.

"Let's face it," Bourke points out, "a client who feels that his or her account has been mishandled wants compensation above all, and that's fair. But we're not the place to provide it. If clients cannot get a settlement from their broker or advisor, or the company they're dealing with, they should talk to the Ombudsman for Banking Services and Investments." If OBSI cannot help the investor gain satisfaction, the IDA will assist in setting up an arbitration process for claims up to $100,000. But don't expect IDA to write you a cheque.

What about discipline for the wayward broker or advisor, assuming that he or she is employed by a member firm of IDA? The association will launch an investigation and impose a penalty, if warranted, which might include fines, a directive for the offender to undergo retraining, and a temporary or permanent ban from employment in an IDA-member company.

Fines remain the most prevalent discipline, with penalties beginning at $10,000. The IDA, however, remains a member-based organization and thus cannot penalize someone who is no longer employed by a member firm, any more than a golf club can penalize a player for cheating on her scorecard if that player resigns from the club. Thus, a broker or advisor hit with a $500,000 fine by the IDA might decide that his future in the business isn't worth a half-million dollar re-entry fee and look for another career. When the going gets tough, a member can simply resign rather than pay the imposed fine. More likely, a tainted broker may find himself personna non grata with the firm even as the firm defends itself against charges by his clients.[4]

One critic of the system estimates that less than 50 percent of all fines levied by the IDA are ever collected. "The advisors have outlived their usefulness at that point and are usually unceremoniously cut adrift by their employers," he says. "Their licence is dependent upon their being employed in the industry, and the regulator does not (perhaps cannot) pursue them for monies due because they are no longer members. That has not prevented many of them from moving to the US and starting the same game all over again."[5]

Other critics of the IDA—and there are many—point out that enforcement of its rules is influenced in favour of the companies making up the organization (who pay the membership dues to keep it operating), and against individual employees. According to its own records, the IDA fined member firms a mere $265,189 in 2003 but nailed individual employees of these firms with $3.2 million in penalties. The implication of lower fines to brokerages than to their employees is clear: Employees can walk away from the association and even the industry, but the association needs those member firms and the fees they provide.

A heavy fine imposed on an individual may persuade him to abandon a career in the industry, but is not likely to result in the resignation of an IDA member firm. Slap a million-dollar penalty on a member firm, however, and it might vote with its feet, preferring to operate outside the organization's bounds. Does this awareness produce lesser fines for member firms and extreme penalties against individuals?

"Any regulatory agency is going to be subject to criticism that it provides too little, too late in some cases," Bourke sighs. "Whatever you do, some people will say you didn't do enough, and others will say you went too far. In our cases, we're dealing with people who expect to be compensated, and if they're not compensated in full, they're not very happy. Having said that, I think we have a good process for taking complaints, investigating them, and moving forward the ones that we believe offer some success in applying discipline. So basically, I think it's a pretty good system."

Does Bourke have any suggestions that may help investors keep out of trouble and away from the need for IDA investigation? "Ask more questions," he offers without hesitation. "If a broker advises putting bank stocks in your RRSP, for example, ask which [bank stock] it should be. Then ask 'Why that one?' People should be more curious, and they shouldn't trust a broker from the outset. The industry works on trust, but brokers should be expected to earn a client's trust by being open with the facts, answering questions directly, and calling the client more than once a year."

The Mutual Fund Dealers Association: Is You Is or Is You Ain't My Dealer?

If you purchase mutual fund units from your broker to insert in your RRSP, does this make your broker a mutual fund dealer? Yes, but this does not mean the brokerage is a member of the Mutual Fund Dealers Association of Canada (MFDA). The distinction between CIBC Wood Gundy and CIBC Securities Inc. may be relatively minor to you, but it is important enough for each to be members of different self-regulating organizations. Wood Gundy is an IDA member, CIBC Securities Inc. is a member of MFDA. Just to make things more complex, both the IDA and MFDA share the same mailing address in Toronto. If your broker or advisor firm is not a member of one, it's probably a member of the other. Or not.

The MFDA began as the kid brother of the IDA in the 1990s, sharing the same president. Since 2003, however, the MFDA has been a stand-alone operation, although they're on the same floor in the same office building. Like the IDA, the MFDA is an SRO. And like the IDA, it fulfills a dual, perhaps contradictory, role of protecting investors from abuses by its members and protecting its members from abuses by whomever.

Leaving regulation of funds and fund sponsors to the 13 securities commissions in Canada, the MFDA restricts itself to regulating only the sale of mutual funds by its members and, in its mission statement, stresses that it "has been created, in part, to protect [the] public confidence." The public confidence, retail investors might suggest, would be protected and perhaps enhanced if the SROs appeared more dedicated to addressing concerns such as inappropriate fund recommendations, questionable sales techniques, excessive fees, and poor fund management.

The MFDA announced with some fanfare on November 5, 2002 that its Investors Complaint Service "… is now fully operational" and that it "… will provide enforcement that is firm, fair and transparent."

Perhaps the MFDA has carried transparency so far that its operations in this area have become invisible because, almost two years later, the same website noted that it had yet to hold any hearings or issue any disciplinary notices.[6]

The Ombudsman for Banking Services and Investments: Nice Guy, But …

Michael Lauber has all the credentials you might expect of a chartered accountant, including more than 20 years with auditing giant KPMG, where he achieved partner status, and a stint as governor of the Canadian Institute of Chartered Accountants, before being appointed (drum roll, please) ombudsman for Banking Services and Investments. Affable and relaxed, Lauber appears to be just the man to balance your budget and weigh the pros and cons of leasing versus buying your next car. But is he the person to count on if things go wrong between you and your broker?

"We're the guys who can recommend compensation from the investment firm," Lauber says in his rather sparsely furnished downtown Toronto office.[7] He works with a lean team of 18, including 15 investigators and 3 support staff. "We don't have any perceived conflict of interest like the IDA, MFDA, and OSC, who are trying to help both investors and the people managing or creating the investments. We're here exclusively to resolve problems between customers and financial institutions, if the two sides have been unable to work things out together. That's why we ask anyone with a complaint to try getting a settlement from their financial provider first. We need to know that people have exhausted all the possibilities of having their bank or brokerage firm deal with their concerns before they come to us."

If the problem with your bank includes banking fees, commissions, interest rates, or credit-granting procedures, or is before the courts, forget about the ombudsman. You might also want to know, going in, that OBSI makes recommendations in favour of substantial compensation for the consumer only about 15 percent of the time, with small adjustments recommended in an additional 5 percent of situations. Why so low?

"By the time a complaint has moved into the formal investigation process, it has already been reviewed at various levels of our members," Lauber explains. He suggests that the low percentage of substantial adjustments proves the system is working because most legitimate claims have been settled before clients encounter the OBSI: "Our existence puts pressure on members to be more responsive to customer concerns and resolve them promptly."

Critics of the OBSI point out that investors should not fool themselves into believing the office maintains strict impartiality, although Lauber undoubtedly attempts to perform this balancing act within his mandate. It's a difficult chore. If Lauber and his people agree to investigate your complaint, its regulations require you to accept that no OBSI ruling or observation can be used as evidence in any other legal action, and that neither Lauber nor any of his staff can be subpoenaed as a witness on your behalf. Nor will OBSI conduct a forensic audit in pursuit of your complaint. It's OBSI's game, after all, so it makes the rules.

Promptness is one aspect where OBSI appears to outpace others in this field, although speed, if that's the word, is relative in these situations. OBSI aims for a 90-day turnaround between accepting a complaint for investigation and issuing a report and recommendations. If OBSI finds in the consumer's favour and a loss of client funds is involved, it is not permitted to recommend payment exceeding $350,000—another OBSI rule, this one designed to limit losses to the banks funding Lauber's operation. Complainants are required to sign an agreement releasing the financial institution from being obligated to pay more than $350,000 regardless of the size of the claim. If your loss totals $500,000, be prepared to forget about recovering $150,000 of the amount, assuming OBSI agrees to investigate the situation and you beat the seven-to-one odds against OBSI finding in your favour.

Lauber stresses that OBSI does not make payments where it rules they are justified; it only recommends that the financial institution make the determined payment, and its proposal is not binding. However, "if a member [financial services provider] does not accept our recommendation," Lauber points out, "we'll make their refusal public. So far, no member has failed to follow our recommendation."

The largest amount recommended for settlement by mid-2004 was $250,000, in a case that involved business loans and guarantees, not investment dealings. "Last year [2003], we had three or four settlements in the $30,000 to $70,000 range in [response to] securities and funds dealer complaints," Lauber says. "In addition, we had two complaints involving investments and/or advice provided by financial planners in bank branches where we recommended settlements in the $125,000 range."

Lauber is undoubtedly qualified for and dedicated to his role as ombudsman. But suspicion remains that he is something of a figurehead assigned primarily to sooth investor concerns. The fact is, too many interlocking positions exist among the various players in the game, all suggesting that strings are subject to being pulled if the industry's assets are at risk. For example, among the directors Lauber reports to is Terry Wright. In addition to his seat on the board of OBSI, Wright is chairman of both the Mutual Fund Dealers Association and the Investment Funds Institute of Canada. Oh—and he is also senior vice-president and general counsel of Investors Group Ltd.[8] If Wright, through Lauber, encounters a serious complaint from you, me, or another retail investor, can any of us count on him to ensure an unbiased, independent opinion?

Canadian Investor Protection Fund: Even If Your Broker Goes Bankrupt, You May Not

You may believe that your chance of going bankrupt is greater than your broker's, and you're probably right. But the possibility still exists. If it helps you sleep at night, about 200 Canadian investment dealers belong to the Canadian Investor Protection Fund (CIPF), which covers members' accounts for up to $1 million each. If you maintain two accounts with a CIPF member—an RRSP/RRIF and an unregistered account—each account qualifies for $1 million coverage.

The most recent broker bankruptcy involved Thomson Kernaghan & Co., which folded in the summer of 2002, leaving a $3.3 million shortfall. Bankruptcy will always be a risk for any business in any industry. While it's a nice feeling to know the CIPF is there to protect you, assuming your investment firm is a member (it will proclaim its membership on its brochures, contracts, and financial statements), most Canadian RRSP/RRIF owners are more concerned about their personal assets than those of their brokerage or investment firm.

Market Regulation Services Inc:
The Backroom Boys Are Watching Out for You

Your broker or advisor is the front end of a chain of functions and responsibilities leading back to the original investment vehicle, whether this is a private company such as Barrick or Petro-Canada issuing shares, or a corporation or government arm selling bonds. So who watches over those guys? Something called Market Regulation Services, which functions as regulatory guardian for the Toronto Stock Exchange (TSX), Toronto Venture Exchange (TSX VN), Bloomberg Tradebook Canada, and Canadian Trading and Quotation System.

Yet another SRO, Market Regulation Services (MRS) Inc., proclaims that it "help[s] protect investors and ensure market integrity by regulating trading on these marketplaces to ensure transactions are executed properly, fairly and in compliance with trading rules. MRS is the only regulator that protects investors in real time. Using sophisticated surveillance systems that provide statistical and rule-based alerts, we monitor each and every trade in real time every day for compliance with the trading rules. If a rule is breached, MRS investigates immediately and, if necessary, has the power to reverse the trade and take disciplinary action."[9]

Most of the activities of MRS involve imposing penalties on people caught buying or selling securities based on insider information, meaning data not available to you or me. This violation is what originally snagged Martha Stewart's hem in a wringer, although her conviction was based on making false statements, rather than illegal gains. MRS also distributes national cease trading orders issued by provincial securities commissions, meaning if the B.C. Securities Commission decides that Vancouver-based Scintillating Snowboards Inc. has not lived up to the commission's rules and regulations, nobody between Nanaimo and Newfoundland will be permitted to trade the stock through licensed brokers.

Wait a minute—couldn't a national securities commission do the job better? Of course it could, if it existed. Which brings us to the Ontario Securities Commission.

The Ontario Securities Commission: Is Big Brother Really on Your Side?

Many people living west of Thunder Bay and east of Cornwall grumble about Ontario's concentration of power, especially where finance and investment are concerned. Some point with justification and reasonable outrage at the Ontario Securities Commission.

On the surface, anything with a province's name in its title should be restricted to that provincial jurisdiction, and that's the official case with the OSC. The practical experience is somewhat different. Like it or not, and most people outside of Ontario do not like it, the OSC sets most of the rules in the investment game.

You may never win a bar bet with this fact, but it's worth knowing anyway: Of all the industrialized countries in the world with a securities industry, only two lack a truly national securities commission. One is Bosnia-Herzegovina. The other is Canada. (By the time you read this, the fact may no longer be true. In April 2004 rumours swept the world, or at least corners where people who care about these things lurk, that Bosnia-Herzegovina was about to finally establish a national securities commission. So was Canada. The smart money is on the Bosnians winning this race.) This drives a lot of people crazy, from Canadian nationalists who are ashamed that one of the world's great capitalist democracies has never been able to agree on a single securities watchdog, to foreign investors who believe they'll be operating a publicly traded company in one jurisdiction and discover they're actually operating in 10. Or more. (For a list of provincial and territorial securities commissions or administrators, see Appendix A.)

When it comes to securities commissions, Canada is like a squabbling family of siblings dominated by a bigger older brother whom everybody respects but nobody likes very much. Each province retains the right to establish and manage its own securities trading operation, but the OSC, by virtue of Ontario's economic clout and the presence of the TSX in Toronto, dominates the scene. It's not purely resentment that prevents smaller provinces from facilitating a national commission, which would continue to be dominated by Ontario anyway. Other provinces, especially Alberta and British Columbia, fear that an Ontario-led national securities commission would have a bias toward large corporations, leading to a failure to recognize the unique needs and concerns of smaller companies in the east and west, and the way they represent regional concerns.

Most dominant of all, perhaps, is the notion that the OSC is poorly administered, to the point of derision by many industry observers. One highly respected academic who has studied securities regulators on an international scale refers to the OSC as "probably the most poorly governed securities regulator among those of the OECD [Organization for Economic Co-operation and Development—the world's 26 most developed nations] countries."[10] The OSC also makes demands from others that it refuses to adhere to itself. For example, it advocates that the majority of a corporation's board members be independent of the company's senior management, yet its own board is composed exclusively of OSC commissioners, who also comprise the compensation committee. Perhaps this is why OSC chairman David Brown's salary is more than two and a half times that of the chairman of the much larger and more powerful Securities and Exchange Commission in the United States. Does David Brown have a legitimate rationale for that particular discrepancy? I don't know; over several months' request for an interview with Brown, I was unfailingly informed that he was too busy for a chat with me.

This would just be business as usual in Canada were it not that the OSC has generated its own coterie of critics and skeptics over the years, many charging that the commission is overpopulated, over-protected, overpaid and underworked.

Susan Wolburgh-Jenah, OSC vice-chairwoman, admits that critics of the OSC have a point regarding its role in investor protection.[11] The solution, she suggests, lies first with investors themselves. "We're not there when they are having the conversation with a broker who is trying to get their business," she explains, suggesting that investors must assume the front line of their own defence against bad invest-ment advice. "We're not expecting people to read long prospectuses. We're just trying to identify areas where people can be the most vulnerable and say, 'Here are things to look out for.' We want [investors] to become our allies in preventing abuses through investor protection." As an example, Wolburgh-Jenah cites elaborate packages of education material made available without charge to retail investors through the OSC.

All well and good—arming investors with knowledge and aware-ness is also the goal of this book. This is the equivalent, however, of telling people to keep their wallets in a safe place and be careful when walking down dark streets. It's good advice, but when you're mugged or attacked, you want the long arm of the law to sweep in and deliver swift justice. When it comes to investor protection, many Canadians feel that the enforcement responsibility has been assumed by members of the same gang who left you broke and beat up in the alley—in this case, the IDA and MFDA. What can these SROs do to convince us that the public concern is being addressed where investor protection is concerned? Well, how about some outside individuals, people like me and you, sitting on the boards of these SROs with a mandate to question policies that do not appear to be in our interests? Wouldn't that be good idea?

Wolburgh-Jenah agrees. In fact, she believes the situation has already been dealt with. "Currently, I think the IDA have a third of their directors representing public interest groups," she suggests. "The IDA's position historically has been, 'We are an industry group, we need to have a lot of representation on our board from industry people.' But you would want to have ... a majority or 50 percent of people on the board, perhaps an academic, who has never worked with the industry, who has no ties to the industry ..."

So in mid-2004, the vice-chairwoman of the OSC believed that one-third of the IDA board consisted of "public interest directors," and that the proportion should be perhaps half. Below is the actual composition of the IDA board of directors for 2004-2005. Can you spot the "public interest people" who have "no ties to the industry"?

INVESTMENT DEALERS ASSOCIATION
BOARD OF DIRECTORS 2004–2005

Brian J. Porter, chairman
executive managing director, Scotia Capital Inc.

S. Ross Sherwood, vice-chairman
president and chief executive officer, Odlum Brown Ltd.

Joseph J. Oliver
president and chief executive officer, Investment Dealers Association of Canada

James C. Baillie
member, executive committee, Investment Dealers Association of Canada

Donald W. Black
chief executive officer, Greystone Managed Investments Inc.

Donald Charter
president, chairman and chief executive officer, Dundee Securities Corp.

Kenneth G. Copland
president, KGC Ltd.

Jacques Daoust
president and chief executive officer, BLC - Edmond de Rothschild Asset Management Inc.

Jean-Pierre De Montigny
president and chief operating officer, Desjardins Securities Inc.

Dale Godsoe, CM
vice-president, external, Dalhousie University

Michael A. Grandin,
chairman and chief executive officer, Fording Canadian Coal Trust

Lonsdale W. Holland
president, Beacon Securities Ltd.

John L. Howard, QC
former senior vice-president, Law and Corporate Affairs, MacMillan Bloedel Ltd.

Robert Jennings
president, Jennings Capital Inc.

Frank Laferriere
chief financial officer and chief operating officer, Berkshire Securities Inc.

Daniel Leclair
vice-president finance and chief financial officer, Hydro-Québec

Ronald Lloyd
president and chief operating officer, Merrill Lynch Canada Inc.

Dean Manjuris
vice-chairman, BMO Nesbitt Burns Inc.

Thomas S. Monahan
managing director, CIBC World Markets Inc.

Colleen J. Moorehead
president, E*Trade Canada Securities Corp.

Gary Reamey
principal, Canadian Operations, Edward Jones

Alain Rhéaume
president and chief operating officer, Microcell Solutions Inc.

G.F. Kym Anthony
president and chief executive officer, National Bank Financial Inc.

SOURCE: IDA WEBSITE, WWW.IDA.CA/ABOUT/ORGANIZATION/DIRECTORS_EN.ASP,
ACCESSED JULY 2004.

Dale Godsoe qualifies for the OSC's definition of someone outside the investment industry and hey! she's an academic as well, suggesting the IDA gets two tokens with one position. But if the admirable Ms. Godsoe represents Canada's public interest groups in questions of investor benefits and protection, everyone else who sits at the table has his or her feet and future firmly planted in the investment industry.

When this is pointed out to her, Susan Wolburgh-Jenah prefers to discuss the results of a 2004 Ipsos-Reid survey on attitudes toward the OSC, stating that its results validate the commission's argument that it is fulfilling its mandate and achieving high rates of satisfaction. A similar survey conducted in 2001 gave the OSC an overall A-minus rating. Three years later, the same cross-section could give the OSC no better than a B or B-plus.

That's still a passing grade, but the OSC may want to pay special attention to actions that respondents identified as priorities when it came to the commission's enforcement and investigation activities. According to the survey, the single top priority for enforcement by the OSC should be—

- Taking proactive steps, such as monitoring market activities to prevent violations (41 percent)
- Punishing those who violate the securities act with fines or imprisonment (27 percent)
- Punishing those who violate the securities act by permanently prohibiting their access to markets (18 percent)
- Where innocent investors have lost money because of a violation, getting and returning their money (13 percent)

The single top priority for investigations by the OSC should be—

- Fraud investigation (47 percent)
- Falsifying financial statements (24 percent)

- Misleading sales practices (11 percent)
- Insider trading (10 percent)

The OSC released the survey findings with great pride, although the responses relating to questions of investor confidence and enforcement suggest that some areas may not be receiving sufficient attention—note that one-quarter of the respondents believe OSC investigators should target the falsifying of financial statements as a priority.

Other OSC critics are surprised that the OSC generates and releases any data at all. Columnist Eric Reguly of the *Globe and Mail*'s Report on Business compared the OSC's activity level "with the reflexes of a superannuated sloth."[12] Reguly was noting that the OSC had been alerted in 1998 to the practice of equity monetization, a trick used by top executives of high-flying companies selling shares to the public. The mechanics are unimportant, but monetization enabled executives who sensed an imminent drop in the value of their company's shares to unload their own shares without publicly declaring it, avoiding hefty tax hits. It took two years for the OSC to acknowledge the problem. Creeping into action, it introduced new regulations riddled with more loopholes than macramé underwear. As a result, almost no incidence of equity monetization was reported until the spring of 2003, about five years after the alarm was raised. Just for fun, some regulations were not made retroactive, meaning that anyone who managed to cheat shareholders, investors, and the taxman in the past could relax. By the time even this vapid ruling was handed down, the bull market that spawned monetization concerns had long faded away.

And while investment industry heavyweights such as the Ontario Teachers' Pension Plan Board were decrying the soft dollars flowing into mutual funds and warning of the conflict of interest they represented in mid-2003, the OSC addressed the problem by promising to "assess the impact of 'soft dollars' on market efficiency, analyst bias and competitiveness."[13] Not a word on investor protection.

Where broker and advisor misconduct is involved, the OSC's reaction is so dawdling as to be almost humorous, except to investors claiming advisor and broker misbehaviour. Seven months after the smooth and devious Patrick Kinlin was convicted and sentenced to prison for defrauding dozens of clients out of millions of dollars, the OSC announced it would hold a hearing into Kinlin's activities. (For details of Kinlin's nefarious activities and ignominious end, see Chapter 11.)

In defence of the OSC, it is not alone in responding to the need for modifying investment rules with all the reflexes of a rusty drawbridge.

Canadian securities commissions have grown notorious for being sluggish to the point of near paralysis. Among the critics is Barbara Stymiest, former CEO of the TSX. Stymiest recalled, as an example of this country's lethargy in this area, an incident concerning the U.S. Securities and Exchange Commission (SEC) when it introduced regulatory changes in mid-2002.[14] The changes were a response in part to investigations into the activities of Enron and Tyco executives. Dubbed the Sarbanes-Oxley Act, the new rules dictated tighter standards and heavier penalties for senior executives who abused their positions at the cost of shareholders.

Acknowledging the cross-border structure of North American corporations, the SEC wrote the Canadian Securities Administrators (CSA) in October 2002, listing the proposed changes to take effect January 30, 2003, and asking for comments and suggestions from the OSC and other CSA members. The CSA, recognizing the meaningful gesture of the SEC and its implications not only for corporations with Canadian links but for the universe of corporate governance generally, leapt into action and managed to reply on February 19, four months after receiving the letter and about three weeks following

the introduction of the legislation. In the Canadian securities industry, this was considered prompt. "One of the [CSA] administrators,"
Stymiest explained, "calculated a couple of years ago that the average
rule change used to take seventeen months."

Eventually OSC chairman David Brown announced new rules,
reflecting the U.S. Sarbanes-Oxley Act, with great fanfare at the end
of March 2004. He also boasted that the average time it took the
OSC to start investigations against a company under investigation
had been reduced from 20 months to just 11 months, suggesting
that the OSC had geared up from the speed of a tranquilized turtle
to that of a snail in heat.[15]

Other criticisms address an apparent buddy-buddy environment
among those entrusted to protect investor interests, suggesting the
possibility that the OSC is more adept at concealing threats to
investor safety than at resolving them.

In 2000, the OSC conducted an audit of the IDA, one that
apparently resulted in the replacement of two top IDA executives
responsible for enforcement, and the launch of a new database to
monitor industry problems. Why *apparently*? Because none of the
25-page audit has been made public nor, in the opinion of both
organizations, should it ever see the light of day. A government-
sanctioned enforcement agency investigates goings-on in a self-
regulated industry association, apparently locates problems serious
enough to dispatch two high-ranking officers into investment
limbo-land and install a monitoring system, and declares the public
has no claim to know of the exposed weaknesses. With rah-rah
encouragement from the IDA, the OSC filed a motion in court to
keep its findings secret and repel demands from the Ontario
Information and Privacy Commissioner to reveal them.[16]

The OSC's defence of its insistence on confidentiality is mired in
legal and legislative guidelines. Only by promising confidentiality,
OSC vice-chairwoman Susan Wolburgh-Jenah explains, could

commission investigators conduct a thorough study of IDA actions. Once having made that promise, it could hardly renege by revealing evidence of poor performance or outright wrongdoing, could it? "Our legislation," Wolburgh-Jenah clarifies, "directs us to rely on SROs to the extent that we can in order to foster fair and efficient capital markets and fulfill our mandate. We must rely on them as much as we possibly can—it's a direction to us, built into the legislation."

In essence, the OSC is playing another dual role, this one acting as both overseer of SRO operations and partners with them to protect investor interests. Can both be achieved with satisfaction? Perhaps. Can they be done without some degree of suspicion that each group takes turns scratching the other's backs? It's doubtful.

In this case, the OSC and its IDA luncheon buddies told Canadians they were better off not knowing about certain aspects of the management of their invested assets, a "trust us" attitude that is all too familiar in this industry. The solution, given broad criticism of SROs in the industry, is called *openness*. More than any element in the investment arena, a broader degree of openness will generate investor confidence. Susan Wolburgh-Jenah lowers her highly competent corporate lawyer persona long enough to nod and admit, "We learned from that experience [the confidential report on the IDA], and would approach things a little differently in the future."

THE BANKS: GATHERING US
BENEATH THEIR UMBRELLA

Sunil and Bharati Kumar[1] were relatively pleased with life. Their two children had just completed university, their small video production business was doing well, and their RRSPs were growing in value.

Their overall financial situation, while not at a critical state, remained somewhat perilous, as it had for several years. They carried a mortgage on their home of almost $200,000, representing about 50 percent of its market value, and maintained a line of credit that frequently nudged their secured limit of $50,000. "Given the cyclical nature of our video production business," Sunil explains, "we were always operating close to the limit. We might get a big production contract, but full payment wouldn't be due for months down the road. Meanwhile, we had expenses to cover, equipment to lease, and so on. Fortunately, our bank manager was understanding, and we had been with the same bank, same branch, for over 20 years. We kept everything there—our household account, our company's current account, our leasing plans, our home mortgage—everything except our RRSP accounts."

The RRSPs, which exceeded $500,000 in 2003, were maintained at the full-service brokerage of a rival bank. "We opened our accounts there years ago," Sunil says, "on the advice of a business associate who had nothing but good things to say about the advisor, a man named Harris. Harris proved as good as our associate said he was. Harris would call every couple of months to discuss things, suggest certain investments, tell us if he was investing in the same thing that he was proposing for us, and let us know when he was getting out of it. We've always made contributions to our RRSPs every year because this is really an unpredictable business. We knew we could sleep better knowing we had money salted away and were investing it wisely."

"He was wonderful, that broker," Bharati adds sadly. She is a dark-haired petite woman, her steadiness balancing her husband's more emotional nature. "He helped make us a lot of money in our RRSP accounts."

In the fall of 1999, a new branch manager arrived at the Kumars' bank. Much younger than the somewhat folksy manager the couple had dealt with for several years, he was friendly and helpful but not nearly as laidback. "He reminded me of somebody who had just stepped out of a motivational meeting," Sunil recalls, "filled with ideas and ambition, and totally dedicated to making you as much of a success as he saw himself to be."

Within a few weeks of arriving on the job, the new branch manager invited Sunil and Bharati in for a chat and a review of their accounts. "Nothing to worry about," he assured them. "You've been a good customer of the bank and I just want to make sure you stay that way."

The bank manager was as positive during the meeting as he had been during the telephone call, looking over the personal financial statements that the Kumars had provided at his request.

"He seemed to fasten on our RRSP balances," Sunil says. "I remember he whistled at the amount on our last statement. Then he asked why we weren't with the bank's brokerage arm."

"We explained that we were happy with our advisor," Bharati adds. "So why change?"

The bank manager noted that his bank-owned brokerage was rated higher for customer satisfaction and performance than the one the Kumars were using. "You should be with us," he said, meaning his bank's brokerage arm. "You won't give up a thing in service, and you'll save money." The manager reminded them that the Kumars' mortgage was scheduled for renewal the following year. Consolidating their financial activities with his bank would put them in a much better bargaining position when it came to negotiating interest rates for their mortgage and operating loan. "I can probably knock at least a quarter-point off the interest rate on your current account overdraft," he said, "and it would make things easier to raise your operating loan credit in the future, if you need it. You've got a lot of clout in your RRSPs—over a half million dollars' worth. You should be using it. Bring everything under one umbrella with us, and we'll bend over backward to save you money and keep you happy."

"It kind of made sense," Bharati says.

"Of course, we owed Harris, our guy at the other company," Sunil says. "We told the branch manager that, but he shrugged and said, 'Business is business. It's your money, and if you can get the same kind of service from our outfit, which is just around the corner from here, and save a few hundred dollars a year on interest charges, why wouldn't you do it?'"

The Kumars promised to give the idea serious thought. Over the next week, the bank branch manager called twice, urging them to make the switch. During his second call, he asked if he could have the registered representative from his bank's brokerage call and make an appointment—"Just to review your account, give you a second opinion." The Kumars agreed.

"To make a long story short, we switched," Sunil says. "The new broker seemed like a pleasant fellow. He made several suggestions about selling some of our mutual funds and buying others. He even brought the papers needed to transfer the account to his brokerage.

So we did. I sent our former broker a letter thanking him for his help in the past. He didn't respond. I didn't expect him to."

None of the new mutual funds appeared to perform better over the next year than those that had previously been held in the Kumars' RRSPs. In fact, returns were mediocre at best. Nor did the new broker contact the Kumars before mid-February, when he called to ask how much the couple would be putting into their RRSP from the previous year's earnings, reminding them that a decision was needed before the end of the month. "I get really busy around then, as you might expect," he said, "so I'd appreciate it if you would get back to me in the next few days."

"Nothing about a review, nothing about strategy or anything like that," Bharati says. "He just wanted to know how much we would be contributing. It was so different from Harris, our other broker."

The Kumars instructed the broker to purchase units in the bank's money market mutual fund while they decided on a longer-term investment.

"We sat down one night in March to talk about it," Sunil says, "and that's when it hit us. Our RRSPs weren't performing as well as they had been and the service—well, there was no service to speak of. We'd given up big potential earnings on over half a million dollars in our RRSPs to save maybe a quarter percent off our bank loan and mortgage. It was a bad deal."

"Friends told us that all the banks were open to negotiating mortgage rates," Bharati adds, "and there's no way they would have let somebody else take over our mortgage if it came down to a competitive battle to keep our business. So why even think of transferring our RRSPs to them? After 20 years with the same bank, we had all the clout we needed."

They decided that night to return their RRSPs to Harris, their previous broker.

"He was a little cool," Sunil says. "And he pointed out that our bank's money market funds couldn't be held in our RRSPs if his bank-owned brokerage was handling our accounts. It sounds like a really stupid law, but it didn't matter much, because we could cash them out and buy something else."

The real blow came when Harris announced that he was no longer accepting new clients. In fact, he was reducing his client load in preparation for moving into semi-retirement. "He said he expected to keep working for another 10 years, but with a reduced client list," Bharati says. "If we had stayed with him, he would have kept us as clients. That's the feeling I got. But ..." She shrugs.

The Kumars were passed on to a junior financial advisor, who failed to impress them. By the end of the year they were searching for another place to take their RRSPs that would have an advisor as good as their old friend Harris, and not having much luck.

The Bank Act prohibits tied selling, defining it as "the practice of linking the purchase of a product or service to a bank loan." Is that what happened here?

"The issue is whether or not there is coercion," banking Ombudsman Mike Lauber explains. The Kumars' experience, he suggests, was something else. "Their situation was not coercive tied selling. It was incentive selling."

Just to confuse things, banks also engage in cross-selling. This involves a bank representative finding a way to sell you two goods or services when you intended to purchase only one. Visit your branch to buy a Canada Savings Bond, for example, and you might receive a sales pitch for a safety deposit box in which to keep it.

Back to tied selling. Is it as major factor for the ombudsman in his role of protecting bank customers?

"We have not had a complaint on this for several years," Lauber replies. "One of the issues that we have considered is, if the customer is approached on a coercive basis and declines the transaction, what are the damages?" No damages, beyond the opportunity for a possible lower interest rate, were linked in this case.

The Kumars fell victim to a powerful sales pitch that cost them potential growth in their RRSP and marked the end of a beneficial relationship. That the idea originated with their bank, which controlled much of the couple's fiscal obligations, added impact to the new manager's proposal. Canada's chartered banks no longer carry the weight of the near imperial authority they held a few decades ago, nor are they the source of last resort for financial assistance. But they continue to represent a repository of trust, leavened with a friendly corporate persona delivered via TV commercials and other media. If the bank claims it can save us money, we tend to believe it. Should we?

Reverse Mortgages: An Expensive Loan Packaged as a Gift

For some time now, no Canadian household with a TV set and a cable linkage has been free from the friendly face and gentle voice of Gordon Pape extolling the virtues of reverse mortgages. Pape, and the smiling clients who appear in the TV commercials featuring him, all fit a comfortable mould of solidly middle-class and late-middle-aged Canadian homeowners intent on getting the most out of the years left for them. And how will they do it? With a reverse mortgage, that's how.

Many people were surprised to see Pape promoting the reverse mortgage concept on behalf of the Canadian Home Income Plan (CHIP). Among the celebrity investment gurus, Pape actually holds an OSC securities trading licence (although he never uses it) because he feels everyone who makes a living dispensing investment advice should be required to pass an examination and be formally licensed.

"Yes, I get some flak from promoting reverse mortgages," Pape
sighs in his Toronto home, "basically from people who do not understand the concept very well."[2] He bristles at the idea that he promotes
reducing the limited amount of capital owned by seniors. "It's a loan
and, just like any loan, your net worth is reduced if you don't pay it
back. The difference is, the money is not taxed, and you don't lose
your home [if you outlive the term of your mortgage]. It's not a
security, it's not a mutual fund, and it has no competition."

That's what it's not. Here's what it is.

A reverse mortgage is essentially a personal loan backed by the
equity in your house. It includes an interest rate applied against the
money you receive through the reverse mortgage. Adjusted semi-
annually, the interest rate hovered between 7 and 8 percent during
2004. The only difference between a reverse mortgage and an equity-
backed personal loan, which you might take from the bank to build
a new recreation room or purchase investments, is the payback
period—and even here the difference is minuscule. In most cases, as
long as the loan's security—the portion of your home equity that you
pledge to back the loan—remains sufficient, you merely have to pay
the interest on the borrowed money. The loan comes firmly due only
when you or your estate sells the house. That's when the bank claims
its portion of the buyer's price. A reverse mortgage contract permits
you to remain in the house indefinitely, while making no interest
payments; you cannot be forced to sell your house to cover either the
principal or interest on the loan. If you are still living there when you
die, however, you cannot pass the property on through your estate
until the bank pockets the money owed to it.

"Aha!" you might say. "Is it possible that the principal plus the
interest generated over the years could exceed the value of the house,
leaving the bank with a loss?"

That's entirely possible. But never forget the difference between
risk and uncertainty. No one is better at assessing and managing risk

than the people who run our chartered banks, and since all the major banks (with the exception of CIBC) and many credit unions participate in CHIP, they have factored risk into the formula quite nicely, thank you.

Under the CHIP program, you must be age 62 or older to qualify, and your home must be substantially mortgage-free. At age 62, CHIP will offer no more than 40 percent of the market value of your home. The actual amount is based on your age—the older you are, the more money the bank will grant you because, let's face it, the less likely it is that you'll be around long enough to generate a loss for the bank. This reduces the bank's risk. If your $240,000 home has no mortgage and you are 63 years old, CHIP might hand you a cheque for $60,000— tax-free, as the advertisements say. The deed stays in your hands, and you remain in the house for as long as you like. You can do whatever you wish with the money—CHIP even provides suggestions:

- Make new investments to generate income and tax benefits.
- Use the cash to take the pressure off managing daily expenses.
- Make home improvements.
- Pay off other borrowing to improve monthly cashflow.
- Provide in-home help or medical care.
- Invest in a hobby or new business.
- Purchase vacation property.
- Make cash gifts to children or heirs.
- Help children/grandchildren with post-secondary tuition.
- Update vehicles [boats, cars, RVs].[3]

Nothing prevents you from paying off the reverse mortgage, principal plus accrued interest, at any time. If you invest the money and make a bundle on the stock market, you can cash in your investments, pay back the bank, pay taxes on your capital gain, and pocket the profits. But do the math: If you managed to get a $50,000 reverse mortgage from your $200,000 home, invested it in a hot stock, and earned 50 percent on your investment over a year, you would now have $75,000. You owe the bank $50,000 plus interest—at 7 percent call it $53,500—leaving you $21,500 profit. Charges to first register your home with CHIP, then deregister it within three years, could chew up $3500 easily, leaving you with $18,000, of which $9000 is taxable (the profit qualifies as capital gains, reducing the tax level). At a 50 percent marginal tax rate, you'll pocket about $13,500. Very nice, but remember that you risked a $200,000 asset to earn it. Nor should we forget that the hot stock tip might just as likely produce a 50 percent loss, which would not be deductible from your taxable income.

A better example might be someone with no need for her home's value to generate an estate and who wants money in the bank to pay for long-term in-home care, should she become incapacitated. The reverse mortgage would permit her to remain living in her home, but only as long as the cash remained.

Pape emphasizes in his TV advertisements, as he did in his meeting with me, that reverse mortgages are not for everyone. This is proven through statistics from CHIP itself. At the end of 2003, after five years of promoting the concept, less than 6000 Canadians had acquired reverse mortgages on their homes. The total value of the homes pledged as security for these deals was $1.2 billion, meaning the average home security hovered around $200,000.[4]

Critics of reverse mortgages—and there are many—point out that you may be cashing out long-term accrued assets to obtain short-term financial benefits. Reverse mortgage interest rates are invariably higher than full mortgages, and unlike long-term first mortgages, a reverse mortgage interest rate cannot be locked in. Twice each year the interest is adjusted to keep pace with the market. If the rates fall, you win. If they rise, you lose.

And the interest keeps compounding. At 8 percent, the reverse mortgage on your home—the amount applied against its value—will double every nine years. If you spent 25 years paying off the mortgage on your house, then took a 40 percent reverse mortgage on it, the bank might recover the total value of your house in less than 15 years.

Even before getting your hands on the reverse mortgage funds, you'll pay a flat fee of $1285 for title insurance, legal fees, and closing costs, plus out-of-pocket expenses—your pocket, of course—for a property appraisal and independent legal advice. If you choose to repay the amount of your reverse mortgage plus interest within three years, you'll be assessed a penalty.

"First the bank makes a bundle when it loans you the money to buy your home," critics say, "and then it makes another bundle from your reverse mortgage, but this time it takes barely half as long. Meanwhile, the bank acts as though it is doing you a favour, handing over a tax-free gift. Well, it's not a gift. It's a hard-nosed business deal, and the bank always makes a profit."

If you need cash and want to reside in your home for several more years, consider more familiar options, like renting out a room or two. You might borrow from your kids, who will eventually inherit the property and would prefer to loan you money and assume the property unencumbered than wrestle with the bank or credit union over the family home after you're gone.

Bank-Owned Brokerages: Wolves in Sheep's Clothing?

The deregulation of banking fostered the entry of chartered banks into the investment industry. When it happened, conservative middle-class Canadians who regarded stockbrokers as alien and unknowable as Afghanistan camel drivers found it more comfortable to deal with their neighbourhood bank branch than with brokerage firms such as Wood Gundy; Richardson Greenshields; Burns Fry; McLeod, Weir, Young; and Dominion Securities. By the early 1990s, when Wood Gundy was absorbed by CIBC; Richardson Greenshields by TD Bank; Burns Fry by Bank of Montreal; McLeod, Weir, Young by ScotiaBank; and Dominion Securities by Royal Bank, they were dealing with them anyway.

Simultaneously, Canada's chartered banks grew more approachable. Everyone, it seemed, wore a friendly smile and had a bundle of cash ready to foist on you. Canadian humorist Stephen Leacock's essay about being rattled every time he entered a bank was no longer simply dated, it was incomprehensible. Why be nervous about entering a bank? Banks were the fiscal equivalent of a neighbourhood pub, the one where everybody knows your name and they all want to buy you a drink, or maybe sell you a savings bond.

Except, in some instances, the bank-owned brokerages.

In recent years, these firms appear to be generating an alarming number of complaints from small investors about the manner in which advisors handle investor accounts. On the surface, this is hardly surprising. Not only do the bank-owned brokerages handle the majority of RRSP and RRIF accounts; their client list is often less sophisticated than those of the few remaining independent brokerages.

This second factor cuts both ways, of course. On one side, it may be argued that unsophisticated investors do not fully appreciate investing philosophies and the inherent risks involved in pursuing a strategy—thus the greater number of unwarranted complaints. It is also true, however, that this very lack of sophistication makes it easier and more tempting for some advisors to place their interests ahead of those of their clients. Not only are the clients less likely to understand or complain about inappropriate investments or misunderstood risks, but they also are less likely to pursue complaints based on unnecessary losses, and are even less prone to launch a legal joust.

Investors who challenge a bank brokerage risk finding themselves financial cannon fodder. Patricia Cosgrove's experience (see Chapter 9) of facing down a senior litigator hired by the bank's investment arm at an hourly fee likely exceeding $1000 in response to a potential $10,000 loss in small claims court is a dramatic illustration of the counterattack small investors risk facing. The only inference to draw from her experience is that the bank could not risk losing even a diminutive challenge to the practices of its brokerage for fear that, like the small Dutch boy removing his finger from the dike, a deluge would follow.

First Rumblings of a Revolution?

No one is suggesting that financial advisors in bank-owned brokerages are about to rise up like the proletariat in rebellion against pressures to generate higher sales and commissions. The industry tends to laugh off claims that this sales pressure is applied at the expense of the well-being of clients, emphasizing that bank-owned brokerages function within the guidelines of the IDA and provincial and territorial securities authorities. But from time to time, someone shines a light on the inner workings of the giant brokerages, with revelations that are neither attractive nor reassuring.

This occurred in April 2003 when finance journalist Jonathan Chevreau printed a resignation letter from a financial advisor in his *Financial Post* column. The advisor, a man in his mid-40s, had built an impressive income-generating portfolio over the years, a tribute to his investing skills. The income this produced, along with the advisor's admittedly frugal lifestyle, enabled him to emphasize benefits to his clients over income for his employers. He had guided most clients into portfolios as low-cost, diversified, and tax efficient as his own. In fact, the annual cost to the broker's clients hovered around 0.65 percent of assets, exceptionally low considering the quality of the service provided.

This was not considered adequate by the bank-owned brokerage, which Chevreau dubbed *BBB* (for Big Bank Brokerage). For some time, Stan, the pseudonym hung on the advisor by Chevreau, had resisted pressure by his superiors to "peddle" wrap accounts and other high-fee investment products. The BBB pressure on Stan and other advisors, he claimed in his letter, was not unique. "As with every other firm on the street," he wrote, "all manner of perverse incentives are in place. All manner of investment pornography is on hand to distract not just clients but advisors too. The most striking thing is not the pilferage of clients' wealth, but how otherwise honest and well-meaning people can be seduced into doing the wrong thing by careful systems design."[5]

The advisor referred to the bank's inactivity fee, which applied a $15 charge each quarter ($60 annually) to non-registered investment accounts in which no trading activity—buying, selling, or exchanging mutual funds, bonds, or stocks—had taken place.

Bank executives defend such a fee by pointing out that they are required to print and mail statements each quarter, along with a tax summary each year. Besides, there were compliance officers to be paid (for sheltering the brokerage from harm), research departments to be maintained (identifying stocks to be bought and sold), executive salaries to be covered ("Churn the old ladies to buy the Mercedes"—sardonic Bay Street poetics), and so on. Were these not accounted for in the bank's existing fee structure? Apparently not—or not well enough. In effect, the bank reversed the concept of user pay into "pay if you don't use it."

Canada's chartered banks are open to another level of criticism, related to multi-levels of power and influence they exert. Consider the following scenario.

A couple in their seventies, persuaded by a well-known investment guru, seek to increase the size of their retirement nest egg through leverage. The man has suffered a heart attack and stroke. His bank-owned brokerage promotes the investment of $100,000 in a tech-based bank-managed mutual fund, purchased at a 9-to-1 leveraged ratio—the elderly couple put up $10,000, and the bank loans them $90,000 secured by the couple's equity in their home. When the fund tanks with the collapse of the high-tech industries, the fund's value is a fraction of its original cost, and the bank demands full payment of the $90,000 loan plus interest.

In effect, the bank has—

1. Made money from the sale of its own fund
2. Made money from interest on the money loaned to purchase the fund
3. Transferred risk (of the fund losing money) from itself to an elderly couple with serious health concerns
4. Obtained virtually 100 percent security via a claim of equity in the couple's home
5. Achieved all of this with a totally inappropriate investment vehicle considering the couple's age and status

Based on the above, a case could be made to impose restrictions on chartered banks involved in such multiple-level actions of advising and financing investments of this kind. By the way, this is not an imaginary event. It is based on an actual case that, unfortunately, cannot be presented in more detail here (to the chagrin of the elderly couple who experienced it) because of a gag order demanded by the bank before any settlement deal could be reached, and a confidentiality agreement certain to be imposed afterward.

For the record, I have dealt with two bank-owned brokerages over the past 14 years, with results ranging from spectacular (thank you, Harley) to frustrating. My current broker is a bright, hard working, and trustworthy guy whose opinion I seek and respect.

The point is not that bank-owned brokerages are to be avoided, but that they are indistinguishable from most of the other players in the game when it comes to 100-percent trustworthy service. Every broker and advisor possesses more means of extracting money from your retirement savings than you are aware, and any advice offered to you may result from pressure on him or her to maximize the bank's revenue rather than an honest desire to maximize the performance of your RRSP or RRIF.

VULTURES, JACKALS, GHOULS, AND EVERYDAY THIEVES

Helen Rentis is not a woman to be trifled with, nor someone you would expect to be easily deceived. As a 16-year-old high school graduate, she began her working career in a secretarial position with Mills, Spence & Co., which metamorphosed first into Burns Fry and eventually to Nesbitt Burns, the brokerage arm of Bank of Montreal. She was also employed in the legal industry, filling a sales position with Butterworths, the leading distributor of law books in Canada. She raised two children as a single mother following the breakup of her marriage, kept a close and supportive relationship with her aging parents, maintained her youthful figure into her 50s, and assembled impressive balances in an RRSP and a non-registered portfolio from years of dutiful contributions and astute management.

These kinds of achievements give a woman confidence in dealing with people, not to mention a sense of independence and self-sufficiency. In short, if you were to choose someone to defraud and swindle, Helen Rentis would not be a good candidate.

She proved this on the day in 1991 when she received a cold call from a young man at Midland Walwyn. "He obtained my name from a list of investors in a popular tax shelter," Rentis recalls. "I had no intention of handing my account over to some stranger via a telephone call, although I recognized that Midland Walwyn was one of the leaders in the brokerage field."

She was, however, considering a new brokerage firm to deal with. Her firm, Richardson Greenshields, had transferred her broker from the downtown Toronto office, convenient to Rentis, north to its suburban Richmond Hill office. The downtown location of the Midland Walwyn office where the cold-calling broker was located was appealing for its convenience, perhaps. But nobody was going to persuade her to move her account on the basis of a single telephone call.

The young broker assured her that he understood her position. "He asked if it would be all right to perform an analysis, at no cost or obligation, of my investments and those of my parents that I was watching over for them," she says. "I went along with the idea, and for several months he gave me his assessment along with examples of the kinds of investments he was doing for other clients.

The young broker explained that, in addition to the usual trading in stocks, bonds, and treasury bills, he employed a unique strategy in commodities trading that was producing excellent results from derivatives—options, puts, and calls. The maximum risk of loss, according to the broker, was 7 percent.

"I was not familiar with that kind of trading," Helen Rentis explains, "but it seemed an acceptable risk to me. He gained my confidence over time, to the point where I thought it might be a good idea to move everything back downtown. Besides, I would be dealing with Midland Walwyn, right?" Better returns were especially appealing to Rentis because she was not a member of her employer's pension plan; this was not a matter of greed but of taking prudent steps to generate a secure financial future, exactly as the investment industry preaches. As a client of Midland Walwyn she also believed that her investments would be secure and that trading in her accounts would be overseen by the brokerage.

Ever cautious, Rentis permitted the broker to use only a portion of the portfolios for his trading system and, with that decision, Michael Holoday, the Bay Street whiz kid, had himself another client.

From the beginning, Holoday reported phenomenal profits with every commodity trade—that is, when Helen could decipher the statements. "I was on the road quite a bit at the time," she says, "and I would come home to piles of statements from Midland Walwyn. I just couldn't understand the ones on options and neither could my accountant. When I complained about them, Michael told me that most of his clients had the same problem so I should just ignore them. He would provide easier to understand summary statements on the multiple trades being made. My accountant could use them to calculate the profits on investments outside my RRSP, report them to Revenue Canada, and pay income tax on them. And that's what we did."

In the early 1990s, Michael Holoday was being portrayed as a kind of boy genius, enjoying special status as the youngest member of Midland Walwyn's Chairman's Club, reserved for the top 5 percent of all Midland Walwyn brokers—an achievement he managed to reach within three years of obtaining his trading licence. How did he rise so far so fast? "Michael's ploy from the beginning was to gain the trust of his clients," Helen Rentis emphasizes. "I had no cause for alarm, nor did I receive any calls from Midland Walwyn informing me that, as I discovered only years later, he had virtually wiped out my account within the first few months of opening it."

Holoday's use of personalized account statements was not limited to Rentis. He used this ruse on all his clients, persuading them to ignore confusing (or distressing) commodity statements and accept his personal assessment of their account status which, of course, was always positive. And all the clients did, through his tenure at Midland Walwyn and his move (under a cloud of suspicion) to aggressive First Marathon Securities, where he was awarded the impressive title of managing director, futures division.

Holoday's lifestyle matched his new title. Instead of the small apartment he occupied when Helen Rentis entrusted her account to him, he now resided in Forest Hill, one of the most exclusive neighbourhoods in Toronto; owned a fleet of cars, including a Jaguar, a Porsche, and a Ferrari; hosted parties at a large cottage on Lake Simcoe; and began construction of a beachfront villa in Barbados. He even married a leggy blonde woman who played the role of Successful Executive's Wife perfectly.

Mistakes happen, but over the next few months, mistakes in Rentis's accounts kept happening over and over. "Finally I told Michael I wanted my money out of my commodity accounts," she recalls. "He promised to do it, but days and weeks went by and nothing happened. Every time I asked about it he had one excuse or another. Finally, I called him just before I was to leave on a business trip. 'I want my money, Michael,' I said. 'No more excuses. Just close out the accounts and send me my money.'"

Holoday protested that he had just doubled the value of Rentis's account.

"I shouted through the telephone, 'So sell the damn thing!'" recalls Helen. "And he promised to. But there was nothing to sell. It took me months to discover that my commodity accounts had been basically empty for years."

It was little consolation, but as events unfolded, Rentis discovered she was not alone in being deluded by Michael Holoday.[1] When he was finally ejected from First Marathon in late 1994, dozens of clients appeared with ransacked accounts and similar stories of Holoday's extensive deception.

As the facts emerged through a long police investigation and criminal trial, it became apparent that Holoday was no ingenious con man. He cheated his victims with any technique at hand, from promising safekeeping for a client's stash of Canada Savings Bonds (promptly cashing them himself) and selling units in a fictitious about-to-be-launched mutual fund, to dispensing promissory notes backed by First Marathon through his position as managing director, futures division.

Nor can his clients be classified as greedy. Almost all were realistic in their expectations, although these expectations were exploited by Holoday's sales pitch and his position at the two brokerages. Without exception, all of the clients relied on Holoday's exalted position within each brokerage to confirm that their investments were appropriate and their statements accurate.

Perhaps most telling was the manner in which the two brokerages that employed Holoday responded to revelations of his frauds. Both steadfastly denied any responsibility for their star broker's antics. Clients who called First Marathon to enquire about the status of their accounts, after news broke of Holoday's dismissal, were told by the firm's compliance officer, "You've been cheated. I suggest you hire a lawyer." No offer was made to replace the money swept from their accounts. When one client protested that he had trusted Holoday because he was First Marathon's managing partner of the futures division, the compliance officer sneered, "That was only a title."

Some clients worked through their emotional distress before throwing up their hands and trying to forget about the experience. Others took legal action, seeking redress through civil suits launched against Holoday's former employers. First Marathon's blanket defence to the lawsuits was to claim the clients were "authors of their own misfortune" for trusting Holoday and his schemes. Two former clients were the subjects of countersuits launched against *them* by First

Marathon, the brokerage claiming $10 million from each to cover damages that the brokerage refused to acknowledge in the first place.

The brokerage fought every claim launched against it with tooth and nail. Most civil cases were eventually settled through arbitration, although a handful remained in dispute a decade later. Thanks to confidentiality agreements, no information on the final settlements, including the proportion of losses reimbursed to the former clients, has been revealed. "I never thought a brokerage could turn on you that way," mused one of the ex-clients.

Why Blame the System When You Can Blame the Victim?

As we have seen, inappropriate investments in your RRSP account (or elsewhere) can lead to losses that you may never recover, with the advisor and brokerage defending themselves in a number of ways, most related to the inevitably of risk and uncertainty.

Fraud and embezzlement differ from bad advice because the proof is often easier to establish and the action can involve criminal courts, where exposure is more widespread and punishment more severe. The common factors, however, are that you lose money and you retain similar low expectations of recovering more than a token amount.[2] Here's one more: Your expectation of protection by the professed guardians of the investment industry should be similarly low, based on past experience.

Remember the OSC? Its stated goals are to "provide protection for investors from unfair, improper or fraudulent practices; foster fair, efficient capital markets; maintain public confidence in the integrity of those markets."[3] Unlike the SROs, the OSC (and related provincial commissions that emulate its structure and objectives) possesses teeth to force settlements, ban participants from the industry (not just member dealers), apply and enforce fines, and generally wield a regulatory club. Securities commissions don't have to limit their muscle to licensed participants in the industry, as they proved with the charges laid against Brian Costello for *not* being licensed (see Chapter 8).

No one expects any regulatory or enforcement body to engage in every corner of its jurisdiction, snooping where it is neither needed nor welcomed, but the OSC and its counterparts across the nation do not inspire confidence in their ability to deter licensed fraud artists from dipping their greasy hands into your hard-won RRSP assets. To many observers, the OSC's attitude toward controlling licensed securities dealers are like a police officer who ignores reports of armed and suspicious-looking characters until the bad guys get around to shooting somebody.

Consider Patrick Kinlin, as notorious as Michael Holoday and cut from the same bolt of cashmere. Like Holoday, Kinlin loved the good life, especially if it was being charged to someone else's tab. He lived in lavish homes, enjoyed expensive clothes, ate at exclusive restaurants, and favoured pricey cars, owning both a Mercedes and a Porsche. He proved especially adept, with his silver mane of hair, elegant bearing, and honeyed voice, at romancing middle-aged women who were in possession of liquid assets. Basically an insurance agent, Kinlin had been licensed by the OSC to sell mutual funds and insurance products exclusively. In the late 1990s, however, he started pushing phoney bonds onto his clients. When word of Kinlin's illegal activities got back to the OSC, it began investigating his actions. In the middle of this investigation, one of Kinlin's clients called the OSC to check on the insurance man, whose profligate living had raised a red flag. Kinlin, the client was told, had "a clean record" at the OSC. Based on that notification, the man handed Kinlin $60,000. Soon afterward, Kinlin fled Toronto and was arrested in a Pennsylvania hospital where he was being treated for an understandable nervous disorder. Needless to say, the client never saw his $60,000 again.

Nothing in OSC policies regarding suspicious activity by licensed dealers seems to have changed. Once again, small investors must take it upon themselves to don their own armour for protection instead of relying on regulators.

They Love Themselves, Not You

Detective Jeff Thomson of the Toronto Police Services Fraud Squad is as familiar with people like Kinlin and Holoday (he was instrumental in investigating and convicting the latter) as anyone, although he probably loathes them more than most. With a powerful physical presence and an expression that can transform itself between warm laughter and threatening scowl in an instant, Thomson has a good deal of sympathy for victims of fraud and embezzlement.

"They don't expect to be taken by these guys," Thomson says over lunch in a sports bar across the street from Toronto Police Services Headquarters.[4] "They expect these fraud artists to help them, because that's how the bad guys present themselves." When someone offers to help you, Thomson points out, your guard is automatically lowered. That's why the victims of fraud and embezzlement can be among the last to recognize and acknowledge that they have been scammed.

Going through life in a highly suspicious state of mind is neither wise nor healthy, Thomson admits. Fortunately, it is also unnecessary. "All you need to remember are a few warning signals," he advises. "Hearing or sensing any of them should turn on a red light somewhere in your mind, and that's when your guard should come up." He is sympathetic with most of the victims and despises the fraud artists. "They all have two characteristics," he says of the fraudsters. "They don't give a damn about other people. And they love themselves."

Here are Thomson's suggestions for avoiding fraud and embezzlement. They're neither infallible nor complete—the scum who prey on trusting elderly people are adept at developing new tricks—but they provide some armour worth wearing whenever you encounter an unfamiliar and promising investment opportunity.

If It Sounds Too Good to Be True, It Probably Is This is the oldest rule in the book. Unfortunately, thousands of people ignore it every day. If anyone tells you they can double your money within a dramatically short period—less than a year, for example—without incurring a major degree of risk, reply with three words: "No, you can't." Or simply walk away.

Do Not Be Overly Impressed with First Impressions You don't know what a swindler looks or sounds like, so do not trust your instincts to warn you about one. They may be smooth and fast-talking, or so shy and soft-spoken that you feel compelled to give them your money. They may boast about their educational achievements, or brag that they were school dropouts who clawed their way to success. They may be men or women, as young as your grandchild or as old as your parents.

One quality shared by many is their lifestyle. Fraud artists almost invariably pursue extravagance in their dress, their possessions, and their social life. Extravagance is the reason they commit fraud in the first place, and the image of success it conveys adds extra appeal to their schemes. Clients begin to believe that an investment advisor making so much money for himself must be able to generate similar wealth for his clients. In reality, the criminals are not just living beyond their means—they are living beyond the means of their clients.

George Nelson Allen, a stockbroker convicted of defrauding several clients out of $7.5 million, lived in a sprawling suburban home (which he transferred to his wife for $2 before investigators could freeze his assets), and drove a Jaguar valued at $110,000.

Allen's embezzlement technique, familiar to Thomson, was to sell "corporate investment certificates" in two fictitious companies. The certificates paid interest far higher than current market rates and could be cashed on 30-days' notice. "It was a classic Ponzi scheme," Thomson recalls. "He was always robbing Peter to pay Paul."[5] Allen had no compunction about grasping money from any source, and no apparent conscience regarding the damage he was inflicting. One of his victims was a young man awarded $600,000 after losing the use of his legs in an auto accident. Allen took every penny. When a married couple saw their entire life savings of $850,000 vanish through Allen's fingers, it almost destroyed the family and nearly drove the husband to suicide.

"He always looked wealthy and successful," Allen's victims would recall. "He was well groomed, well dressed, and drove that flashy Jaguar."

Upon conviction, Allen was sentenced to four years in prison. The courtroom audience, mostly comprising Allen's victims, broke into applause as he was handcuffed, and one ex-client shouted, "You're a scumbag!" at the ex-broker's back.

"In 27 years as a police officer, I've never seen cheering in the courtroom before," says Jeff Thomson. His wry smile suggested that it was well deserved.

If "You Have to Act Now!"—Don't Con artists do not want you thinking too much before you hand over your money. If someone insists that you "act now!" and sneers at your insistence on thinking things over, take a hike.

Michael Holoday was brilliant at persuading people to jump at his schemes, many of them short-term investments—as short as one week—providing promissory notes indicating that he would be paying 5 percent interest for a seven-day loan, which works out to an annual interest rate of 250 percent. When his scheme collapsed around him, one element of Holoday's defence was to point out, correctly, that this interest rate was illegal under the Criminal Code of Canada and, as a result, he was not obligated to pay it. Besides, he argued, non-payment of a loan is a civil, not a criminal, matter, and he should not be subject to criminal charges as a result.

This illustrates one more quality to expect from these people: chutzpah.

Never, Ever Fall for a Scheme to Extract Money from Your RRSP, RRIF, or LIRA Tax-Free

The money in your RRSP or RRIF is free of income tax until you withdraw it as cash. This is fair, since you did not pay income tax on the contributions you made nor on any growth that took place over the years. Still, it hurts to find Canada Customs and Revenue (CCR) standing there with its hand out when you're ready to enjoy the benefits of all that saving and investing.

Enter the fraud artists.

While you cannot withdraw funds from your registered plan without triggering income tax, you can move the investments within it, perhaps selling bonds to purchase shares in a company, assuming they are eligible as an RRSP investment. This rule inspired a number of scams in which investors were offered the opportunity to invest in a growing company with RRSP assets, and the company would return as much as 75 percent of the share price in cash to the investor. Newspaper advertisements still appear from time to time, offering an RRSP loan free of tax. Buy $100,000 worth of shares in Ungava Enterprises Inc. and receive $75,000 in cash that CCR needn't know about. Boy, is this a good deal or what?

You probably know the answer. Unfortunately, hundreds of people each year discover too late that their money has covered only a transaction fee or a down payment, in the case of legitimate corporations. Even if shares are transferred into the RRSP, their actual value will be more apparent than real, and clients eventually discover that $100,000 has effectively vanished from their retirement savings. Then things get worse.

CCR takes a dim view of any attempt to avoid paying taxes. They'll demand immediate payment plus interest and perhaps a penalty as well when such activity is suspected. While the bilked investor is dealing with this blow, there is always the risk that the shaky company whose shares the investor purchased goes bankrupt. If this occurs, the corporation's creditors may appear on the investor's doorsteps demanding payment, even though the purchased shares are now worthless. Yes, it has happened.

Do Not Trust the Internet   To those engaged in fraud and embezzlement, the internet is like a commuter train delivering them to work each day. "Work," in this case, means persuading trusting citizens to part with their money, which vanishes into cyberspace before being deposited in offshore bank accounts.

That's what happened to about 13,000 people in 60 countries around the world who invested in a "bank debenture trading program" promising 120 percent annualized returns. The "program," operated by an organization calling itself the Tri-West Investment Club, claimed to be associated with Haarlem Bank via something called the Haarlem Universal Corporation, and included among its directors a vice-president of Lloyd's of London. All of this could be accessed on the Tri-West website, where investors could obtain every bit of information needed to participate, including instructions on transferring their deposits.

It was, of course, yet another variation of the old Ponzi scheme. The alleged kingpins behind Tri-West, including Canadian Alyn Richard Waage, were eventually collared. Waage admitted his guilt and promised to make restitution to his victims, who should not be hanging by their thumbs waiting for it.

You wouldn't fall for a deal pledging such high returns, would you? Not unless you were among the people who responded to a fictitious website launched by the OSC in March 2001 as a means of alerting people to the dangers of investing blindly through the internet. The website promised monthly returns of 30 percent or more from "international debentures" eligible for RRSPs. Within six weeks the site scored over 16,000 hits. Many visitors expressed keen interest in the prospect, and some offered to send $50,000 or more in cash without obtaining more information. P.T. Barnum would be pleased.

Never Invest in Something You Do Not Understand Stay clear of anyone who promises substantial earnings while being unable to explain the deal in terms you can understand.

This goes for friends, relatives, and colleagues who rave about the returns they are receiving, or more likely are expecting to receive, from an investment. "I don't know how it works," they may say, "but it's making me money and that's all I care about."

Your grasp of the investment's mechanics will be about the same as your eventual grasp of any profits.

Beware of Investments Sold through Affinity Groups Fraud artists feed on your trust. Unless you believe and trust their promises, they won't collect a penny from you.

We place our deepest trust in those whose values and culture we share, and this represents prime feeding ground for vultures who dine on our investment assets. Religious groups, service clubs, and community organizations are typically composed of people who enjoy each other's company and confer their trust easily. The members of a Toronto mosque did just that in the summer of 2000 when a charming young man named Salim Mohammed Damji began discussing a new investment opportunity. Damji, who told some people he was a dentist and others he was a physician—in reality he was neither—claimed his company, Strategic Trading Systems, had developed a teeth-whitening product called Instant White. Colgate Palmolive was prepared to buy the rights to Instant White for $400 million, and

Damji was offering friends, relatives, and almost everyone in the close-knit Islamic community an opportunity to purchase shares in Strategic Trading Systems. "When Colgate buys us," he promised, "you get back $20 for every dollar you invested."

He had little except his word to back up his promises, but that was enough to persuade over 5000 people to hand Damji a total of $70 to $80 million before the scheme collapsed 18 months later. Less than $5 million was recovered; much of the balance was lost by Damji through bad investments, real estate purchases, and internet gambling.

How could one person scam so much money from so many people on such a flimsy promise?

"It's the nature of an affinity group," Detective Jeff Thomson explains, "plus the special character of the Islamic community. In their culture, a handshake is a binding contract. Damji took advantage of that, plus the trust placed in him by members of his mosque and even members of his own family. That's the power that fraud artists have inside their own ethnic and religious group."

In November 2002, Damji was sentenced to prison for six years and three months, with no directive for him to make restitution. Many of his victims were forced to sell their houses to settle loans made for their investment in Damji's scheme, and some required treatment for mental and physical hardships directly related to their experience.

Viatical Investments—Betting on Someone Else's Death

The Oxford dictionary says *viatical* "relates to a journey; articles for use on a journey." The word is derived from *viaticum,* the Eucharist when administered to or received by one who is dying or in danger of death. The practical sense borders on the ghoulish.

Some insurance companies offer a terminally ill policyholder up to 80 percent of the policy's death benefit in cash during the last year of his or her projected life. The balance of the coverage is paid to the estate after the person's death. A viatical settlement is a means of providing funds for treatment, physical comforts, or any other purpose that the dying person may choose. On the surface it appears fair and humanitarian, and it is, until processed by the criminal mind.

The practice of offering viatical settlements to terminally ill patients is not universal among insurers, and it can involve complex paperwork and processing time—not an appealing thought to people who may be measuring their remaining lifespan in months. This has launched a ghoulish mini-industry of brokers acting as intermediaries between the policyholders and third parties, who bid to be named beneficiary of the policies. The highest bidder pays the policyholder. For $100,000 in coverage, the bidder may offer $60,000 to the patient, with the prospect of receiving the full amount of the policy when the patient dies, less a finder's fee paid to the broker. In 1999 alone, an estimated $1 billion of life insurance policies were transferred in the United States under viatical agreements.

Viatical settlements are a foggy issue in Canada. While prohibited in Ontario (though motions have been made to change the law and permit them), the provinces of Nova Scotia, New Brunswick, Quebec, and Saskatchewan have no provision addressing them, and arguments can be made both in favour of and in opposition to the idea. Whether you agree with the morality of it or not, they are an honest business proposition. Or should be. Whenever large amounts of money are changing hands, someone looks for an illegal way of cashing in on it, and this is no exception.

In both the United States and Canada, potential investors are being offered a 100 percent return by purchasing a policy on a terminally ill person, with the investor named as the beneficiary. Spend $50,000 now and pocket $100,000 in a year or two. To relieve your suspicions, if not quell your moral concerns, the deal may include an option of selling your policy after two years for 70 percent of its face value. If the insurance company refuses to honour the coverage or challenges payment, you will be provided with a new policy for equal or greater coverage through a "replacement policy trust" managed by the viatical brokerage. The deals are promoted with the best (or worst) of Madison Avenue–style sales lines:

Full liquidity at maturity from rock-solid A-rated insurance companies! Zero risk to principal—a totally safe investment with no load and no fees!

Short holding periods with early buy-out options available!

Supposedly, you are making a humanitarian investment, permitting the patient to purchase improved health care, pay off debts, reduce family strife, take a vacation, or enjoy some other benefit that would not be possible without your combination of compassion and astute investment style. Will you really grow wealthy while enjoying the warm glow of fellowship and charity? Is it snowing in Miami?

Here is what usually happens:

- The patient, whose cooperation is obviously vital, might receive only 10 or 15 percent of your investment after the brokers deduct their fees and commissions. Hand $50,000 to the broker and perhaps $7500 reaches the patient.

- You may discover that the policy was purchased without informing the insurance company of the patient's illness. Insurance companies will refuse to pay coverage on someone who conceals a pre-existing condition.

- The patient may survive well beyond the projected lifespan. If you discover that he or she is still around after three or four years, do you feel uplifted at their good fortune or deflated at your bad investment?

- Even when things go as planned, you may find that the insurance payment is challenged by family members, creditors, or other claimants.

- Some viatical contracts direct your investment toward the insurance policy premiums, some require you to pay the premiums, and others assure you that the brokers will maintain the premium payments for you. Needless to say, lapsed premiums mean no benefit for you.

Whether or not viatical contracts become legal and widely available across Canada, it is difficult to imagine them being acceptable within an RRSP or RRIF ... or eagerly sought by anyone with substantial ethics.

When the Punishment Fails to Fit the Crime

Our justice system makes a clear distinction between crimes committed with a stroke of the pen (or computer key) and those committed with the use of a threat, a fist, a knife, or a gun. Rob a bank of $20,000 and you may receive a nine-year prison sentence; with acceptable behaviour you will be eligible for parole in three years. Steal $20 million from trusting citizens through scams and embezzlement and you may also receive a nine-year sentence; behave in the same manner, however, and you'll be back on the street in just one and a half years because your crime was "non-violent."

That's assuming, of course, that you are caught and convicted in the first place. To give it a hip-hop beat: Crimes in the street get you more time than crimes in the suite, and, the punishment is lighter when your collar is whiter. There are practical reasons for this. No offence to neighbourhood muggers, but white-collar criminals are a little higher on the intellectual level and work with more sophisticated tools than a lead pipe. Tracking a street thug employs snitches and descriptions. Tracking an investment mugger may take months or even years of following paper trails and computer records.

A study conducted by Osgoode Hall Law School noted that "people from poor and working-class backgrounds charged with committing street crimes are less able to resist the use of criminal law, whereas the business and professional classes who engage in corporate [or financial] wrongdoing are better able to avoid the criminal label as a result of their influence and financial resources."[6]

The entire legal process tends to favour a softer, more complacent treatment of white-collar criminals, beyond the distinction between supposedly passive and violent methods of stealing other people's money. Under the federal Criminal Code, a conviction of breaking-and-entering carries a potential life sentence for the offender even if nothing more valuable than a beer is taken from the fridge. The same man committing fraud faces a maximum sentence of 10 years, no matter how many tens of millions of dollars he stole and how many lives he devastated. And while Statistics Canada spews detailed figures on street crime every year, it produces only a smattering of statistics on white-collar crime.[7]

The underlining philosophy suggests that white-collar crime is either victimless or merely a crime against property exclusively, with no link to personal suffering. Anyone who has endured a severe loss in their life savings, especially in their middle years or beyond, will reject this as nonsense. Virtually every conviction of fraud and embezzlement conducted against trusting individuals leaves the victims feeling twice-abused—first by the fraud artist and then by the legal system.

The victims of Michael Holoday received some satisfaction when he was sentenced to a total of seven and a half years for his misdeeds at brokerages Midland Walwyn and First Marathon, plus another 15 months for writing bad cheques while awaiting trial on the earlier charges. They were less than thrilled, however, to learn that Holoday served most of his time at the minimum-security Beaver Creek facility set among the lakes and woodlands of Muskoka, where inmates reside in winterized log cabins and cook their own meals in a communal kitchen. "That's not prison, it's summer camp," sneered one of Holoday's victims. And many were further appalled to learn that Holoday was released to a downtown Toronto halfway house in August 2002, having served just 16 months.

Patrick Kinlin, who carried out scams similar to Holoday's, was released on day parole after serving less than a year of his five-year sentence. Salim Damji's immense fraud, which cost friends, relatives, and members of his Islamic community an estimated $80 million, served barely a year of his six-year three-month sentence before receiving day parole, leaving him free to walk among people whose lives he had damaged to such an enormous extent. Nelson Allen's four-year sentence for pocketing $7.5 million of investor funds meant he would be back on the street in just eight months. Those are Canada's parole rules; non-violent crimes qualify first offenders for release after just one-sixth of the sentence has been served.

David Blow, who masqueraded for years as an insurance agent in a Toronto suburb, avoided trial by admitting he had defrauded 65 victims of $7.3 million. When sentenced to 43 months in prison in February 2001, the court considered that he had been held in a detention centre for five and a half months, all of which qualified him for day parole after serving about seven months behind bars. If you care to look at it from a salary or wage angle, that's about $1 million a month.

The rationale for this lenient treatment is based on the apparently lesser impact of white-collar crimes versus those of appalling offences such as sexual assault, robbery with a weapon, and murder. That's reasonable, but it fails to address the true impact of crimes in which victims lose virtually all their worldly possessions. Fraud artists lacking financial resources receive a court-appointed attorney to defend them against criminal charges, while their victims are frequently left too destitute to retain a lawyer and recover their losses (or attempt to) in civil court.

Victims are often left defenceless in other ways. "Over 80 percent of all frauds involve people more than 60 years of age," states fraud investigator Jeff Thomson. "They had assets saved for their retirement, and they came from a generation when people were more trusting of others. That's what makes them the favoured target. Of course, they are also the least able to recover their losses, so they are also the most tragic."

Whatever the age and status of the victims, the shock of losing a substantial portion of their life savings often results in depression, family strife, divorce, and even suicide. White-collar offences are "victimless crimes"? Says who?

Admittedly, prison sentences are ineffective as a deterrent to these scam artists. Investigators claim the rate of recidivism with fraud artists and embezzlers is among the highest of any criminal activity, including murder and armed robbery. Within months of being released onto the streets of Toronto, Michael Holoday was found collaborating with an internationally sought fraudster who had set up internet sites promising high returns for investors and employing good old Ponzi-scheme principles. Patrick Kinlin was even brasher. He spent his day parole hours chatting on pay telephones, promoting a phoney retirement home and picking up donation cheques at mail drops. When the scam was discovered, Kinlin's parole rights were revoked and he languished in a prison cell for a few weeks before succumbing to a heart attack. Few mourned his passing.

"These guys never learn," said one investigator familiar with both the Kinlin and Holoday cases. "They consider their time behind bars as an educational opportunity, where they can pick up new ideas and maybe meet new partners in crime."

If incarceration provides neither deterrent to the fraudsters nor gratification for their victims, perhaps our best course of action as citizens is to assume responsibility for preventing scams. It will cost us something in trust, normally an admirable and beneficial human characteristic, and require us to temper our greed to a substantial degree, which is not a bad goal in itself. In this manner, we can avoid being victims and prevent the fraudsters and embezzlers from succeeding. It is, like it or not, our best defence.

12

LOOKING OUT FOR YOURSELF
AND YOUR MONEY

"I'm not an angry guy," Stan Buell insists. "I may be outraged, but I'm not angry."

We are relaxing over coffee on a promising spring day in the affluent Toronto suburb of Unionville. Buell's real estate office is a short walk up the street from Starbucks. He has arrived at my request to discuss the Small Investor Protection Association (SIPA), an organization Buell launched in 1998. Trim and stylishly dressed, Buell appears substantially younger than his 66 years, and the spring in his step is that of a more youthful man.

Like most of SIPA's 500 members, Buell was the victim first of broker malfeasance and later of the failure of regulatory bodies and the legal system to support him. "I prefer not to discuss my own experience because people will assume I launched SIPA as some sort of revenge," Buell says, "but I didn't. I started SIPA to help others, after I went through my own nightmare."

Buell's nightmare consisted of returning from a five-week trip abroad to discover that his six-figure investment portfolio entrusted to his broker in his absence had vanished, leaving him a $70,000 debt. He spent years attempting to recover his losses, encountering unhelpful industry regulators and the brokerage's attempts to prevent the case from being heard in civil court. Meanwhile, Buell remained distracted from earning a living, drawing on the remainder of his personal savings to cover his living expenses. Thanks to unflagging energy and unfailing optimism, he managed to put the incident behind him, but the experience left him sensitized to problems of small investors who are at the mercy of the investment industry. When he heard a story of advisor wrongdoing in 1998 that was even more devastating in its impact than his own situation, he decided to do something about it.

"It concerned an elderly man and woman who had worked together all their lives to build a thriving business," Buell relates. "When the husband was stricken with terminal cancer they sold the business. Soon after, the husband died, believing that at least his widow would live her life in financial comfort and security. But that wasn't the case. The widow put her money, which included the proceeds from the sale of the business, the sale of their house, and their last $160,000 of savings—a total of over $900,000— in the hands of a financial advisor she trusted. The entire amount was gone within three years, placed in high-risk investments that benefited only the advisor through commissions. It was terrible, and it got worse when nobody seemed able or willing to assist her. Nobody really cared."

Buell cared enough to start SIPA, holding the organization's first meeting in the basement of his church. "About a dozen people showed up," he recalls, "and we've been building slowly but steadily ever since. Now we have about 500 members in nine provinces."

Instead of bragging about the organization he spawned, Buell regrets the necessity for his group. "Investors need an organization with the power to offer them protection," he suggests, "and that power will not come from the SROs. An industry-sponsored association cannot properly look after the concerns of individual investors, because its focus is on the people who pay the association dues—and that's the brokerages and mutual fund companies."

No one representing small investors sits on the board of directors of the SROs or the provincial securities commissions, Buell points out. He notes that the industry giants are very effective, however, at defending their own interests: "The larger companies protect themselves from anything that might affect their image. The financial press may cover frauds and scam in details, but when a bank-owned brokerage is taken to court over its involvement in the Bre-X fiasco, which cost small investors untold millions of dollars after it collapsed, very little is heard about it."

Buell's denunciation of large financial firms represents the root of his criticisms about the industry. He is not an advocate, for example, of do-it-yourself investing by most RRSP/RRIF owners. "Investors need good brokers and financial advisors," he suggests, "and I really believe most advisors are bright, hard-working people. Many problems are caused not by individuals but by a system that forces advisors and brokers to compromise their principles in the name of pushing profits higher and higher." When the pressure gets strong enough, Buell says, even good people will bend both the rules and their own principles to satisfy upper-management demands to produce more profits. "The first place to fix things is at the top, not the bottom," he suggests.

Buell drains his coffee and prepares to return to his work as a successful realtor. Is he still sensitized to investor horror stories? "Oh yes," he sighs. "And I still hear about them. A few weeks ago I received a call from a doctor who worked hard all of his life with the goal of retiring at 55. He set aside every dollar he could spare through his working career only to discover, in his 50s, that it had vanished through his broker's hands. He had nothing whatever to show for it. When I spoke to him he sounded suicidal, so I made a point of driving to his home to lend him support.

Buell understands the pain the doctor experienced—how much it hurts to face the realization of loss and the refusal of an industry to address the situation.

How many Canadians have been victims of bad investment advice that produced intolerable and unnecessary drain on assets in their retirement portfolios? It depends on whom you consult. The investment industry claims the number is minimal, and that victims are the product of their own excessive greed, or that the number reflects the same degree of criminal activity found in every profession.

No one knows the extent of abuse suffered by Canadian investors at the hands of brokers and advisors or by the system as a whole, thanks in part to the veil of secrecy created by confidentiality clauses inserted into settlements and supported by the investment industry. It does not take deep undercover detective work, however, to deduce that thousands of Canadians endure preventable losses in their retirement portfolios year after year. Many are told their losses represent normal investment risk levels, and they are cowed into accepting this explanation by their advisor. Others blame themselves or are too embarrassed to acknowledge the evaporation of substantial portions of their assets. Those who take their cases to the SROs, the provincial securities commissions, or the civil courts and obtain little or no redress assume the attitude "You can't fight City Hall" and try to erase the experience from their memory.

Nothing drove this realization home more dramatically than my research and preparations for this book. Several more accounts of fiscal abuse by financial advisors could have been included here, many representing flagrant exploitation of investor trust and unacceptable behaviour by advisors. Stories included the promotion of risky age-inappropriate instruments to elderly investors, the use of bank loans on a highly leveraged basis for investors persuaded to purchase funds managed by the same bank (a nice win-win situation for the bank), performance awards for brokerage advisors who elevated their production through such actions, and so on. In all these cases, the wounded investors were willing and often eager to provide me with details of their experiences. Wherever the investors had retained legal counsel, however, they were directed—sometimes harshly—by their lawyers to say nothing about their claims publicly until a settlement was reached. In the event of a settlement, of course, they would be subject to a similar gag order, and thus the secrets are maintained ad infinitum.

Lawyers will argue that such confidentiality is critical to launching a successful suit against an advisor or brokerage, ignoring protests from investor groups that operating behind an opaque curtain of secrecy enables the investment industry to claim that abuses are limited in extent and impact. Nor can the actions of some law firms on behalf of their small-investor clients be considered altruistic—not when the same firm plays on both sides of the fence, acting on behalf of brokerages against investors and investors against brokerages, and prefers not to be publicly identified with either side for fear of restricting its earnings opportunities.

Of course, the gag orders do not keep settlement terms totally secret from observers—only from those who might criticize the industry's policies. A typical directive used to keep investors from discussing their lawsuits before and after settlement might read:

> [The plaintiff] will not disclose terms and conditions of the settlement offer to any third party except financial advisors or lawyers, except as required by law and excepting any communication with securities regulatory or other enforcement authorities and self-regulatory organizations.

In case you missed it, this means everyone in the industry with an interest in the facts, including lawyers, brokers, advisors, the IDA, and other SROs, can be privy to the details, but not the press and the public.

Given the concern of law firms not to be associated with one position over another lest it limit their potential client lists, how can we avoid suspicions of self-interest when they direct their small-investor clients to avoid public discussion of their cases? One investor who had been eager to describe his experience to me was directed by his lawyer to not only to avoid any media contact but also refrain from identifying the firm representing him. Why? Because this same firm had defended one of Canada's celebrity gurus in a legal case, arguing against charges that its client's actions had been detrimental to the interests of investors. The legal team obviously wishes to ride two horses at once, with each trotting in opposite directions. Nothing prohibits lawyers from doing this, and the legal profession can make a strong case against such restrictions. Some firms, however, focus on either one side or the other, choosing to fight battles for small investors exclusively, or be retained by brokerages and advisors to repel investor charges of inappropriate actions. They, at least, deserve some respect for choosing an ethical position (ethics are, of course, a moral quality and not a legal one).

How Many Anecdotes Does It Take to Make a Statistic?

During presentations I make to community and service groups on the subject of mistreatment of RRSP holders by the investment industry, I ask if anyone with an RRSP or RRIF has felt that her account was mismanaged, or believed he had suffered unacceptable losses in his portfolio. Typically more than half of those present raise their hands. It's easy to locate malcontents in any gathering, but the stories narrated to me during and after the meetings indicate that the majority of these people are neither perpetually disgruntled nor excessively greedy. Too often, their losses are the apparent product of a commission-based sales system that rewards industry practitioners first and investors only incidentally.

When investor horror stories spill onto the financial pages of newspapers, how many private experiences does each publicized tale represent? A dozen? A hundred? A thousand? No one knows, but while each tale differs in character and setting, all are similar in the unfolding of the plot. Consider these, culled at random:

- A Toronto man and wife in their mid-70s had their retirement portfolio invested in quality bonds and stocks in large established corporations. Encountering an affable stockbroker at a social event, the couple was persuaded to transfer their account to his firm, with substantial cash added from the couple's non-registered account. After selling much of the couple's blue-chip investments, the broker began trading in penny-stock shares of gold mines, audio-cassette producers, and other high-risk ventures. From 1996 to 2001, while stock markets were recording some of the biggest gains in history, the couple's portfolio fell one-third in value. Their complaints led to an investigation by the IDA, which could dispense punishment to the broker but could not recover their losses. After spending three years attempting to obtain some degree of compensation, all the couple, now in their 80s, had to show for it was a thick file of correspondence.[1]

- In July 2000, a new financial advisor was assigned to handle the accounts of a retired Mississauga, Ontario, couple. This advisor severely criticized the emphasis on conservative fixed-income RRIFs pursued by the previous advisor and persuaded the couple to transfer $330,000 into several high-MER funds such as Global Science and Technology, and Global e.Commerce. The husband, aged 75, was suffering from terminal cancer; his wife was scheduled for major heart surgery. Following the husband's death and her recovery from surgery, the woman noted that the values of their RRIFs, which had never before lost money, had declined by more than $100,000. As the RRIFs spiralled downward with the collapse of the tech industry, the widow called her advisor to express her concern. In response, the advisor suggested she put away her account statements and pick up a good book instead. In November 2002, the widow finally transferred her account to another securities firm and demanded the first company review her case. When no review was submitted after six months, the widow contacted the Ontario Securities Commission, which yielded a telephone call from an independent adjuster who had been assigned to her case. By year's end, nothing had yet been resolved, although a proposed settlement letter arrived in December 2003 in which the brokerage offered a settlement of just $7461. The amount, less than one-tenth of the widow's claimed loss, was based on a KYC form allegedly signed by the husband. Unfortunately, the date on the KYC form was one year after the man's death.[2]

- An 83-year-old retired printing-paper salesman in Pointe Claire, Quebec, was annoyed to discover that his RRIF was docked almost 4 percent of its total value in redemption fees and termination fees when he transferred the account to another brokerage. His complaint letter generated a rejection from the first brokerage's director of business standards, who wrote: *"It appears you are aware that* [the brokerage] *may charge fees and, on review of the client application, I note that you have initialled this provision, as well as that having to do with the simplified prospectus. The applicability of redemption fees are* [sic] *disclosed in the prospectus and outline the formula used to make the calculation."* The former client noted that the agreement he signed said the company "may" charge fees on redemption, that he had never received a prospectus, and that he had never been charged fees for moving his account in the past. He abandoned hope of recovering the fees.[3]

- An Ottawa man fought for years to have his bank-owned brokerage accept responsibility for losses suffered when the registered representative placed substantial portions of the man's portfolio into high-risk investments that included gold and diamond exploration companies, debt-heavy conglomerates, and the notorious Bre-X Minerals Limited. Whenever the man questioned the wisdom of these investments, especially the Bre-X ones, the broker told him to relax, adding assurances such as, "I have your best interests at heart," and "Our analysts have checked this company thoroughly." When a hefty portion of his portfolio was lost in the collapse of Bre-X and other dubious investments, the client launched a vigorous battle to recover at least a portion of his losses, to no avail. Working his way through a convoluted trail of compliance officers, branch managers, ombudsman's office, MPs, cabinet ministers, and senators failed to penetrate the brokerage's defence that he was an experienced investor, had approved the investment choices, knew the risks involved, and had no right to claim restitution. Seeking $250,000 in damages, he partnered with other former clients who had suffered comparable losses, all alleging breach of contract, negligence, and breach of fiduciary duty, in a class-action suit. A settlement was finally reached years later, with details unavailable because of a confidentiality order.

- In Kitchener, Ontario, Melville and Marion Hunt won a court decision against their advisor for selling a substantial portion of their investment in BCE Inc. without their permission or direction. The judge agreed that the brokerage breached its fiduciary obligation and instructed the brokerage to pay losses and damages. The brokerage appealed and won, the appellate court ruling that the brokerage did *not* owe the Hunts a fiduciary duty because they had opened a non-discretionary account, and thus had "an obligation to mitigate their losses." Undeterred, the Hunts decided to take their case to the Supreme Court of Canada on the basis that "by denying the existence of a fiduciary relationship between the broker and the client in this case the appellate decision results in financial advisory relationships being treated differently in Ontario than in the rest of the country."[4] In March 2004, the Supreme Court declined to deal with the matter, apparently confirming the Ontario Court of Appeal ruling that the advisor did nothing wrong in selling the Hunts' BCE shares without their permission.

Road Maps, Detours, and Scenic Routes

Canadians need to invest their RRSPs wisely, not salt them away in Canada Savings Bonds or bank savings accounts paying minuscule interest. Investing is all about risk, and risk, as discussed earlier, can be managed.

We need a broader view of risk, especially for RRSP/RRIF holders 60 years of age and older, people whose trust levels and RRSP assets are highest. As a result, they are most prone to suffering unnecessary losses rooted in broker and advisor actions, both passive (DSC-based mutual funds with high MERs, unsuitable allocation of assets, insufficient portfolio updates) and active (account churning, frauds, embezzlement).

Some critics of the investment industry suggest that RRSP/RRIF owners should assume full management of their investments, drawing on articles in the news media and a constantly expanding library of books for guidance. Others disagree. "People with RRSPs still need professional assistance managing their plans," says Stan Buell. "The ordinary Canadian just doesn't have the proper training, expertise, and facilities to make wise investment decisions." Yet trading the risk of making poor investment decisions on one's own for the risk of encountering an incompetent, avaricious, or criminally minded advisor is not an ideal solution either, especially when the prospect of retrieving losses through the convoluted channels of compliance officers, SROs, securities commissions, and civil law is so discouraging. (One self-management strategy that has gained favour in recent years is the so-called Couch Potato Portfolio, detailed in Appendix B.)

A third choice can be described with a simple but effective analogy: View the management of your RRSP or RRIF as an extended journey you have never taken before—perhaps a coast-to-coast motor trip.

Your plan is to follow the main highway, where most people travel. There is a risk, of course, of traffic jams during which you hardly move at all, or of being forced to take a detour until the road ahead becomes clear. Over the course of the journey you'll likely pass scenic sites that tempt you off the main path to admire the view. From time to time you'll encounter other travellers who will rave about a short cut that you shouldn't pass up. Billboards will suggest you turn off at the next junction for an experience you can't afford to miss. You'll consider each, remaining aware of the risk that these diversions and detours might leave you stuck in the mud and spinning your wheels, or direct you into a blind alley from which you may never escape.

The road map is drawn not in lines but in rules familiar to every qualified financial advisor and knowledgeable investor. There is nothing new and revolutionary here, nor should there be—you are not blazing the Northwest Passage after all. This is the Trans-Canada Highway, the main route you follow unless you have a good reason for diverting your path.

Preserving Your RRSP/RRIF Capital While Pursuing Growth

1. Match Your Age to the Guaranteed Fixed-Income Portion of Your Retirement Portfolio
At age 60, the portion of your portfolio comprising government bonds, GICs, or cash (including money market funds) should be about 60 percent, rising as time passes. This tactic is designed to preserve your hard-earned capital, not to generate spectacular short-term growth. Simply put, the older you get, the less time you have to

rebuild your portfolio if it suffers from major market setbacks or inappropriate investments.

Here is how a conservative approach to your portfolio might be charted (short-term assets are cash or money market funds).

	AGE-BASED INVESTMENT GUIDELINE			
AGE	GROWTH (EQUITY) (%)	GROWTH AND FIXED INCOME (%)	BONDS/FIXED INCOME (%)	SHORT-TERM ASSETS (%)
55–65	10	20	55	15
45–55	20	25	40	15
35–45	30	30	30	10
25–35	50	20	20	10

The growth/equity portion could be a low-MER mutual fund, perhaps a combination of managed and indexed plans. For growth/fixed income, consider a balanced fund or quality income trust.

Once committed to this strategy, evaluate government-backed strip bonds for your bonds and fixed-income source. Strip bonds are the interest coupons clipped from long-term (15-plus years to maturity) bonds. High-quality strip bonds are exchanged like currency among brokers. You can purchase and redeem them in just about any amount. You don't actually take possession of the bond or coupons. Your ownership is registered in your name as a *book entry* and purchases or redemptions are recorded in the *book,* held by a trustee.

The stripped coupon shows its price at maturity, the date when the bond issuer will replace it with cash. You purchase the strip bond at a discount from its face value. The amount of the discount determines the annual interest rate you will earn. A $10,000 coupon maturing five years from today may carry a discount price of $8000. Your total profit of $2000, divided by the five-year period, produces annual earnings of $400 or 5 percent—about average in mid-2003. Remember that these are government guaranteed, meaning that the federal or provincial government will be there to redeem them, reducing your risk to its lowest attainable level and raising your ability to preserve capital.

Some advisors may propose bond funds rather than the bonds themselves, noting that an active manager can trade bonds for short-term profits while providing long-term security. This loses sight of the goal to preserve capital, although several bond funds have managed to exceed bond yields over the long term. Bond funds can and do lose money from time to time, so choose one carefully and, if your RRSP assets are sufficient to justify it, combine both bonds and a track-proven bond fund.

2. Treat Risk Like Saturated Fats, to Be Avoided or at Least Minimized

Remember that high reward demands risk in similar proportion. While it may be tempting to goose your RRSP or RRIF with potential double-digit returns by shifting a substantial portion of its assets to a sector fund or some other vehicle, the risk is almost never worth it. Losses are inevitable with risky ventures, and losses inside your RRSP/RRIF bring an extra measure of pain. Lose investment money outside your RRSP and you will at least receive a tax deduction to soothe the blow. No such balm is available to soften the loss inside a registered plan. In addition, a key benefit of RRSPs and RRIFs is their ability to generate compound earnings free of taxation. Once a loss occurs in your RRSP or RRIF, you lose the immediate asset plus potential future earnings as well. Manage your risk.

3. Be Realistic in Your Expectations for Growth

Events of the late 1990s, when mutual funds recorded annual returns of 20 percent or more, convinced investors and RRSP/RRIF owners that such earnings were possible year after year. Well, they're not, unless you are prepared to micromanage your investment and extend your risk tolerance substantially. History suggests that 10 to 12 percent returns are closer to reality, with the higher figure requiring a larger proportion of investments based on equities. The farther you reach for long-term earnings beyond the historical average, the more you wander from the safe and proven path.

4. When Making New RRSP Investments in Equities, Avoid Lump-sum Purchases

Take advantage of dollar-cost averaging wherever possible. Instead of dumping a lump-sum contribution into a mutual fund, or purchasing a large block of blue-chip stocks, make your investment in equal amounts over several months. If you have $3000 to contribute for the coming year (and your cash flow can handle it), make one $500 stock or fund purchase each month for six months. Since mutual fund and stock prices vary—sometimes widely—from day to day, this ensures that you purchase fewer units or shares when prices are high, and more when they are lower.

5. Never Purchase a DSC Mutual Fund
There should be no exceptions.

6. Pass on Any Mutual Fund That Charges More Than the Median MER for Its Category
Generally, MERs and fund performance move in opposite directions—the more of one, the less of the other. Morningstar, one of the leading investment research firms, awards from one to five stars for mutual funds based on performance versus others within their own category. In 2003, Morningstar related its ratings, with three stars indicating average performance, against the MERs for funds in each category.

AVERAGE MER BY STAR RATING				
	4–5 STARS	3 STARS	1–2 STARS	N/A*	ALL
All Categories	2.30	2.50	2.78	2.73	2.62
Cdn. Balanced	2.31	2.45	2.81	2.63	2.55
Cdn. Bond	1.23	2.05	2.35	1.95	1.94
Cdn. Equity	2.65	2.77	2.93	2.80	2.78
Cdn. Money Market	0.62	0.97	1.54	1.17	1.12
Global Equity	2.78	2.72	3.09	3.00	2.93
Science & Tech	3.08	2.95	2.86	2.88	2.92
U.S. Equity	2.29	2.60	3.10	2.76	2.70

* N/A: Unrated funds (due to limited reports, etc.)

SOURCE: MORNINGSTAR CANADA, OCTOBER 2003. REPRODUCED WITH PERMISSION.

In every category, with the exception of Global Equity 3-star ratings, fund performance declined with an increase in MER levels. Keep in mind that Morningstar looks beyond immediate past performance levels to other areas, including volatility (less is more).

This stretch of the road may present a side trip or two, because among the thousands of mutual funds available, an exception is certain to arise. The Sprott Gold and Precious Metals Fund, for example, has a MER of (hold your breath) 10.5 percent. In almost any other situation, this would border on criminal, but the highly specialized Sprott fund actually manages to validate its high MER with equally high (but wildly volatile) performance. In fact, much of the Sprott MER is hitched to a performance bonus earned by Sprott for reaching specific return thresholds. When Sprott's unit holders win big, so does Sprott management, which is reasonable. The proof is in the performance: Over the 12 months ending July 31, 2004, the fund returned 26.2 percent, more than triple the precious metals index.[5] Sector funds such as this one should not account for more than 10 percent of your retirement portfolio, so the general rule still applies: When evaluating mutual funds, reject any with a higher-than-average MER unless it represents an extraordinary sector.

7. Be Dumb Enough to Ask the Smart Questions The smartest people I know are the ones who never, ever pretend they know something when they do not. It takes courage to admit ignorance or unfamiliarity with facts before making a decision. Do not permit your pride to overcome your need to know when your financial advisor presents you with investment alternatives. The smart questions worth asking are—

- Why are you recommending this mutual fund/bond/stock?
- How does it fit my current investment strategy?
- What is the management expense ratio for this mutual fund? (If the MER is above the median for this group: What justifies its high expense?)
- Is this a DSC mutual fund?
- What is the fee or commission you will charge for me to buy or sell this bond/stock?

8. Favour No-load/low-MER Mutual Funds Lest some of the foregoing criticisms and observations on mutual funds have totally dissuaded you from using them, fear not. For small investors with more to do than follow the stock market like a hungry hound after a hare, quality mutual funds remain the best choice for growth. Some of the finest mutual funds are rarely, if ever, recommended by financial advisors, *because they do not offer sales commissions and pay very low, if any, trailer fees.* Chalk up another blow against the commission-based system.

Among the most highly regarded no-load/low-MER fund companies are Altamira, McLean Budden, Saxon, and Philips, Hager & North.

One drawback of no-load low-MER fund companies can be a limited selection of investment styles. Saxon, for example, offered just five funds in 2004, with more promised in 2005. This need not represent a major obstacle since the five established Saxon funds—Balanced, High Income, Small Cap, Stock, and World Growth—meet about 90 percent of your investment needs. Some no-load fund families require higher initial investments to play in their backyard—typically $5000 to get started (compared with $500 or less for the glitzier operations). Larger opening sums help the funds operate more efficiently, as do frugal marketing and communications policies. I don't know about you, but when a company is spending my money, frugal is fine.

A commission-based financial advisor will require a transaction fee of perhaps $100 to obtain units in no-load funds for your portfolio, and that's reasonable. It's wise to establish this fee beforehand.

9. Do Not Hold More Than Six to Eight Mutual Funds in Your Portfolio

Investment advisors arm-wrestle over the optimum number, some proposing as few as 4 or 5, others suggesting 10 or 12. Let's be Canadian and compromise.

Why not hold more funds in your plan? Because you don't need more if the ones you own are chosen carefully, and because too many funds can dilute the benefits of diversification.

The top 10 holdings of large Canadian equity mutual funds are remarkably similar in content and structure. All fund managers draw from the same warehouse of statistics, so it is inevitable that their selections are alike. The secret to effective diversification among funds lies in choosing different sectors, and different fund management styles within the same broad sectors.

Sector selection identifies basic industries or companies assessed by the fund manager as the best available, given the fund's mandate. A Canadian large-cap fund will invest at least 70 percent in companies headquartered in Canada, each with a capitalization—the total value of all shares available for investors—of $500 million or more. Small-cap funds will choose among companies with capitalization under $500 million. Global funds invest around the world; international funds restrict their investments to a slightly narrower range. Emerging market funds target areas such as China, Latin America, and Asia-Pacific. Other funds whose descriptions identify their focus include Health Care, Gold and Precious Metals, Resources, and Bonds.

Management styles are associated with broader equity-based funds, and are categorized as growth or value. Growth funds choose companies with limited assets or earnings but with the promise of a bright future. Tech-based companies such as Nortel were sweethearts of growth funds in the 1990s, and we know what happened to them. Value funds favour proven companies whose share price may be temporarily squashed because of market conditions, bad publicity, momentary disasters, or other reasons. Value fund managers like to say they are shopping for bargains, and the best manage to do so with impressive frequency.

Do not trust a fund's name alone to indicate its management style. Example: One of the largest and oldest mutual funds, Templeton Growth Fund Ltd., is actually a conservative value fund. Best solution: Read the prospectus (snore), ask a trusted financial advisor, or do some investigations on your own.

It's wise to have representation from various sectors and styles in your RRSP/RRIF portfolio along these lines, applying the suggested percentage of total equity investment values:

SUGGESTED BASIC FUND SELECTION		
NUMBER PER SECTOR	**SECTOR/STYLE**	**VALUE (%)**
1–2	Canadian growth-based equity funds*	20–30
1–2	Canadian value-based equity funds*	30–40
1	Global/International equity fund	15–30
1	Canadian small-cap fund	10–20
1–2	Sector funds: resources, emerging markets, etc.	10–15

* One of these could be a broadly based index fund instead of growth or value.

Why so few Canadian equity funds when there are literally thousands to choose from? First, because it's easier to track and manage a fewer number of quality funds. Second, because of the indexing effect. An indexed fund, as you know, tracks the companies making up a major index such as the TSX 300, holding equal proportions of the same companies as the index it mirrors. Advantage: Low MERs, because management expense is literally minimal. Disadvantage: An index fund cannot, by definition, outperform the index itself. This is not necessarily bad, since most actively managed funds actually *underperform* a comparable index. Here's the point: Since the universe of Canadian equity funds is limited, and competent fund managers easily winnow out the losers, by the time you assemble six or eight funds drawing from the same equity base, you have substantial duplication among the best companies, which amounts to a modified index fund and dilutes the whole impact of diversification. Of course, you're probably paying 10 times the MER for the actively managed funds than for an index fund. So why not purchase one index fund instead?

Foreign investments in RRSPs and RRIFs have long been a thorny issue for the investment industry. For years, Ottawa dictated that the foreign content in registered plans must not exceed 20 percent, raising it to 30 percent after intense lobbying from brokers and financial planners. Many of these same people insist that the foreign content limit should be eliminated, leaving Canadians free to invest 100 percent of their retirement assets beyond our borders. Canada's capital markets, they point out, represent barely 2 percent of the world's total investment opportunities. Why shouldn't we be free to take full advantage of the remaining 98 percent?

Perhaps we should. But foreign investment opportunities for your RRSP/RRIF involve the risk of currency fluctuation, which everyone with substantial investments in U.S. companies has encountered recently. From 2001 through 2004, the high-flying U.S. dollar fell more than 20 percent against the loonie. No matter how well a U.S.–based equity fund might have performed over that period, its bottom line was slashed by about one-fifth when converted to Canadian dollars. The more you have invested in foreign equities, the greater your exposure to currency fluctuations.

By all means, incorporate foreign holdings in your retirement account, perhaps to the current 30 percent limit. Just remember that you may be trading one risk—underperformance of the Canadian market versus elsewhere in the world—for another risk, based on currency fluctuations. Thirty percent foreign content is not bad. Fifty percent might be better. One hundred percent is casino and race track territory.

10. Never Forget Whose Money It Is It's not theirs, it's not his, and it's not hers. It's *yours*, and you have more than a right to know where it is going, how much is being siphoned off, and to whom. You have a responsibility to yourself and your family, especially where RRSP/RRIF investments are concerned, to ensure that as much of it as possible remains in your hands.

Managing your money effectively involves maintaining a good relationship with your financial advisor. Like all relationships, this one depends on full and open communication for its success, and an understanding of each partner's rights.

You have the right to pay the lowest fee possible, consistent with the advisor receiving reasonable remuneration for the work done on your behalf.

The advisor has a right to earn a living, and to provide service commensurate with the amount she is earning from your account. In summary: Find an advisor you can trust. Expect openness and honesty on both sides. Locate a space between vigilance and relaxation, and settle into it.

Through discussions with dozens of Canadians who suffered devastating losses in their retirement savings, I have been struck by the manner in which many blamed their misfortune on themselves. True, better diligence might have helped avoid disaster in several instances. Blaming the system, with its commission-based remuneration, unrelenting pressure on advisors to generate ever-higher earnings, and lax regulatory procedures, may be justified, but it brings little consolation. We can only hope that industry disturbers such as Joe Killoran, Glorianne Stromberg, and John De Goey, partnered with principled advisors such as Hans Merkelbach and others placing their clients' needs foremost, will stimulate a structure in tune with the concerns of those relying on their registered savings plans for future security.

It is my view that avoidable RRSP/RRIF losses are rooted deeper than investor inattention and advisor malfeasance. They represent an attitude that permeates the industry at the top levels of many brokerages, including those owned by Canada's chartered banks. The evidence seems to indicate that pressure is applied on individual brokers to maximize their commissions to the detriment of other, more critical, concerns, including the growth and security of the client's investment portfolio.

Big producers of commissions, such as Michael Holoday, are stroked with special perks and recognition. Holoday was feted and praised for rising to become among the top 5 percent commission producers at his brokerage within three years of earning his broker's licence. No one noticed, until red lights began flashing from other directions, that almost without exception all of Holoday's clients had lost substantial portions of their portfolios, and some had been wiped out within months of entrusting Holoday with their investments. Did no one care that virtually all of his clients were losing money? Apparently not.

Holoday and others of his ilk do not lurk in every brokerage cubicle. If it need be said, brokers and advisors are neither more nor less honest than others in similar circumstances. But when the industry drives itself according to the generation of wealth for itself rather than the success of its clients, and rewards are made not as a reflection of the growth in client assets but by quarterly increases in sales commissions, *every decision, every nugget of advice, and every broker-influenced transaction will be subject to suspicion regarding the ultimate recipient of profit and earnings.* How can it be otherwise?

A final observation on two aspects of life that everyone 50 years and older can confirm and that sanction the activities of advisors who place their own interests ahead of those of their clients.

Canadians 50 years and older may be the last generation to harbour a tangible definition of *trust,* having grown up with the concept that a man or woman's promise was as solid as any contract written in dense legalese. They may recall the years of their childhood when every neighbourhood had a corner grocery store where families sent their children to request "a loaf of bread, a quart of milk, and a pound of sugar, and put it on our bill, please." The grocer duly recorded the order, the child returned home with the food, and every Saturday one of the parents—usually the mother—arrived at the grocer's to settle the bill. The grocer trusted the families to pay what they owed. The families trusted the grocer to record the purchases accurately. It was all achieved without credit cards, ATMs, or promissory notes because it was based on mutual trust. Both the neighbourhood grocery stores and that kind of trust are gone.

The other contributing factor is ignorance of financial and investment basics. Today's seven-year-old child likely knows more about sex than her parents and grandparents know about the investments that make up their retirement savings. Our schools appear to consider the subject of finance and investment considerably less respectable than the use and abuse of sexual organs. As adults, the ignorance is reinforced by too many commissioned salespeople assuring us that we are incapable of understanding the means of nurturing our retirement savings, and that our only salvation resides in giving them our money and our ... trust.

Do they deserve either?

I love and trust my wife. But when we play gin, I always cut the cards.

APPENDIX A

Provincial Securities Commissions

ALBERTA

Alberta Securities Commission
4th Floor
300 - 5th Avenue SW
Calgary, AB T2P 3C4

BRITISH COLUMBIA

British Columbia Securities Commission
701 West Georgia Street
PO Box 10142, Pacific Centre
Vancouver, BC V7Y 1L2
inquiries@bcsc.bc.ca

MANITOBA

Manitoba Securities Commission
1130 - 405 Broadway
Winnipeg, MB R3C 3L6
securities@gov.mb.ca

NEW BRUNSWICK

New Brunswick Securities Commission
Centennial Building
670 King Street
Fredericton, NB E3B 1G1

NEWFOUNDLAND AND LABRADOR

Securities Commission of Newfoundland and Labrador
Department of Government Services and Lands
PO Box 8700
St. John's, NF A1B 4J6

NORTHWEST TERRITORIES

Securities Registry, Department of Justice
Government of the Northwest Territories
PO Box 1320
Yellowknife, NT X1A 2L9

NOVA SCOTIA

Nova Scotia Securities Commission
2nd Floor, Joseph Howe Building
1690 Hollis Street
Halifax, NS B3J 3J9

NUNAVUT

Government of Nunavut Communications
Iqaluit, NU
Tel.: (867) 975-6000

ONTARIO

Ontario Securities Commission
Inquiries and Contact Centre
20 Queen Street West, Suite 1903
Toronto, ON M5H 3S8

PRINCE EDWARD ISLAND

Consumer, Corporate and Insurance Services Division
Office of the Attorney General
PO Box 2000
Charlottetown, PEI C1A 7N8

QUEBEC

Autorité des marchés financiers
800, Square Victoria, 22e étage
C.P. 246, Tour de la Bourse
Montreal, QC H4Z 1G3

SASKATCHEWAN

Saskatchewan Securities Commission
6th Floor
1919 Saskatchewan Drive
Regina, SK S4P 3V7

YUKON

Securities Registrar Corporate Affairs
Department of Community Services
Box 2703
Whitehorse, YT Y1A 2C6 (J-9)

APPENDIX B

While several Couch Potato Portfolios appear in financial and investment columns, most are variations on this system:

1. Divide the value of your existing portfolio into three equal portions:

   - Invest one portion in an RRSP-eligible foreign-based index fund such as Barclays iUnits S&P 500 Index RSP or the Altamira Precision American U.S. RSP Index.
   - Invest a second portion in an index fund that tracks the S&P/TSX 60 such as Barclays iUnits S&P TSX 60 Capped Index Fund.
   - Invest a third portion either in laddered strip bonds, a Canadian bond index fund such as Legg Mason Canadian Index Plus Bond Fund (MER = 0.69), or a solidly based active bond fund such as Mackenzie Sentinel Real Return Bond Fund (MER = 1.88) or TD Real Return Bond Fund (MER = 1.65).

2. Once each year, buy or sell the assets as necessary to maintain the one-third/one-third/one-third balance.

Purists will question the use of an active bond fund rather than pure strip bonds or an index fund. Both the actively managed funds shown invest heavily in government bonds (as of mid-2004), so you are trading secure instruments against active cost risks—not a bad compromise. Besides, the Mackenzie fund managed to achieve almost 12 percent return in one year ending June 30, 2004. Can it keep up the pace? That's the risk quotient.

Proponents of the Couch Potato Portfolio point out that it addresses three principles of good portfolio management: It diversifies your investment across different types of investments; it minimizes your costs with low-MER funds; and it involves annual rebalancing to ensure that you buy low and sell high.

How well does it work? A fully indexed Couch Potato Portfolio tracked by MoneySense magazine and posted April 30, 2004, on its website www.MoneySense.ca, noted that $100 invested in the Canadian Stock Index in 1976 would be worth $1742.64 in March 2004, while the same amount invested in its version of the Couch Potato Portfolio would cash out at $2402.57—an extra 38 percent.

If you choose to apply the Couch Potato Portfolio to your RRSP, use a self-directed account in a discount brokerage. You won't be using financial advice, so why pay for an advisor?

NOTES

Chapter 1: You Are David, They Are Goliath, and You Don't Have a Slingshot

1. All the data and quotations for the Laflamme tale herein are derived from the written judgment of Supreme Court Justice J. Gonthier in the ruling of *PA Laflamme Inc.* v. *Roy,* May 3, 2000.

Chapter 2: Of Foxes and Hedgehogs

1. "Make Mutual Funds Bare All!" *Wall Street Journal,* January 16, 2004.

2. *Roles, Rights & Responsibilities—A Guide to Investors from the Ontario Securities Commission* (April 2003), p. 1.

3. General Social Survey, Statistics Canada, 2003; Financial Planners Standards Council.

Chapter 3: Brokers and Advisors

1. A pseudonym.

2. As defined in the Glossary, short selling involves borrowing someone else's securities, usually shares in common stock, and selling them at a current high price with the strategy of buying them at an expected lower price in the future. Dealing in "shorts" is a sophisticated and highly risky method of investing unsuitable for anyone without extensive experience, deep pockets, and loads of nerve.

3. The complete saga of Holoday's career is told in my book *Free Rider: How a Bay Street Whiz Kid Stole and Spent $20 Million* (Toronto: McArthur and Co., 2001).

4. IDA Compliance Interpretation Bulletin #C-130.

5. Personal interview with John J. De Goey, Oakville, Ontario, January 13, 2004.

6. Advocis news release, January 29, 2004.

7. As quoted in John Craig, "Advisors Urged to Protest OSC's Fair Dealing Model," *Globe and Mail,* November 7, 2002.

Chapter 4: Mutual Funds

1. A pseudonym.

2. A dramatic exception to the policy of annual distributions is Warren Buffet's Berkshire Hathaway operation, whose unit/share value began at U.S.$19 in 1965 and was valued at U.S.$50,498 in March 2004, an average annual return of 22.2 percent. Buffet's operation differs from garden-variety mutual funds because of its closed-end structure, meaning that its shares (not units) are traded on the market just as common shares of corporations are. You invest in the company by purchasing shares from other shareholders, not from the management company.

3. Investment Funds Institute of Canada.

4. The lunch bill gets even bigger if the fund company applies the back-end fee not to your initial investment but to the market value of the fund when you cash it in, assuming the market value is substantially higher than your purchase cost.

5. For those with a mathematical bent: the formula involved taking the median MER for all mutual funds in the Canadian equity asset category (2.7 percent), expressing it as a percentage of the median of pre-MER returns averaged over the previous five years (6.99 percent), and applying it to the 366 days in 2004.

6. Morningstar Canada.

7. In May 2004, AIM Trimark announced that the Select Growth Fund would no longer exactly mirror the original Trimark Fund.

8. AIC picked up more than Buffet's investment guideline. AIC founder and president Michael Lee-Chin also adapted Buffet's company's name, Berkshire Hathaway, for Lee-Chin's Canadian securities operation, The Berkshire Group, which includes Berkshire Investment Group Inc. and Berkshire Securities Inc., and describes itself as "an independent investment dealer offering a full range of registered and non-registered products and services including mutual funds, stocks, bonds, tax-assisted investments and other specialty investment products." Since Berkshire and AIC share both top management and a head office location in Burlington, Ontario, some observers question the degree of independent advice provided to its clients.

9. Personal interview with Glorianne Stromberg, Toronto, February 23, 2004.

10. Power Corporation of Canada/Investors Group financial report.

11. The CSA comprises 13 provincial and territorial securities commissions, a loose-jointed method of functioning in the same manner as the Securities and Exchange Commission (SEC) in the United States and similar organizations elsewhere in the world. In reality, it lacks the power and political clout that a truly efficient national securities organization should have. (For more on the OSC and Canada's disgraceful lack of a national securities commissions, see Chapter 8.)

Chapter 5: It Shouldn't Be Complex—It Should Be Open

1. A pseudonym.

2. The duplication is not as impressive as it appears. The CFP designation is awarded by the Financial Planners Standards Council and the RFP by the Institute of Advanced Financial Planning. In terms of feeling confident about the advice being rendered, for most investors this would be like flying in an airplane whose pilot graduated from two flying schools. In reality, some of the most successful advisors, as measured by the growth of client assets in RRSP/RRIF accounts, have neither designation.

3. Statement on file with the author. Figures rounded off to the nearest $5.

4. I am indebted to Doug Steiner, managing partner of Ventura VGI, who first described this formula in a column appearing in the April 2003 issue of *Report on Business*.

5. "Select Few Reap Unfair Gain," *Globe and Mail,* June 21, 2004, p. B4.

6. Letter, from OSC chairman David Brown to all publicly traded mutual funds under OSC jurisdiction, November 5, 2003.

7. "Hard Line on Soft Dollars," *Globe and Mail,* April 5, 2004, p. B1.

8. "Soft Dollars Unveiled," *Benefits Canada,* October 1998, p. 1.

9. "Hard Line on Soft Dollars."

10. Ibid., quoting Bob Bertram, executive vice-president, Ontario Teachers' Pension Plan Board.

11. Derek DeCloet, "Investor Complaints to IDA Tripled from 1996 to 2000," *Financial Post,* May 12, 2001.

12. "Securities Regulators Assailed," *Globe and Mail,* April 19, 2004, p. B1.

13. Ibid.

14. Glorianne Stromberg, "A Wake-Up Call to the Fund Industry," *Investment Executive,* February 19, 2004.

Chapter 6: Investment Pornography and Red Suits

1. A pseudonym. I am indebted to Ken Kivenko for providing basic facts on this case; some details have been altered.

2. The mutual funds strategy of "I'm the expert and you're the fool" was never more clearly illustrated than during a pitch made to me by a mutual fund salesman who scorned my relatively conservative RRSP portfolio, telling me that I should be 100 percent invested in equity-based mutual funds. "Which funds?" I asked. "You transfer your account to me and I'll tell you," he sneered. At that point I showed him the door.

3. Russell 4, www.russell.com/CA/Investor_Services/Sovereign_investment_Program, accessed April 19, 2004.

4. Some wrap accounts appear to deliver good performance. Here are comparable returns for two of the largest operations (to June 30, 2004):

	1 YEAR	3 YEARS	5 YEARS
Seamark Canadian Equity	23.5	8.8	13.7
Jarislowsky & Fraser Canadian Equity	24.2	11.0	15.0

While these are satisfactory, they are not extraordinary for the periods covered (2003 saw strong returns everywhere), and the same concerns regarding lack of flexibility and high expenses apply.

5. Globefund, March 31, 2004.

Chapter 7: A Guide to Investment Divorce

1. Personal interview with Hans Merkelbach, Bowen Island, B.C., March 2, 2004.

Chapter 8: Celebrity Bingo

1. Personal telephone interview with Neil Gross, September 16, 2002.

2. Personal interview with William Sloper, Burlington, Ontario, September 23, 2002.

3. For a detailed critique of reverse mortgages, see Chapter 10.

4. "Financial analyst fined in store theft," *Hamilton Spectator,* June 28, 1982.

5. Dollar-cost averaging is the process of purchasing investments such as mutual fund units across an extended period. Instead of making a lump-sum investment of $12,000, for example, dollar-cost adherents propose investing $1000 each month for 12 months, especially in equity-based investments in which the price might fluctuate widely from month to month. Under this theory, you purchase more units when the price is depressed and fewer units when the price rises, thus lowering the average cost per unit.

6. Interview with Garth Turner, Toronto, August 15, 2002. Proactive maybe; active, maybe not. Turner's website lists only six seminars all through 2003 and none thereafter. What's more, his seminar-booking website SpeakerSolutions.com is not only closed, its address is for sale.

7. Garth Turner, *The Strategy: A Homeowner's Guide to Wealth Creation* (Toronto: Key Porter, 1997), p. 52.

8. "More Advice from a Cocky and Dangerous Source." Garth Turner column, December 4, 2000, www.garth.ca.

9. "Here Are Two Harbingers of Much Better Times to Come." Garth Turner column, March 26, 2001, www.garth.ca.

10. Turner continued to demonstrate bullish behaviour in 2004 when, in a March column of that year, he reiterated his proposals of converting equity in the family home into cash for stock-market based investments.

11. Rod McQueen, "Physician Heal Thyself," *Financial Post,* October 12, 1996.

12. The listed charities included Feed the Children U.S. and U.K., Canadian Physicians for Aid and Relief (CPAR), Canadian Health and Environment Project, and Children's Emergency Foundation (CEF). CGI's description of their "highly skilled professionals" is derived from information posted on their website, at www.canadiangift.ca/index.php.

13. James Daw, "Tax System Squanders Donations," *Toronto Star,* December 6, 2003.

14. Posted on Cestnick's website, Waterstreet.ca, September 18, 2003.

Chapter 9: SRO or SOL?

1. The broker has since retired.

2. Personal interview with Paul Bourke, IDA offices, Toronto, January 14, 2004.

3. "Report Seeks IDA Revamp," *Report on Business,* December 13, 2003.

4. As of mid-2004, the IDA had obtained the authority in Alberta to obtain a court order enforcing fines against individuals no longer associated with an IDA-member firm or out of the industry completely rather than pay the fine. It remains to be seen whether the IDA can obtain similar authority in other provinces and just how effective it may be, if and when this authority is granted.

5. Personal email correspondence with James Roache, August 12–18, 2004.

6. MFDA website, www.mfda.ca/NewsReleases/Mediareleasecomplaints.pdf and www.mfda.ca/DisciplinaryNotices.html, accessed September 14, 2004.

7. Personal interview with Michael Lauber, Toronto, March 31, 2004, and follow-up correspondence.

8. *MFDA Completes Corporate Governance Restructuring and Appoints New Board, Chair and President.* News release, Mutual Fund Dealers Association of Canada, Toronto, December 9, 2003.

9. MRS Inc. website, www.rs.ca.

10. Prof. Joel Fried (University of Western Ontario), "The OSC Swamp: Sobering Thoughts for a Legislative Standing Committee Investigating Problems at the Ontario Securities Commission," *Financial Post,* August 28, 2004.

11. Personal interview with Susan Wolburgh-Jenah, Toronto, July 29, 2004.

12. Eric Reguly, "OSC Slothlike over Monetization," *Globe and Mail,* March 4, 2003.

13. OSC Statement of Priorities for Fiscal 2003/2004, June 2003.

14. "Brown Launches Securities Crusade," *Toronto Star,* April 16, 2003.

15. "Governance Rules Go into Effect Today," *Toronto Star,* March 30, 2004.

16. "OSC Tries to Block Release of Report on Brokerage Watchdog," *Globe and Mail,* July 20, 2004.

Chapter 10: The Banks

1. Pseudonyms.

2. Personal interview with Gordon Pape, Toronto, August 13, 2002.

3. www.chip.ca/new/how_seniors.asp.

4. "How Seniors Use the Money," CHIP website, www.chip.ca/new/how_seniors.asp, accessed April 8, 2004.

5. Jonathan Chevreau, "Advisor Quits Big Bank in Disgust," *Financial Post*, April 22, 2003.

Chapter 11: Vultures, Jackals, Ghouls, and Everyday Thieves

1. The complete sordid story of Michael Holoday is related in my book *Free Rider: How a Bay Street Whiz Kid Stole and Spent $20 Million* (Toronto: McArthur and Co., 2001).

2. There are exceptions. When RBC Dominion Securities broker Christopher Horne duped his clients out of $7 million, the brokerage reimbursed his clients for their losses, plus interest, and paid legal fees for clients to investigate RBC Dominion's actions to confirm that the company acted in a correct manner. It also paid a $250,000 fine to the IDA for failing to adequately supervise their star broker. (The complete story of Horne's deception is related in Deborah Thompson's *Greed: Investment Fraud in Canada and Around the Globe* [Toronto: Viking, 1997].) RBC Dominion's actions in this case are considered exemplary. They are also, unfortunately, extraordinary.

3. *Financial Disclosure: What You Need to Know,* OSC, September 2000.

4. Personal interview with Detective Jeff Thomson, Toronto, May 6, 2003.

5. Ponzi schemes are named for their inventor, Charles Ponzi, who in 1920 launched a Boston-based company supposedly dealing in U.S. postal reply coupons. When Ponzi promised 50 percent profit in 45 days, and delivered these earnings to the first wave of investors, others joined in, and soon Ponzi was sitting on more than $10 million. In reality, of course, the fraud artist was paying early investors with money from late arrivals. The scheme eventually collapsed, and Ponzi fled to South America, where he died in poverty. His sole legacy was to have his name associated to any fraud similar to the one he masterminded.

6. "White Collar Crime Lament," *Toronto Star,* March 3, 2003.

7. Ibid.

Chapter 12: Looking Out for Yourself and Your Money

1. Rob Carrick, "Financial Services Consumers Need a Court of Last Resort," *Globe and Mail,* November 8, 2001.

2. Rudy Luukko, "74-Year-Old Widow's Case Just Drags On," *Toronto Star,* December 7, 2003.

3. Paul Delean, "Feeling Burned and Bitter About It," *Montreal Gazette,* July 22, 2002.

4. Supreme Court of Canada, *Bulletin of Proceedings,* March 12, 2004, pp. 415–32.

5. Globefund, September 1, 2004.

GLOSSARY

Asset   Something of value. Your home is your asset (or at least the portion that is free of mortgage), as is your RRSP or RRIF.

Asset allocation   The process of dividing your assets over various options, including cash, fixed income (e.g., bonds, GICs), equity (stock market shares), and real estate according to an investment strategy.

Back-end load   *See* Deferred sales charge.

Balanced fund   A mutual fund investing in a combination of equities and fixed-income investments, seeking growth with limited volatility.

Bear market   A phase in the stock market when prices decline over an extended period.

Beta   A measure of price volatility compared with similar investments such as an index fund. If the benchmark investment is set at 1.0, investments with wide price fluctuations will exceed a beta rating of 1.0; those with less volatility will be rated less than 1.0.

Blue chip   Large, well-known publicly traded companies with long records of earning profits and paying dividends.

Bond   A means of borrowing money over a long term (up to 30 years). Bonds are issued by governments and corporations and pay a declared rate of interest, usually on a semi-annual basis.

Broker   An individual who arranges the purchase and sale of assets.

Bull market   A phase in the stock market when prices rise over an extended period.

Canada Deposit Insurance Corporation (CDIC)   A government agency guaranteeing deposits in member financial institutions to a maximum of $100,000 per account.

Canada Pension Plan (CPP)   A federally sponsored pension plan requiring mandatory contributions from earned income during your working years and providing monthly income for your retirement (Quebec residents contribute to the QPP).

Capital gains/losses   The difference between the price you pay to purchase a security and the price you receive when you sell it. Income from capital gains is taxed on only 50 percent of the profit earned. Capital losses may be deducted from taxable income (outside of an RRSP or RRIF).

Capitalization   In stock market terms, the total value of all publicly traded shares in a corporation. Companies with capitalization of $500 million or over are considered large cap; those under $500 million are assessed as small cap.

Churning   The illegal practice of making multiple unnecessary trades in a client account for the purpose of generating commissions for the broker and the brokerage.

Closed-end fund   A mutual fund that accepts no new investors. Its units may be traded like shares of common stocks.

Commodities   Any product or material traded publicly, usually in the futures market.

Common shares   Ownership shares in a publicly traded corporation. They provide voting rights and dividends, if available.

Coupon   Portions of a bond removed and submitted in exchange for earned interest.

Deferred sales charge (DSC)   A fee levied on mutual fund unit holders who redeem their investment before a fixed period—usually five to seven years. The redemption fee, expressed as a percentage of either the original investment or the value of the investment at the point of redemption, is reduced for each year the fund is held. DSCs are used to generate front-load commissions (or "loads) to brokers and advisors, recovered with higher MERs (which remain in effect after the DSC redemption-penalty period has passed).

Derivatives   Financial arrangements between two parties based on the performance of a security or asset.

Discount broker   A firm that will buy and sell securities for its clients at a lower cost without providing investment advice.

Diversification   The strategy of spreading an investment portfolio over a wide range of alternatives, industries, and countries. The goal is to avoid wide fluctuations in value over the investment period.

Dividend   Payment to shareholders of a public company based on the amount of profit earned and subject to directives from the board of directors.

Equity fund   A mutual fund investing primarily in shares of publicly traded companies.

Exchange traded funds (ETF)   Units of a mutual fund traded as though they were common shares.

Fixed income   An asset paying a determined level of interest for a specific period. Bonds, GICs, savings accounts are examples of fixed-income vehicles.

Front-end load   In mutual funds, when the sales commission is immediately deducted from the investor's assets placed in the fund.

Futures   The expectation of earning a profit by bidding for contracts to deliver items—usually commodities such as wheat, minerals, or energy—at a date in the future.

Global fund   A mutual fund investing in companies throughout the world with no (or limited) geographical restrictions.

Growth fund   A mutual fund investing in companies with little or no current income but prospects for substantial earnings in the future. Generally considered high-risk investments.

Guaranteed investment certificate (GIC)   Certificate issued by financial institutions guaranteeing a predetermined level of interest to the purchaser over a fixed period—usually one to five years. Redemption before that date may result in penalties.

Index fund   A mutual fund whose investments exactly match that of the index (e.g., S&P/TSX 300, Dow Jones) it is copying. Indexed funds are considered passively managed because the fund manager makes no investment decisions.

Initial public offering (IPO)   The first time a publicly traded stock is made available to investors.

International fund   A mutual fund investing in countries throughout the world with the exception of North America.

Investment Dealers Association (IDA) of Canada   A self-regulated organization funded by member brokerages and securities dealers to promote the industry's goals and positions.

Load   The commission cost of purchasing units in a mutual fund.

Leverage   Borrowing money to maximize the size of an investment. If $90,000 is borrowed to add to $10,000 in assets, the resulting $100,000 investment is leveraged at a 9-to-1 ratio.

Liquidity   A measure of how quickly and easily an asset can be converted to cash.

Management expense ratio (MER)   The portion of a mutual fund's assets deducted annually to cover the fund's expenses.

Margin   An account in which the investor adds leverage to the investment by borrowing funds from the brokerage.

Market timing   Trading shares in anticipation of a major price change, based on statistics, intuition, experience, and so on.

Mutual fund   A vehicle in which contributions by large numbers of small investors are pooled and invested by professional managers, who are paid by a portion of the MER.

Mutual Fund Dealers Association (MFDA) of Canada   A spinoff of the Investment Dealers Association focusing on the goals of mutual fund dealers in Canada.

Net asset value per share (NAVPS)   Total assets of a mutual fund divided by the number of units owned by its investors. A mutual fund with $1 million in assets and 100,000 units owned by investors has a NAVPS of $10.

Ombudsman for Banking Services and Investment (OBSI)   An organization that investigates customer complaints against financial services providers, including banks and other deposit-taking organizations, investment dealers, mutual fund dealers, and mutual fund companies.

Open-end fund   A mutual fund accepting investments by unit holders with no limit to size or number.

Preferred shares   Shares that earn a fixed or variable dividend without voting privileges but with first claim to a portion of profits.

Price/earnings ratio   The ratio of a stock's price to its earnings per share.

Principal   The amount of an investor's capital that is at risk.

Sector investing   Assigning a portion of your assets to a relatively limited part of the investment universe. Examples are mutual funds or companies operating in emerging markets or specific geographical areas (Japan, Asia-Pacific, China), specific markets (gold and precious metals, health care, internet-based industries), or investment philosophies. Sector investments tend to be highly volatile and should represent only a small proportion of a total investment strategy—typically 10 percent or less.

Self-dealing   The actions of a parent company of a mutual fund to ensure its economic well-being. Corporation A, the parent company of Mutual Fund B, may spearhead an equity offering by a client company, Corporation C, to ensure that C is able to pay debts owed to A, then pressures its Mutual Fund B to purchase substantial amounts of the share offering and ensure success.

Self-regulated organization (SRO)   An association of industry members whose goal includes policing the members' operations in lieu of direct government oversight.

Short selling   The strategy of borrowing publicly traded shares and selling them immediately with the prospect of purchasing later at a lower price and thus earning a profit.

Small Investor Protection Agency (SIPA)   A private organization that acts in the interests of retail investors, alerting its members to investment risks and acting on their behalf to influence regulations and procedures.

Strip bond   A bond with interest coupons removed, or the coupons itself. Strip bonds are sold at a discount to the face value of the bond or the coupons; the discount and the maturity date (or due date) of the bond or coupon determine the annual interest earned.

Trailer fee   A fee (actually, a commission) paid annually to a financial advisor by a mutual fund company whose units the advisor has sold to clients who continue to hold them.

Value fund   A mutual fund that purchases shares in a company on the basis that the share price is less than its true value.

Volatility   Wide swings in value of an investment over time. High volatility brings increased potential reward at an increased level of risk.

ACKNOWLEDGMENTS

The goal of this book was to go beyond the familiar RRSP investment guides and address the hazards faced by Canadians with substantial assets and limited investment knowledge. To achieve this, I needed actual experiences from real people telling their real stories, holding back neither the mechanical details nor the emotional trauma. Their cooperation, more than anything else, made this book possible. My debt to Stan Buell, Patricia Cosgrove, Joe Killoran, Jean and Lindsay King, Carol MacKinnon, and Helen Rentis is enormous; those who were just as forthcoming but prefer to conceal their identities know of my gratitude.

Others provided an essential fount of information, views, sources, and commentary. Among them are John De Goey, Larry Elford, Ken Kivenko, Robert Kyle, Hans and Shannon Merkelbach, Jim Roache, Glorianne Stromberg, and Jeff Thomson. Thanks as well to Ted Mumford for his assistance in preparing a feature for *ROB Magazine* that formed the basis of Chapter 8; Matthew Elder at Morningstar Canada; Larry Wade, for his lectures on RRSP investing; and Bill Sloper and Neil Gross for their professional insights. Paul Bourke of the Investment Dealers Association and Michael Lauber, Ombudsman for Banking Services and Investment, were gracious with their time, as were a quartet of sources at the Ontario Securities Commission: Wendy Dey, Eric Pelletier, Perry Quinton, and Susan Wolburgh-Jenah.

I have been associated with Penguin Group (Canada) for almost 20 years and over that period their high publishing standards have never wavered. I am indebted to Editorial Director Diane Turbide for her initial confidence in the idea and Susan Folkins for her editorial guidance. Catherine Dorton, Tracy Bordian, and Judy Phillips did what all good editors do: They made this a better book.

Finally, love and appreciation: the latter to my agent Hilary MacMahon of Westwood Creative Artists, whose warm outlook never fails to lift my spirits; and the former to my wife, Judy, whose most foolish act in life may have been to marry a writer.

INDEX